N

Martha Raye

Film and Television Clown

DAVID C. TUCKER

McFarland & Company, Inc., Publishers
Jefferson, North Carolina

ALSO BY DAVID C. TUCKER
AND FROM MCFARLAND

*Joan Davis: America's Queen of Film, Radio
and Television Comedy* (2014)

*Eve Arden: A Chronicle of All Film, Television,
Radio and Stage Performances* (2012)

*Lost Laughs of '50s and '60s Television:
Thirty Sitcoms That Faded Off Screen* (2010)

Shirley Booth: A Biography and Career Record (2008)

*The Women Who Made Television Funny:
Ten Stars of 1950s Sitcoms* (2007)

Frontispiece: Martha rips into her rendition of "Pig Foot Pete" in *Keep 'Em Flying.*

LIBRARY OF CONGRESS CATALOGUING-IN-PUBLICATION DATA

Names: Tucker, David C., 1962– author.
Title: Martha Raye : film and television clown / David C. Tucker.
Description: Jefferson, N.C. : McFarland & Company, Inc., Publishers,
2016. | Includes bibliographical references and index.
Identifiers: LCCN 2016021271 | ISBN 9780786495832
(softcover : acid free paper) ∞
Subjects: LCSH: Raye, Martha. | Actors—United States—
Biography. | Entertainers—United States—Biography.
Classification: LCC PN2287.R248 T83 2016 | DDC 791.4302/8092 [B]—dc23
LC record available at https://lccn.loc.gov/2016021271

BRITISH LIBRARY CATALOGUING DATA ARE AVAILABLE

ISBN (print) 978-0-7864-9583-2
ISBN (ebook) 978-1-4766-2427-3

Front cover: Martha dodges slings and
arrows in *Hellzapoppin'* (author's collection)

Printed in the United States of America

*McFarland & Company, Inc., Publishers
Box 611, Jefferson, North Carolina 28640
www.mcfarlandpub.com*

To James Robert Parish,
who led the way.

Acknowledgments

My thanks to the staff of the Margaret Herrick Library in Los Angeles for access to the Martha Raye papers, generously donated to that institution by Martha's widower. I am likewise grateful to those who knew Martha Raye, and granted me interviews.

TV historian Wesley Hyatt kindly shared information about Martha's appearances on *The Carol Burnett Show*. Garry Berman and Eddie Lucas steered me in the direction of some helpful research material. Scot Lockman and Ken McCullers are able proofreaders who did my manuscript more than a few favors.

Lynn Kear and James Robert Parish continue to be supportive friends and colleagues whose help I greatly value. I also appreciate the encouragement and assistance of Danny Proctor, a longtime fan of Martha's who has done much to keep her memory alive.

Table of Contents

Preface

Comedienne, comic actress, funny lady—perhaps the most accurate term that describes Martha Raye, professionally, is "clown." She understood that it was a privilege to give people pure, uncomplicated laughs, and from a young age she showed herself uniquely gifted to do so. Still, the careers of female comics were rarely nurtured like those of their male counterparts. As film historian Leonard Maltin said, "Martha Raye and Joan Davis proved their brilliance in spite of their film vehicles and not because of them.... It remained for television to give Miss Raye, Miss Davis and, of course, Lucy the kind of showcase they deserved."[1]

Most previous works about Miss Raye have understandably focused on one of two undeniably interesting aspects of her life: her chaotic personal relationships—evidenced by seven trips to the altar—or her efforts in entertaining American troops during wartime. While those topics are covered here, the emphasis is on her career as a comic actress-singer. First stepping on stage as a child, alongside her vaudevillian parents, Martha was a professional entertainer for more than 60 years, slowing down only in the mid–1980s when her health began to give way. Though she appeared in motion pictures for more than forty years, her most productive period was her late 1930s stint as a Paramount contract player.

In the early 1950s, she began to make her mark on the still-new medium of television. Within a few years, *The Martha Raye Show* was a popular attraction for NBC-TV, whose executives signed her to a long-term exclusive contract. Then what should have been the most secure period of her frantic life came to an abrupt end, because of problems that were at least in part of her own making.

Because her television comedy shows of the 1950s were typically broadcast live, Martha did not receive the attention given in later years to Lucille Ball and others whose filmed shows were rerun many times after their initial airings. During the 1960s and 1970s, she was a popular guest star on the variety shows of Carol Burnett, Red Skelton, Perry Como, and others, played recurring roles on *McMillan & Wife* and *Alice,* and had a starring role on the Saturday morning children's show *The Bugaloos.* But younger viewers may know her best for a commercial campaign in which she endorsed a denture cleanser.

Published to coincide with the centennial of Martha Raye's birth, this book opens with a biography of Miss Raye. The second section is an extensively annotated filmography of her motion picture career, which had an auspicious beginning with *Rhythm on the Range* in 1936, and continued through her last film role, in *The Concorde: Airport '79*. As that section makes evident, Hollywood did not always make the best use of her talents, and in some ways her movie career is marked by unrealized potential. Nonetheless, she left behind many energetic, enthusiastic performances for us to enjoy, and in the best of those films her comic talent and ability to put over a song still shine brightly.

The third section discusses her television career, including her popular variety shows of the 1950s, culminating in *The Martha Raye Show*. Guest appearances are covered as well. Also found in this section is information about Martha's unsold pilots for two weekly television comedy series, *Baby Snooks* (1957) and *Bill and Martha* (1964), missing from most previous accounts of her career. She remained a frequent television performer until her retirement in the mid–1980s.

There was little about Martha Raye that was subtle, either in her professional or personal life. Though she was a relatively petite woman, everything else about her was big: her emotions, her mugging style of comedy, and her appetite for life. Watching Raye at work also shows a performer whose sheer delight at being onstage comes across strongly. Yet there is an undeniable strain of vulnerability to be seen in her performances. Few performers have ever matched her hunger to be liked, to please the audience members who watched her at work. Insecure about her lack of formal education, reminded often that she was not traditionally beautiful, and lacking confidence in her own abilities, Martha did her best to overcome these deficits through sheer force of will.

In her personal life, she often made decisions that could call her judgment into question. Her relationship with her only daughter hovered somewhere between guarded and openly adversarial for much of her life. Though she would make headlines late in life by marrying a man many years her junior, it was nothing out of the ordinary for the woman who'd already been divorced six times. For all her romantic complications, however, her most sustained love affair may have been with the men and women who served in the United States armed forces, especially those who were overseas during the Vietnam War.

Martha Raye has been the subject of two previous books. Jean Maddern

Pitrone's *Take It from the Big Mouth: The Life of Martha Raye* (University Press of Kentucky, 1999) benefits from the participation of Martha's daughter Melodye Condos, who provided some family background. Unfortunately, the book lacks complete scholarly documentation; given the author's tendency to describe events in her own voice, it is sometimes difficult to tell what her sources of information were, and Condos herself has disavowed it. Pitrone's book also lacks detail about Martha's career, mostly summing up her Paramount films in terms of what was said about them in *New York Times* reviews.

Noonie Fortin's *Memories of Maggie: Martha Raye, A Legend Spanning Three Wars* (Langmarc, 1995) is required reading for anyone interested in Martha's dedication to military service. The author's own career in the U.S. Army makes her uniquely qualified to gather and assess information, which she collected from dozens of veterans who crossed paths with Martha during the Vietnam War years.

A key source in researching this book was the collection of Martha Raye Papers, donated to the Margaret Herrick Library of the Academy of Motion Picture Arts and Sciences by her widower Mark Harris. Included in that collection are correspondence from Martha's agent Abe Lastfogel, documents concerning her divorce from her sixth husband Robert O'Shea, and records of a publicity tour she undertook as a Paramount contract player. Genealogical records were helpful in verifying her family background, details of her seven marriages, and the lives of her siblings Buddy and Melodye.

I was fortunate to be able to interview several professional colleagues of Martha's from various points in her career. As might be said of most of us who pursued a career, regardless of the field, some who worked with Martha spoke highly of her; others did not. There is a marked difference between Martha as one co-star described her in the 1960s, versus the recollections of another colleague from nearly 20 years later. I leave it to the reader to determine the reasons for those differences.

Others whom I contacted chose not to participate in this project, for undoubtedly valid reasons of their own. Martha's daughter Melodye Condos is wary of authors and interviewers, having been disillusioned by previous experiences, and politely declined an interview. She indicated to me that some previous published accounts misrepresented her views. Rather than risk repeating disputed information, I have not written extensively about her relationship with her mother, which I hope does not diminish its importance in the reader's mind. I respect her desire for privacy and wish her every happiness. Others simply didn't respond to my communications, or said they had no information to share.

One final note: "Martha Raye" is a stage name, one adopted by young

Margy Reed and her mother during the up-and-coming performer's teenage years. In private life, the star preferred to be addressed as "Maggie." In this book, I have mostly chosen to use her professional name when referring to her, in keeping with my focus on her performing career. That is not to say that, given the chance, I would not have welcomed the opportunity to know her, and hoped that I might be instructed to use the name that her friends used.

And now, ladies and gentlemen, Miss Martha Raye....

I. Margy Reed

Looking back on her tumultuous life from late middle age, Martha Raye told an interviewer, "With all the ups and downs, I wouldn't change my life for one minute. It's been—and is—very colorful. Sure, it's sad, but more happy than sad. I think you've got to have a certain amount of sadness to appreciate the happiness."[1]

The future Martha Raye was born August 27, 1916, to Peter F. Reed, Jr., and Maybelle Hooper Reed, at St. James Hospital in Butte, Montana. Her impending arrival may well have been the motivation for the marriage. At the time of her birth, her parents had been married for only a few weeks—Peter and Maybelle were married July 19, 1916, in Bozeman, Montana. Peter was 24, Maybelle 20. Martha's father was a Britisher by birth, having been born in Manchester, England, in 1893, to Peter Reed, Sr., and Catherine Finnigan. Maybelle, known in the family as Peggy, was a native of Milwaukee, Wisconsin, daughter of Samuel and Theresa Hooper. The baby's full name, as recorded on the birth certificate, was Margy Reed.

"I wasn't born in a trunk," Martha said nearly 60 years later. "It was in the charity ward of the hospital in Butte, Montana. My parents, Pete Reed, a putty-nose comic, and Peggy Hooper, a singer, were both from Ireland and had a vaudeville act, Reed and Hooper. They never made the big time. The night before I arrived, my father stole a can of condensed milk to feed my mother."[2] Unable to afford time off from work, Mrs. Reed continued to appear onstage nightly, doing her best to disguise her condition with costuming, until just before Margy was born.

Surviving on the lower rungs of show business, the Reeds brought their new daughter into a life they couldn't make entirely secure. "My first cradle was the tray of a trunk," she later wrote. "My first memory is looking up at the ceiling of a dressing room, with the paint hanging down where it had peeled, and hearing Mama thumping away at a piano on stage while I bawled with loneliness."[3] Given the family into which she was born, a show business career was virtually inevitable. "I didn't have to work until I was three," she later liked to say. "But after that I never stopped."[4]

When Martha later spoke about her upbringing, she sometimes felt compelled to explain what she considered some of her shortcomings as an adult. "As a child, there was no city, no town, no house I could ever call home," she

said. "My mother taught me how to read and write, and after that, whatever education I picked up I just got on the fly. I learned a lot about life in the backstages of theaters, and I can tell you that's not the easiest or the most digni-fied way of getting an education. Maybe if I'd gone to school with other children I would have become more perceptive about judging people or human rela-tionships."[5] Instead, Margy (or Margie, as the family later spelled it) received an education focused primarily on mastering stage business and technique. For the rest of her life, she would be sen-sitive about her lack of education and her reading difficulties.

As the Reeds' vaudeville tour continued through the first years of their daughter's life, the

Baby Margy Reed, who would grow up to become Martha Raye.

family continued to expand. Margie's brother Douglas Haid Reed, who would be known as "Buddy," arrived October 21, 1918. Sister Melodye Jeanne was born August 27, 1920, four years to the day after Margie. Of the three, only Melodye would not find a place in the family act.

By the early 1920s, Margie had become an important player in the act, often receiving her own mention in billings at vaudeville houses. Occasionally, however, this led to complications, as in 1921, when five-year-old Margie's act ran afoul of child welfare authorities in Kansas. Learning of her scheduled appearance at the Strand Theater in Emporia, members of the local Women's City Club filed a protest. "It is against the child labor law of Kansas," said Mrs. J.R. Wilkie, chair of the Club's child welfare committee, "for a child under 14 years old to appear on the stage professionally at any time, or for a child between 14 and 16 years old to appear on the stage after 6 o'clock."[6] Juve-nile Court Judge I.T. Richardson concurred, and the theater management was notified that Margie could not perform.

When she did appear, young Margie's publicity made claims on her behalf that are difficult to validate nearly 100 years later. Reed and Hooper were billing their young daughter as someone audiences should recognize from visits to their local movie houses. When the Reeds appeared at Fischer's Theater in Appleton, Wisconsin, in September 1922, a local newspaper ad promised customers "Little Mary [sic] Reed, the Popular Movie Star."

In Moberly, Missouri, theatergoers were advised: "The management of the Grand has been fortunate in arranging to hold over for the big matinee Monday and the three shows Tuesday, clever Baby Margie Reed, the child movie star in a complete change of songs and dances. She captivated the large audiences at the Grand Friday and Saturday."[7] During a Wisconsin engagement, a newspaper write-up provided more details of Margie's purported movie credits: "In the second act, Baby Margie Reed, seen in juvenile parts with Anita Stewart [and] Norma Talmadge, appears in a clever sketch with her mother, father and little brother. The brother runs away with much of the honors with his clever drumming and dancing, while the little girl and her parents are also good in their program of songs, piano numbers and dances."[8]

Montana audiences saw an advertisement for "The Marlow, Helena's Coolest Spot," that promised, "Featuring Baby Margie, the $100,000 movie star, in person, assisted by 3-year-old Buddy Reed. You have seen 5-year-old Baby Margie on screen with Mary Pickford, Norma Talmadge and others. Now see her in person.... Little Buddy and Margie Reed are two of the cleverest child entertainers we have ever seen." In Iowa, an advertisement in the *Fort Madison Evening Democrat* (May 8, 1922) said, "Margie Reed has appeared in *Once to Every Woman, Yes or No* featuring Norma Tlmadge [sic] and the Booth Tarkington pictures." As an adult, however, Martha Raye would never repeat the claim that she had worked in Hollywood as a child, and all indications are that she did not.

Possible résumé-padding aside, reviewers did generally agree that the Reed kids showed talent: "Reed and Hooper, who are former Great Falls people, [and] their two children participate in the act and are considered unusually brilliant for youngsters."[9] Margie, said a reviewer in 1922, "looks like a doll, has a charming personality and a sweet voice."[10] Buddy's contribution to the act was said to be as a comedian and drummer. When the family opened in Billings, Montana, a *Billings Gazette* advertisement (August 24, 1924) attributed movie experience to not only Margie but her brother: "A couple of little movie stars—brother and sister with their mother and father in a musical and comedy act.... [T]he cleverest juveniles in vaudeville." By 1925, Margie, Buddy, and their parents were billed as "The Famous Reed Hooper Four."

For much of the 1920s, the Reeds went wherever the best bookings could be found. In 1928, the family was working the Palace in Bridgeport, Connecticut—"the Reed and Hooper Revue, featuring Baby Margie the juvenile movie star in songs and dances of her own creation."[11] In Ohio, "Bud, the younger who still possesses his boyish voice, engages in a fast line of cross fire comedy with the older man of the company as well as with Margie.... Margie sings and gives several clever readings while both children do acrobatic feats."[12]

But Margie, who would soon be a teenager, was outgrowing the act. By the end of the 1920s, Margie Reed was beginning to grow into Martha Raye, the busty woman with shapely legs, and the "child act" would have to be retired.

By 13, Margie had matured beyond the routines she had done most successfully in vaudeville, so she and her mother decided a fresh start was in order, and picked her new professional name from the telephone book. Originally gaining attention for her singing ability, the newly christened Martha Raye fell by accident into another show business specialty. "I started doing comedy when I was 15 by just lucking into it," she said. "My father was a comic, and I thought he was so good that I wanted to be one, too."[13] "At the age of 15, she began a single [act]," one journalist explained, "and this was largely because the family act wasn't very good and the family income wasn't very high."[14] Her energetic way of selling a song, often leavened with a tinge of comic flair, made her popular. According to a 1930s fan magazine account, "When she was 16, Orchestra Leader Paul Ash wired Martha an offer to join his show. The salary proffered was better than the combined earnings of the entire Reed family. Pete and Peg agreed to take a short vacation, and Martha wired her acceptance."[15]

By the early 1930s, Martha was beginning to be noticed in revues and vaudeville performances around the New York area. It was lucky timing for the young performer, as vaudeville engagements around the country were growing scarce. Part of the "Lou Holtz and Company" troupe in the spring of 1932, she received brief notice from the *New York Times* (April 19): "Martha Raye sings ... in a somewhat eccentric manner." The show overall, however, was described as "a bill which was quite often neither good vaudeville nor good revue." That summer, she was featured in the "Benny Davis and Gang" stage show as one of several "coming stars." *Billboard* (July 16, 1932) said, "Martha Raye, pretty blues singer, has a robust voice and peppy delivery." Onstage in Salt Lake City in the fall of 1933, she was deemed "an energetic blues singer whose work met favor."[16]

Years later, after her stardom was firmly established and Martha was commanding $5000 per week for her nightclub bookings, columnist Jack O'Brian recalled seeing a then-teenage Miss Raye perform with Paul Ash's swing band in the early 1930s, during the Chicago World's Fair. He recalled "a bashful—yes, bashful—little youngster whose looks could not be described honestly as beautiful, nor even as pretty, but who was cute nevertheless."[17] While on the East Coast, with Hollywood still in her future, Martha was seen as a singer in two short films, *Melody Makers: Benny Davis* (1932) and *A Nite in a Nite Club* (1934).

In 1934, Martha joined the cast of a Broadway-bound musical comedy revue, *Calling All Stars*. Comedian Jimmy Durante was originally intended as the show's headliner, but a Hollywood commitment forced him to bow out, leaving the leads in the hands of Phil Baker and Lou Holtz. The comedy was being handled by actress Ella Logan, until an unexpected incident opened a door for Martha. "I was song-and-dance," Martha recalled. "At the out-of-town opening in Boston, Ella was very sick.... [Her pianist] told me to do one of Ella's skits, a drunk woman at a Hollywood party. That did it. From then on I did comedy."[18] Thomas Mitchell, later an acclaimed Hollywood character actor, was at that time a Broadway performer also noted for his ability to write comic skits, and he was summoned to help Martha develop and polish her comedy routines in the show. As a reporter noted some years later, "Mitchell helped head Martha down her immediately explosive road to low comedy success."[19]

The musical revue opened at the Hollywood Theatre on December 13, 1934. Aside from Baker and Holtz, its other leading attractions included Judy Canova, Mitzi Mayfair (Martha's movie co-star in 1944's *Four Jills in a Jeep*), and Jack Whiting (seen with Martha in 1938's *Give Me a Sailor*). Although the show, reportedly staged at a cost of $100,000, had been well received during Boston tryouts a few weeks earlier, New York critics were less impressed. Brooks Atkinson of the *New York Times* (December 14, 1934) wrote, "Much of this revue is unsavory ... most of the material is hackneyed and tasteless." After only 36 performances, it closed on January 12, 1935.

After *Calling All Stars* closed, producer Lew Brown helped Martha land a nightclub gig with Jimmy Durante. "Jimmy was so nice—let me have good lines and helped me a lot," she remembered.[20] The two troupers became good friends, and more than a quarter-century later, Raye and Durante worked together again in the film *Billy Rose's Jumbo*.

While Martha's adult career was beginning to come together nicely, the same could not be said of the Hooper family. In September 1935, Martha's parents legally separated, and soon divorce proceedings were underway. More than one chapter in her life was coming to a close, and more than ever the family fortunes depended on what Pete and Peggy's elder daughter could accomplish.

II. Paramount Player

In January 1936, Martha began a booking at a Los Angeles club—one that would have a monumental impact on her career. "Martha Raye, late of the New York Central Park Casino, thrilled a big crowd at her opening at the Century Club last night," reported Read Kendall of the *Los Angeles Times*.[1] A few days later, Kendall noted, "B.P. Schulberg and Sylvia Sidney and Harry Cohen [sic] and a big party laughed for hours watching that hot singer, Martha Raye, and Billy Gray and Jerry Bergen, perform at the Century Club."[2]

Over the next few weeks, a stream of customers, many of them Hollywood notables, saw her act, which now showcased both her blues singing and her comedy. Among the paying customers whose visits were reported in Hollywood gossip columns were Lupe Velez and her then-husband Johnny Weissmuller, Barbara Stanwyck, and George Raft.

As it turned out, the most important visitors were Paramount Pictures talent scout Jack Votion and director Norman Taurog—coincidentally both there on the same night. Taurog was then at work on a musical comedy film, *Rhythm on the Range,* starring Bing Crosby and Frances Farmer. Taurog and Votion took note of Martha, "with a funny face, a huge mouth and an ability to wisecrack and put over a song."[3]

Being booked in a club frequented by Hollywood types could be a heaven-sent opportunity for an ambitious young performer, and discovering new talent was big business in the 1930s. As reporter John Scott noted, "Scouting operatives delve into school plays, college debating societies, nightclubs, little theaters, radio stations and even amateur performances. They appear quietly and depart just as unostentatiously. You don't know who they are, unless you are lucky enough to be singled out as a prospect for a test."[4]

Crossing paths after Martha's performance, Votion and Taurog agreed they were onto something, even though the object of their admiration was still a teenager. Within a day or so, in February 1936, Martha was offered a featured role in the latter's current film. Because *Rhythm on the Range* production was already underway, Martha was shoehorned into the plot as a love interest for co-star Bob Burns. There was little time to generate script pages for her, so material from her nightclub act was dropped in, and her musical abilities were showcased. She was comforted to find that many of her scenes were played with comedian Burns, whom she had known when she was a little girl in vaudeville. Songwriter Sam Coslow, under contract to Paramount, also provided a musical number that would become one of Martha's staples, "(If You Can't Sing It) You'll Have to Swing It," more commonly known as "Mr. Paganini."

When *Rhythm on the Range* opened that summer, reaction to Paramount's newest discovery was immediate and intense. Frank S. Nugent of the *New York Times* (July 30, 1936) was impressed by her motion picture debut, writing, "Hollywood has found a remarkable pantomimist, an actress who can glare in several languages, become lovelorn in Esperanto and register beatific delight in facial pothooks and flourishes." Nugent also took note of her ability to perform "swing music in a voice with saxophonic overtones and an occasional trace of pure fog horn."

Aware they had stumbled onto a promising new talent, Paramount signed Martha to a five-year contract in June 1936. This allowed her to buy a ten-room house in Hollywood, as well as financially support her parents— heady experiences for one who had grown up deprived of so much. "It was not many months before some people in the movie colony were snickering at the way she had 'gone Hollywood' with a prodigal display of gowns and jewels and furs. Miss Raye didn't bother about defending herself; she was having too much fun buying things."[5] Having experienced real poverty and hunger, Martha appreciated her sudden success even more than other performers might have. "No more one-night stands, no more hamburgers, no more rinsing out my one pair of stockings in the washroom," she said happily.[6]

"I used to envy folks who lived in one place—girls who could go to school and have friends," she told an interviewer in 1937. "I look back at 17 hard years in show business. Life consisted of lay-offs with little or nothing to eat, sandwiched in between engagements in strange theaters with cold, dirty dressing rooms. There never was anyone my own age to play with."[7]

After the summertime success of *Rhythm on the Range,* Paramount gave moviegoers three more chances to see Martha before the year was out, as *The Big Broadcast of 1937, College Holiday,* and *Hideaway Girl* landed in theaters. Paramount frequently gave its customers musical comedy revues, with thin storylines holding together the best singers, comics, and dancers from its contract roster. Martha more than held her own when thrown into this mix.

Rhythm on the Range had established Martha's screen persona—a brassy, clumsy, loud-mouthed yet likable girl who was looking for love, or chasing it as it ran in the other direction. Subsequent roles for the next several years would vary little from the pattern her first film had set. Although she was an attractive young woman, her comedy roles emphasized the size of her mouth and the power of her lungs. Paramount scriptwriters invited audiences to laugh at her supposedly eccentric features, but Martha claimed she didn't take offense. "I know I can't be pretty," she said in 1936, "but there are lots of pretty girls. My face, funny as it is, helps me to get laughs."[8] Around the same time, she was quoted as saying, "Go ahead and laugh. It's my face and I guess I'm stuck with it, but what of it? It got me a contract at Paramount Studios. What has your face done for you lately?"[9] Paramount publicists planted newspaper items embellishing her comic persona, such as one in which she supposedly challenged Joe E. Brown, the popular wide-mouthed comedian, to a mugging contest, to determine who actually had the bigger kisser.

At the age of 20 a Paramount contract player and budding movie star, Martha was happy to undertake whatever publicity tasks the studio assigned her. Early December found her making a whirlwind two-day tour of the Denver and Salt Lake City areas, where Paramount publicity men kept her hopping. On Monday, in Denver, she gave newspaper interviews and spoke at a Junior Chamber of Commerce luncheon; according to Paramount's Hugh Braly, "I do not know of anyone who could have done a better job than did Miss Raye, and I know that at least 300 new patrons were made a certainty on any Raye picture which plays Denver in the future." From there, she was presented to both the governor of California and the mayor of Denver, posing for more photographs to be published in local newspapers. That same day she squeezed in an appearance at a local theater, where she greeted moviegoers and signed autographs. At a local Veterans' Hospital, she addressed some 300 patients—"that being all that were able to get into the auditorium and for those that were confined to their beds, a microphone was set up and a loudspeaker system carried her speech and stories." Braly reported.[10] She finished her day's activities with a radio interview.

Though her schedule allowed little time for frivolities, Martha did make a brief stop that evening at the Denver dog pound, where she adopted a puppy "on a bet she made with Glenda Farrell," reported Braly. Her touring schedule never having allowed her to be a pet owner before, Martha took joy in being able to adopt a dog. Passing one cage, she spotted "the sorriest looking little dog she'd ever seen. He was dirty and he was sad…. [H]er heart went out to this sorrowful little creature, and she asked for him." (Back in Hollywood, after he had been seen by a veterinarian and groomed, she would learn that he was a wire-haired terrier.[11]) Tuesday found her in Salt Lake City, where she greeted employees at the local Paramount theater and gave more newspaper interviews. Afterwards, she was hustled onto a California-bound train.

Throughout, as Braly reported in a letter to Paramount's Chris Dunphy, "she was a swell sport and did everything possible to make a success of her visit."[12]

During the 1936–37 radio season, she began making regular appearances on Al Jolson's Tuesday night show, sponsored by Lifebuoy ("America's leading bath soap"). The show's original cast had her and comedian Sid Silvers supporting the star, with most episodes giving her the opportunity to belt out a song. A reporter who attended rehearsals noted, "Both of them listen attentively to [Jolson]. They admire and respect Al as well as like him—and they're both perfectly aware that he's been making hit shows longer than they've been around to hear them."[13]

Working in radio didn't much change Martha's style of performing. She delivered a song much as she had grown accustomed to doing onstage:

> She waltzes around the mike, slapping her thighs and swinging her hips in time to the music. She rolls up the sleeves of her velvet dress, tosses off a shoe, and waves her arms wildly about her. It's a singing style that Martha created when producers used to tell her they liked her singing, but her mouth was too large, and—well, she just wasn't good-looking enough.[14]

Despite the talent's best efforts, the CBS show had a rocky beginning: "The half hour seemed to lack coordination and zip. Critics throughout the country jumped on it almost gleefully, and for a time the show and Jolson's radio future hung in a precarious position.... Martha Raye, who had sky-rocketed to fame in the motion pictures, was still inexperienced in radio, and she was trying too hard to attain perfection."[15] Silvers soon left the cast, and was replaced by comedian Parkyakarkus, otherwise known as Harry Einstein, father of Albert Brooks. The announcer was also changed. After these cast modifications, the show began to coalesce, and Martha was well-received by listeners and critics alike. The show that preceded it, Edward G. Robinson's *Big Town,* grew in popularity, and the Jolson show benefitted from the exposure to a larger audience. Raye remained a regular until 1939, helping to make it one of Jolson's most successful radio efforts. She was also a welcome guest on other popular radio shows of the late 1930s and early 1940s, among them Bob Hope's *Pepsodent Show, The Rudy Vallee Sealtest Show,* and Fred Allen's *Texaco Star Theatre.*

Alongside her film and radio commitments, Martha took time to enjoy her private life as well. Not long after arriving in Hollywood, she had been romanced by dancer Johnny Torrence, and in the summer of 1936 they were reportedly engaged—for one day. "We had a spat," she explained to reporters who noticed that she was no longer sporting her ruby engagement ring. "I told him I never wanted to see him again and he said that was all right with him. So I guess that's that."[16] In January 1937, she was wearing a sizable sapphire ring, and told a reporter, "Yes, I'm engaged. But nobody was supposed

Al Jolson's not the only one who can get on his knees and belt out a number, as Martha demonstrates on his CBS radio show.

to know until the formal engagement." She identified her mystery fiancé as Jerry Hopper (1907–1988), a cousin of actress Glenda Farrell.[17] Hopper was then working as assistant to Paramount musical director Boris Morros. Columnist Leo Townsend described Martha's fiancé in a fan magazine as "a personable and intelligent young man [who is] genuinely in love with her."[18]

By the time that issue hit the newsstands, however, columnist Paul Harrison reported that the young lovebirds had "called it quits." Hopper, who would go on to have a substantial career as a film and television director (*Wagon Train*, *Perry Mason*, *Voyage to the Bottom of the Sea*), married actress Marsha Hunt in 1938.

More serious romance came into her life a few weeks later, once again on a Paramount soundstage. "One day, the famous Paramount makeup man, Perc Westmore, introduced me to his young brother, Buddy," she wrote some years later. Both Westmores were already accomplished in the family trade as movie makeup artists, along with siblings Monte and Ern. Remembered Martha, "Buddy was 20, looked like 17, and from the very first I saw him through rose-colored glasses. When he asked me for a date, I almost fainted."[19] Another Westmore brother, Frank, would write years later that Buddy "was so handsome that he became a romantic target for nearly every aspiring actress."[20] The attraction between Martha and Buddy was immediate.

She married Buddy, more formally known as George Hamilton Westmore (1918–1973), on May 30, 1937, in a civil ceremony held in Las Vegas. The couple eloped, with Martha sporting a blue chiffon evening gown. Martha was 20 years old; her new husband was still a teenager, though he gave his age as 21. Journalists noted that Martha's mother "was reported in a state of near collapse because the wedding was so sudden."[21] "They promised me they would not marry for two years," Mrs. Reed told reporters tearfully.[22] As Martha later admitted, her elopement temporarily caused an estrangement from her mother. "She was hurt at what I had done," she explained. "And it was kind of abrupt. But everything is all right now. We're living in our own home, though, which is as it should be. Marriage is tough enough without interested bystanders."[23]

Once Martha had landed a well-paying motion picture gig, her parents followed her to Hollywood, though not as a unit. Thanks to radio and the movies, vaudeville was essentially dead by the mid–1930s, and Mr. and Mrs. Reed, weary in early middle age from years on the road, were only too happy to escort their daughter through the pitfalls of a lucrative film career. Both felt they deserved some credit for Martha's newfound success, and exercised their parental privileges to remain deeply involved in her life. Their marriage of some 20 years neared its end when Mrs. Reed filed for divorce, on the grounds of desertion, in March 1937. Her complaint alleged that Peter Reed had "threatened her, necessitating the intervention of neighbors, and … received money after he had threatened to make statements about her which would have an unfavorable effect on the career of her daughter."[24]

The newly unattached Peggy became involved with a man named Pete

Balma, who pursued his Hollywood ambitions under the name Pete Bau-mann. Peter responded to his ex-wife's new romance by filing an alienation of affections suit against Baumann. Both Martha's parents and Peggy's boyfriend kicked up a fuss when Martha showed signs of incipient adulthood. Baumann, who had taken it upon himself to advise Martha in her career moves, reportedly expressed his resentment in the strongest way: "He broke into the honeymoon apartment brandishing a revolver and threatening to kill Miss Raye and Westmore for getting married and interfering with his plans."[25]

Martha's professional obligations allowed no time for the newly married couple to have a honeymoon, and despite her infatuation with her new hus-band, Buddy was often sidelined while she worked long hours. In July, she was in Boston, pulling down a reported $6000 per week for a stage show. A journalist who interviewed her there called her "a sweet kid. She hasn't yet grown up." Though screenwriters had fun depicting her as a homely young lady, her Boston correspondent wrote, "Martha is really a pretty girl, despite the fact that Hollywood makeup men would have you believe to the contrary. Something of a gasp went up in the audience when she appeared on the stage, and still later when she met the theater managers and members of the press."[26]

Whatever her motives for saying so, Mrs. Reed may have been correct when she insisted that her daughter was too young to make a good wife. "I was in the first flush of success, with professional demands on my time 24 hours each day," Martha later explained of her life as a newlywed. "Buddy expected a normal married life. When the two forces came into conflict, I was utterly unprepared to handle them. Instead, I felt crushed and broken-hearted."[27] Buddy's older brother would claim that Martha, just out of her teens, was not prepared for the expectations of a marital relationship. "His bride was so much under Peggy's influence that she slept with a gun under her pillow and an apple pie in the bed between them lest he 'try to get at her' during the night."[28] When this anecdote, which appeared in Frank's 1976 memoir, was called to Martha's attention, she laughed it off, claiming she had learned plenty about the facts of life in the course of some 15 years in and around vaudeville theaters.

Nonetheless, the first year of Martha's marriage to Bud Westmore was proving to be a rocky one. Martha later testified that, on one occasion when she arrived home from a long day at the studio, her new husband "bawled me out for being late and said I thought more of my work than I did of him. I tried to explain that I had obligations and a contract with the studio, but we had a heated argument. I tried to call my mother, but he took the phone away from me and slapped me."[29] Said Martha's maid, Eunice Patterson, "They went to bed, and I fixed them some pie to eat in bed. Then they argued all night long." Raye testified that Westmore had taken to carrying a gun on his person, and on more than one occasion threatened her with it during marital spats. She filed for divorce in September 1937, citing cruelty. Westmore's response depicted Pete Baumann as part of the problem, with his "charges that a male friend of Miss Raye's mother insisted upon being present at all business confabs and that this was 'highly objectionable and detrimental to [Raye's] career.'"[30]

That same month, police were summoned to a Hollywood nightclub where Westmore and Baumann engaged in fisticuffs. The scuffle, which took place in the club's washroom, resulted in injuries only to the unfortunate waiter who tried to break it up. Westmore downplayed it to reporters: "There was nothing to it. It was just a private fight and couldn't possibly be of any interest to the police."[31] In the wake of that incident, Martha's attorney Vincent A. Marco filed for a restraining order against Westmore. However, she failed to appear for a court date later that month to settle the matter, and Marco stated, "Miss Raye feels it is no longer necessary."[32]

With both parties agreeing to the divorce, Martha's six-month marriage was dissolved. In January 1938, columnist Erskine Johnson reported that Raye and Westmore "celebrated the annulment of their marriage by having dinner together." Many years later, she would say, "We were both a couple of kids. We didn't know what marriage was all about. I didn't, anyway. He was my first serious date, and I thought I loved him. He was a very nice attractive person. But we both realized very quickly that we were incompatible."[33] Westmore, known in later years as Bud, would go on to marry actress Rosemary Lane and serve as head of Universal's makeup department for nearly 25 years. According to his brother Frank, one factor that helped Bud secure that job was revealed when Universal executive William Goetz told him, "Anyone who could make Martha Raye look that good can't be all bad."[34] At the time of his death from a heart ailment in 1973, he was married to his third wife, Jeanne.

Fractious as her private life was during this time, Martha continued churning out Paramount films as quickly as executives could find roles for her. She appeared in four films released in 1937. One of them, *Mountain Music,* teaming her yet again with Bob Burns, represented the studio's first attempt to find out whether she could advance from featured roles to headlining her own comedy vehicles.

In September 1937, she resumed her job as vocalist on Al Jolson's radio show, which also continued to feature comedian Parkyakarkus. Reviewing the September season opener of Jolson's show on CBS, with guest star George

Jessel, *Variety* (September 15) reported that Martha's participation was disappointingly slim—"she was almost totally overlooked on [the] program caught.... Both her versatility and name value warrant more attention." Among those booked as guest stars for the show's second season were Edward Everett Horton, Louise Fazenda and John Barrymore. Listeners had the opportunity to hear Martha sing a number of songs, including "My Reverie," "Shoeshine Boy," and, of course, "Mr. Paganini." Scripts also called for her to have a running feud with Parky, in which they traded insults. Said he of Martha, "Look at her, with that mouth! Why, in her last picture she yawned and I couldn't see Bing Crosby!" In return, Martha told her co-star, "[I]f there was a sales tax on brains you'd get a refund."[35]

Studio heads watched closely to see how the careers of young contract players like Martha advanced, and what names on a marquee sold tickets. Said executive William LeBaron,

> Single picture success means that the public is going to flock to see the second picture, just as people who have read an intriguing novel want to read the sequel. But this second picture must be as good or better than the first. And the third must keep to the standard of the first two. I think the issue is not how many pictures establish a star, but how many bad pictures destroy a reputation. This is the issue which we are interested in and must guard against.[36]

Though LeBaron's comments would seem to suggest that the studio meant to take a measured, thoughtful approach to developing Martha's career, the sheer number of films into which she was shoved in the first two years of her contract left this open to question. As film historian Richard Zoglin noted, "What Paramount wasn't especially good at was nurturing and grooming its stars. In contrast to a studio like MGM, Paramount's modus operandi, all too often, was simply to throw stars into projects willy-nilly and see what stuck."[37]

For a time, though, it appeared that all was well with Martha's career at Paramount. While she was shooting *Double or Nothing, Daily Variety* (May 3, 1937) reported, "Martha Raye's Paramount contract has been renewed with a pay hike that brings her up into the four figure paychecks." Though the studio kept her busy, she also found time to make lucrative personal appearances. Her July 1937 appearance at the Metropolitan Theatre in Boston broke house records, taking in $56,000. In late 1937 Martha's growing fame was noted when she was spoofed, as "Moutha Bray," in the Looney Tunes cartoon "The Woods Are Full of Cuckoos."

Swept along by her unexpected success, Martha had little time, and perhaps lacked the perspective, to assess whether her career was being handled well. For all that she loved clowning, there was also a price to be paid for the not-always-flattering screen image Paramount had given her. Many years later, Martha's friend, actress Jane Dulo, commented, "As a woman the movie thing pained her. She was surrounded by the great beauties of her time. She was the ugly one. Even worse, she had no live audience to play to. She needed to feel its love."[38]

As Martha continued to earn sizable weekly paychecks as a movie performer, several of the people close to her continued to clamor for what they considered their fair share of the proceeds. In April 1938, Martha's father filed suit against his daughter, asking $50 a month in support, $500 for clothing and dental work, and $100 for attorney's fees. In legal papers he claimed that he and his former wife "trained their daughter for the stage and that through this training she now makes $2500 a week in film and radio work."[39] Reed asked for an accounting of Martha's earnings in the time prior to her reaching legal adulthood, valuing the training he had provided her at $50,000.

Given Martha's popularity, the lawsuit inevitably attracted publicity, some of it implying that she had enthusiastically feathered her own nest while leaving her family out in the cold. Martha admitted that she resented some of what was written. As a journalist put it, "What really hurts, she said, are the small, malicious digs one columnist takes at her about slinging away money on dozens of fur coats and other finery. Actually, she has two fur coats, a white fox and an undistinguished brown one." In fact, she claimed, she had been helping her father financially since she had first had the means to do so. "But it doesn't make you feel any better when all your pals say, 'You know, this suit is bad publicity for you, Martha,'" she added.[40] The suit was dropped shortly afterwards, though not without a commitment from Martha to help support her father.

That same month, Martha's mother announced that she had married Peter Baumann. According to Peggy, the ceremony took place on March 17, 1938, in Phoenix, Arizona, only days after her divorce became final. "Yes, we are married and very happy," she told reporters in April.[41] In a move that echoed Martha's father's alienation of affections lawsuit, Nancy C. Dixon, a stenographer from St. Louis, filed a $75,000 suit against Peter Balma (Baumann's real name), charging that "Balma promised to marry her and then betrayed her."[42] She testified that she met him on a blind date in 1935, and refused his initial proposals of marriage because she was too young.

In court, Dixon supported her claim by producing two rings, which she said had been given her by Balma, as well as a telegram in which he reportedly wrote, "Will always love you." Balma testified that he had enjoyed her companionship but "emphatically denied" that he had ever promised to wed her.[43] The case grew odder as it played out. Testimony from Dixon elicited the admission that "she was married at the time she claims Peter Balma proposed marriage."[44] She claimed to have already been planning to divorce her husband, Samuel S. Butler, whom she had married in 1936. Despite that revelation, Dixon won the initial judgment, but Balma hauled her back into court in 1939, producing new evidence. Ultimately, a Los Angeles judge ordered Balma to pay a $2500 settlement to Dixon.

At around the same time, Martha's sister Melodye came west to live with the family. Never pressed into working onstage as her older siblings had been, the teenager nonetheless craved her own chance for the spotlight. "Melodye hasn't had any experience singing or dancing," Louella O. Parsons reported, "but Martha thinks she has talent and is going to try to get her in the movies."[45] Attaining that goal proved difficult, in part because Martha's sister was not in good health. That fall, a columnist reported, "Martha Raye always takes her parties to the It Café where Maestro Bill Roberts has a telephone hook-up and sings songs to her sister Melodye, who is ill in the Good Samaritan Hospital."[46] In 1942, columnist Jimmie Fidler noted, "Melodye Raye

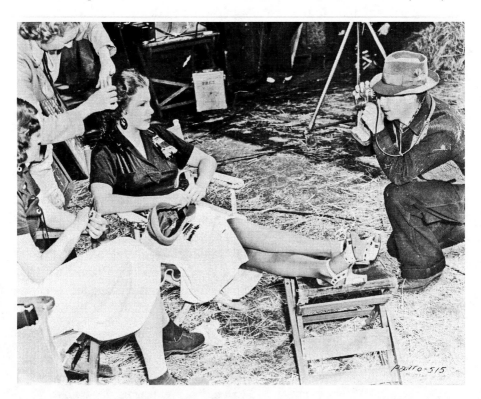

Busy Paramount player Martha is photographed by Bill Wallace (right) as she's prepped for a scene in *Tropic Holiday* (1938).

(Martha's sister), who was in a sanitarium for months, is well and joining Gene Austin's band as a singer."[47]

As she had done in 1937, Martha spent much of 1938 acting in whatever films Paramount could find to exploit her popularity. Her billing, and the size of her roles, grew, but a new effort was underway to glamorize her image. Being married to a makeup man had shown her that she could be quite pretty, and many fans noticed her curvy figure and shapely legs as well. Could Martha be made over into a woman who was funny, yet pretty enough to win the leading man in the last reel? Paramount decided to find out.

Musically, too, she was receiving encouragement and assistance from someone who strengthened her belief in her talent. On the set of *The Big Broadcast of 1938,* Martha renewed an old acquaintance with music arranger David Rose (1910–1990); they had known each other slightly some years earlier, in Chicago. As they worked to perfect her songs on the soundstage, romance bloomed.

Give Me a Sailor, which teamed her with Bob Hope, represented audiences' first look at the "new" Martha Raye. While there was still plenty of physical comedy in her performance, publicity largely centered on playing up her lovely legs, and the film story contrasted her with an atypically bratty Betty Grable. Martha, the screenwriters made clear, had come into her own as a woman who could attract and hold a man. Said Louella O. Parsons, "It's Mr. [Adolph] Zukor's plan to make a comedy starring team of Martha (who has gone glamorous on us and no longer does her loud-mouthed type of nonsense) and the very able Mr. Hope."[48]

Off-screen, of course, her allure with men had already been established, and her romance with David Rose progressed rapidly. In June 1938, columnist Harrison Carroll reported, "Martha Raye is telling friends that she'll marry her arranger, David Rose, as soon as she gets her final papers. September 28 is the day she can [be] free."[49] Within weeks, she was sporting a diamond and ruby engagement ring that Rose had given her, and asking reporters of her fiancé, "Don't you think he's cute?"[50] In September 1938, she officially announced her engagement, though she was forced to postpone the ceremony when she was summoned back to work at Paramount. Their togetherness extended to her appearances on Al Jolson's radio show, for which David provided arrangements when his wife sang.

He also helped her record 12 musical sides in 1939; many regard them as her best singing ever captured on wax. Jazz critic Will Friedwald attributes her reputation as a fine jazz artist to these recordings. "They amount to barely 35 minutes of music altogether, yet this is an overpoweringly excellent, if frustratingly brief, canon of music." These songs would be reissued multiple times over the years, including a 1955 album called *Here's Martha Raye*. Added Friedwald, "The power of her voice and the skill of her musical and comic imagination make it hard to believe that she wasn't regarded more seriously as a musical artist in her prime."[51]

Martha became Mrs. David Rose in a ceremony performed by a justice of the peace on the afternoon of Saturday, October 8, 1938, at Ensenada in Baja California. Witnesses were columnist Jimmie Fidler and his wife. Raye believed that her second marriage would coalesce in a way the first one never had, bolstered by their shared interests and his greater maturity.

After a short honeymoon, Martha returned to work at the studio to complete her latest picture, *Never Say Die,* again with Bob Hope. She was at the apex of her Paramount career, being groomed for starring roles, and billed above the promising Hope, whose radio popularity hadn't yet translated to full-fledged movie success. Even before *Never Say Die* was in the can, Louella O. Parsons reported that Adolph Zukor had acquired another screenplay for Martha and Bob Hope, *The Lady Is Charmed*. Parsons said that the Nat Perrin screenplay "will be put on the screen exactly as written."[52] But time would show a different outcome.

In January 1939, Paramount presented her with the keys to a glamorous new star dressing room, formerly inhabited by Marlene Dietrich. But the wind was soon to change for Raye, now said to be earning $2000 a week. That spring, the Al Jolson radio program was winding down. And public reaction made it clear that the image change the studio had envisioned for her wasn't panning out. "Glamour girls became the craze," Martha later explained. "Somebody thought I had nice legs and they tried to make a glamour girl out of me."[53] The planned teaming with Bob Hope went by the wayside; *Never Say Die* was their final joint effort. He went on to establish his own stardom with hit movies such as *The Ghost Breakers* (1940).

When her chance at top movie stardom came crashing down, it happened fast. Audience response to her leading roles of the late 1930s had been disappointing, and before long she was no longer being considered for the studio's better films. Martha's fan mail made it clear that audiences didn't want to see her glamorized at the expense of her comedy. While Martha continued to work in 1939, it was obvious that advancing her career was no longer Paramount's top priority. Instead, the studio seemed intent on making what money it could off her before her popularity cooled altogether. Her pictures *$1,000 a Touchdown* and *The Farmer's Daughter* were cheaply and hastily made, and looked it. The former teamed her with Joe E. Brown, with whom she had often been compared, but it was a second-rate vehicle, short on laughs. *The Farmer's Daughter,* clocking in at a modest 60 minutes, was clearly destined for the bottom of a double bill, and that's where it usually landed.

Having been delightedly surprised by her fast ascent to popularity in Hollywood, Martha was ill-equipped to understand why, in her early twenties, the tide turned just as quickly. She was beginning to learn the hard way about the less appealing aspects of life in the movies. "[W]hat really got me down," she explained years later, "was the terrible caste system where your salary was what made the difference as to who your friends were. You went around with the people who got the same amount of money you did. If your best friend lost her contract she couldn't be your best friend any more, according to *their* rules."[54]

Though she kept up the pretense that all was well, by the summer of 1939 trade paper reports were making it plain that Martha's status as a Paramount contract player was shaky. In late June, *Variety* reported "her option has been lifted." On August 5 the same publication added, "Martha Raye's Paramount contract expires Sept. 7, with actress skedded to go on week-to-week basis." As summer gave way to fall, her future in the movies was looking insecure. Clearly, her four-figure weekly salary was no longer looking like a good deal to executives counting box office receipts. Nor could she look forward to steady radio employment. According to *Variety* (July 13, 1939), Raye and Parkyakarkus "will be missing from Lifebuoy's *Tuesday Night Party* when it goes back on the air after the summer layoff."

Aside from the career troubles, there were also rumors that her second marriage was floundering. During a personal appearance in Salt Lake City, Martha exuded enthusiasm for David, her spouse of six months, saying, "This time it's permanent. He's too grand to lose."[55] In defiant response to rumors of a marital rift, Martha, according to columnist Jimmie Fidler, had her Paramount dressing room door marked "Mrs. David Rose" in huge letters. Martha's second marriage was the subject of a cover story in *Radio Mirror,* "Why Make Those Marriage Mistakes?" The article was under her byline, though it's doubtful she did more than give an interview for it; she provided advice on how two people with busy careers can have a successful marriage: "Work together when you can. When the job at hand is something you have to do alone, then do it *alone.* Don't drag the other fellow in, just to stand around and wait for you. Guard a free hour together, as though it was your last hour on earth. And don't let *anybody* intrude on it."[56] The article concluded with Martha expressing hope that she and David had made a match for life, adding, "You've no idea how hard it is to write with your fingers crossed."

When it rained, it poured. In September 1939, with her second marriage shaky, her stint as a Paramount contract player came to an end. Though her career setbacks had been reported, the final word came while she was filming *The Farmer's Daughter.* As she told the story some years later, "Right in the middle of the picture, I was making up in my dressing room one day when I heard a noise at the door, turned, and watched a pink envelope slide onto the carpet.... I was fired without even an interview or a personal word. And I had to go out and be funny for the rest of the picture."[57]

With every reason to believe that she had been a loyal and hardworking contract player, she understandably felt disrespected. Jimmie Fidler blamed the studio's handling of her for the career woes. He decried the studio's efforts to give her a star buildup, believing that Paramount could have better used her as a featured player, much as Fox used Joan Davis in the late 1930s. "Her comedy relief, thrown in here and there, was worth thousands of dollars at the box office," Fidler wrote of Raye. "But the trick mannerisms which were so funny when seen occasionally became boresome when over-emphasized by stardom."[58]

Some years later, Raye admitted that the termination, and the months that followed, were painful. "I packed my things and left. For a year, I hung around Hollywood, trying to find work. I couldn't find any. I'd invite people to a party. They didn't even have the courtesy to call and say they weren't coming."[59]

The first few months of 1940 found Martha keeping busy with radio work (she made two appearances that spring on *The Rudy Vallee Sealtest Show*) and personal appearances. She was still a popular attraction in nightclubs, so when work dried up in Hollywood she went on the road. Meanwhile, her final Paramount picture, *The Farmer's Daughter,* landed in theaters to indifferent response, and she began proceedings to divorce David Rose.

While Paramount dropped her, Martha's days as a top-billed star seemed to be over. In late March, after several months of film unemployment, Universal signed her, for a substantially smaller salary than she had commanded at Paramount. Her first assignment was a featured role in *The Boys from Syracuse,* adapted from a Broadway show of 1938–39, opposite radio comedian Joe Penner.

Despite their estrangement, Martha and David were not quick to part ways. Only weeks before they split, Louella O. Parsons reported them "apparently as happy as can be," noting that he entertained at a large party for his wife.[60] "The Martha Raye–David Rose situation intrigues the gossips," reported syndicated columnist Harrison Carroll. "Although she has filed suit for divorce, Rose still is acting as her arranger and as her accompanist in rehearsals for the Universal picture, *The Boys from Syracuse.*"[61]

In May 1940, Martha was granted a divorce on the grounds of extreme cruelty. She described Rose in testimony as "sullen and abusive," and often absent from home.[62] The couple reached a property settlement out of court, allowing the hearing to end in a matter of minutes. It soon became apparent that Rose's romantic attentions had been otherwise engaged. As soon as he was legally free to do so, Rose married Judy Garland in Las Vegas. "Judy came into David's life just after his break with his wife and at a time when they had quarreled violently," Louella O. Parsons wrote in June 1941, shortly before he and Garland married. "Rose has a gracious, charming personality. His hair is prematurely gray and he is, in the opinion of most women, extremely handsome."[63] That marriage worked out no better than his union with Martha. Rose and Garland separated in early 1943, and the couple was divorced in 1944. Some 20 years later, Martha would work amicably with Rose when he was serving as musical director on Red Skelton's television show.

Disillusioned with the way Hollywood had shown her the door, and with her marriage to Rose kaput, she was pleased by an offer from her friend Al Jolson to co-star in a Broadway musical comedy, *Hold On to Your Hats.* The show's plot concerned a radio star famous as a singing cowboy, and the adventures he encounters when he goes out West and becomes entangled with genuine desperados. Jolson was majority owner of the show, which was being mounted on a budget reported at $100,000, and quickly offered Martha the featured role of Mamie. It would mark his first Broadway appearance in ten years, and a welcome opportunity for Martha to be back in front of live, responsive audiences. *Hold On to Your Hats* featured music by E.Y. Harburg and lyrics by Burton Lane, with the book attributed to Guy Bolton, Matt Brooks and Eddie Davis.

The Broadway-bound show opened in Detroit on June 30, 1940. Also in the original cast was Jolson's estranged wife, actress-dancer Ruby Keeler, a situation which quickly turned tense. Despite their breakup, Jolson and Keeler had believed they could work together as friendly colleagues, each leaving the other to conduct his or her personal life. But it quickly became evident to the company that Jolson felt resentful toward his former wife, and couldn't resist acting it out in ways that made her and other company members uncomfortable.

Chicago performances of the show found Jolson hobbling on crutches, and later with a cane, after twisting his ankle. Nonetheless, according to *Variety* (July 18, 1940), business was strong. "Both Jolson and Martha Raye got rave critical notices." In Chicago, Keeler finally left the company, and the backstage tension eased somewhat.

Life magazine caught a preview performance in Chicago, and praised

"Martha Raye from Hollywood whose ample talents, both musical and muscular, keep the customers happy."[64] Critic Martin Yoseloff noted, "She played the role of a stagecoach driver, and was undoubtedly the most irrepressible stagecoach driver ever to explode on the American stage.... [She] brought a lot of energy and her own little cyclone of mirth to the musical."[65] After an engagement in Philadelphia, the show was deemed ready to hit the Great White Way.

The show opened on September 11, 1940, at the Shubert Theatre. Audience members paid $8.80 for opening night tickets. Aside from Jolson and Raye, the cast included Jack Whiting, who had appeared with Martha in *Give Me a Sailor,* Bert Gordon ("The Mad Russian") and comedian Gil Lamb. Among the pretty young ladies seen in lesser roles as "Dudettes" were Jinx Falkenburg and Joyce Matthews (the future Mrs. Milton Berle). Among the musical numbers in which Martha took part were "Would You Be So Kindly," "Life Was Pie for the Pioneer," "Down on the Dude Ranch" and "She Came, She Saw, She Can Canned."

Some years later, Martha credited actress Marie Dressler with the advice given in her memoirs that performers should not set limits on themselves, but take on new challenges when they were encouraged to do so. "I had never done much legit acting on the stage before," Martha noted. "Friends told me to forget it, but I paid them no heed because Jolson told me I could handle the part.... For that, I will always be grateful to Jolson's memory."[66] Taking on the challenge, Martha impressed even those who had previously been left cold by her work. Said a critic,

> As one who used to think that Miss Raye was, as a 'movie' actress, just about the most annoying comic of either sex he had ever encountered, you cannot expect to take it all back at once. I must say, however, that Miss Raye on the stage is an infinitely more skillful and likable player than she ever seemed to me on the screen, and that she adds an agreeable note of heartiness and zest to the show.... Her clowning was received with an enthusiasm second only to that accorded the great man himself.[67]

Hold On to Your Hats closed in February 1941, reportedly due to Jolson's doctor's orders to rest after a bout with pneumonia. Cast members signed a petition pleading with Jolson to continue, rather than throwing them out of work midway through the Broadway season, but to no avail. Though box office returns had been strong, the show did not run long enough to reap much profit for its investors, and Jolson was slapped with a lawsuit by his producing partner George Hale for decamping. An angry Hale, who arranged for the star to be served legal papers on the night of his final New York performance, told the press, "Jolson's not sick. He's got plenty of money and he just got tired of the show. I figure it's costing me $100,000 in profits if the show doesn't continue in New York or go on the road."[68]

Jolson did subsequently take the show on tour, but another actress stepped in to assume Martha's role. Louella O. Parsons reported in March 1941 that the picture rights to *Hold On to Your Hats* had been sold to Universal, and that Martha would reprise her stage role, but this did not pan out.

In March 1941, Martha, back in Hollywood, announced that she would marry for the third time. The new man in her life was hotel executive Neal Lang, whom she had reportedly met while on a personal appearance tour several months earlier. Not for the first time, though, Martha's marital plans would have to be arranged so as to accommodate her professional life. Her stage success, while short-lived, had served to remind Hollywood producers of her talent, and she once again found herself in demand for movie work. Warner Brothers cast her in a featured role in *Navy Blues,* with shooting scheduled to start in April 1941. While filming was underway, Martha and Lang were said to be house hunting in preparation for their new life together.

Rather than waiting until *Navy Blues* was in the can, Martha and her fiancé employed some creative scheduling.

Miss Raye ... indicated that the ceremony will necessarily have to take place with almost time-clock precision. Her wedding party will board a Western Air Express plane at 7:30 tomorrow night, which means Miss Raye will have to leave a set at Warners, greasepaint and all. The couple will go to Las Vegas, obtain a marriage license around 9:30 p.m., and drive about ten miles to the El Rancho Vegas, smart resort, for the ceremony.[69]

She married Lang in Las Vegas on May 25, 1941, at midnight. The bride was 24 years old, the groom 38. Upon her return to Hollywood, Martha's marriage was celebrated with a party at Slapsie Maxie's nightclub, emceed by Ben Blue. Jack Oakie, Jackie

Martha with husband Neal Lang, in 1941. By year's end their marriage had fallen apart.

Gleason and Ann Sheridan, all from the cast of *Navy Blues*, were in attendance.

Within weeks, however, a familiar pattern began to emerge. Rumors were swirling that there was trouble in the marriage. In August, Dorothy Kilgallen quoted a letter from Lang, who wrote, "To the contrary, we are very happy, re-arranging an old ranch house that we recently took in Encino. It's large and livable and we are having lots of fun puttering around, when circumstances permit Martha to get away from the studio."[70] The project underway was *Hellzapoppin'*, a frenetic Universal comedy adapted from the long-running stage hit starring Ole Olsen and Chic Johnson.

Her *Hellzapoppin'* role was so demanding that columnist Ken Morgan reported her "in a state of near collapse after working for weeks with Olsen and Johnson." Expected in Chicago to take part in a charity baseball game, an exhausted Martha reportedly "entered Cedars of Lebanon Hospital ... under an assumed name [to be] worked on by doctors who will get her in good enough shape to attend the game."[71] That fall, Lang, making a career switch, took a sales position in the radio department of General Amusement Corporation in New York. Martha was hard at work supporting Abbott and Costello in *Keep 'Em Flying*.

By late 1941, the predictions of a separation between Martha and her third husband had come to pass. In December, Jimmie Fidler reported that a reconciliation was expected. Dorothy Kilgallen reported that Martha and Lang "are twosoming about town, but they say she's turned down his offers of reconciliation."[72] Many years later, with the benefit of hindsight, Martha said, "I should never have married Neal.... I did a great injustice by marrying him. He's such a nice man [but] I was torching for Dave."[73]

Neal Lang joined the war effort and was sent overseas. In the spring of 1942, columnists were writing about Martha's involvement with a new man, dancer Nick Condos (1915–1988). Born January 26, 1915, as Nicholas Kontas, Nick, along with brothers Steve and Frank, were popular as a dance troupe, the Condos Brothers, whose tap routines were much admired. They had appeared not only in theaters but in several films, especially at 20th Century-Fox, where studio boss Darryl F. Zanuck was a fan. Martha and her new beau met when they shared the bill on a vaudeville engagement in 1941. Louella O. Parsons reported in May that Martha had told "intimates" that she and Nick "would consult a preacher soon."[74] Other reporters noted that she was making bookings for personal appearances so as to coincide with Nick's work schedule as much as possible.

Martha announced her impending marriage in June 1942. "I sure love that man," she said. "I'll go wherever he goes to be near him."[75] That might be easier said than done, since Condos expected to be called up for military service at any time. Nor was she yet free to wed, as her marriage to Lang was still in the process of being dissolved. Meanwhile, a personal loss came when Martha's sister Melodye died on November 6, 1942, at the Los Angeles area sanitarium where she had been a patient for some time. Never having made major inroads toward a performing career, Melodye's short life came to a difficult end at the age of 22.

As World War II escalated, Martha unexpectedly plunged into what would become her unofficial second profession for many years to come. She was invited to take part in a USO tour overseas, entertaining troops, and eagerly accepted. The tour paired her with actresses Kay Francis and Carole Landis and dancer Mitzi Mayfair. In time, Martha would estimate she had traveled some 100,000 miles by airplane, and another 50,000 by train, car, or Jeep in the process. In late November, Martha and her fellow USO entertainers gave a command performance at Windsor Palace for Queen Elizabeth and the royal princesses, with an audience composed of some 1500 British servicemen. By then, Nick was urging her to come home. In December 1942, her agent Abe Lastfogel telegraphed her at the Savoy Hotel in London, advising that he had been keeping both Nick and her mother updated on her activities while she was overseas. In addition, he noted, "Working on couple pictures for you. Planning in addition [to] pictures that you will continue doing work you now doing."[76]

In her memoir about the tour, Landis would write, "Martha is a born comedienne. Everything she says, her every move, electrifies the audience, whether she's telling a story, singing a song, or merely wrapping her leg around the microphone."[77] Early 1943 found the tour wending its way to Africa, where the accommodations and the work were anything but glamorous. Said famed war correspondent Ernie Pyle, "These gals work themselves to a frazzle. They travel dangerously. They live and work under mighty unpleasant conditions. They don't get a dime. They are losing a lot and they have nothing to gain—nothing material, that is."[78]

Though both Martha and her estranged husband Neal were involved in the war effort, their marriage was essentially over. In January 1943, Louella O. Parsons reported that there was no possibility of a reconciliation "even though she did see [Lang] when she went overseas to entertain the service men."[79] "They're still the best of enemies," concurred Parsons' rival Erskine Johnson.[80] By long distance, while she was in London, Martha filed papers to end the marriage. In later years, however, Neal Lang would be one of the few men Martha felt had not exploited her financially, and she would speak kindly of him.

By that time, Nick was urging Martha to come home from the front, both from a desire to get married as well as his concern for her safety. One writer reported,

> Martha Raye met with dangers more than once. She was blown out of bed during an air raid; she was in a plane when it was fired on; she spent three days in a slit trench and saw "plenty of blood." These people have given shows in prize rings, submarines, by candlelight. They do their own laundry when there is water. They are subject to Army regulations and they live on Army rations. And they are doing these things either for no pay at all, or for a fraction of the money they would be making if they stayed at home.[81]

(According to the Office of War Information, they received only $10 in expenses per day.)

Not surprisingly, movie and radio audiences heard little from Martha Raye in 1942, and she continued entertaining the troops into the early months of 1943. If she was doing so at the expense of advancing her career back home, she seemingly didn't care. She found the work enormously fulfilling, and the soldiers sensed her genuine commitment and regard. Journalist Inez Robb noted, "In the winter of 1943 in North Africa, Martha Raye could have run for president on a straight GI ticket and won in a walk."[82]

When she did find her way home, plans were percolating to make a feature film based on the wartime experiences of Martha, Kay Francis, Mitzi Mayfair and Carole Landis. The film would ultimately be released by 20th Century-Fox in March 1944 as *Four Jills in a Jeep,* accompanied by a same-name book carrying Landis' byline. Though the film substantially glamorized the ladies' experiences, patriotic audiences responded kindly to it.

Safely back home, Martha worked to resolve the lingering issue of her third marriage. In May 1943, she told Louella O. Parsons, "I talked with Neal when I was in England and he agreed to give me my freedom. You see I never got a divorce and you cannot divorce a man in service unless he agrees. I am going to marry Nick just the minute I get my freedom."[83] Her efforts to secure a divorce would drag on throughout the summer.

In September, the Condos Brothers were signed to be featured in Martha's new picture *Pin-Up Girl.* As filming got underway at 20th Century-Fox, she was trying to obtain a divorce in Mexico, with the grounds listed as incompatibility. "Neal and I have been separated for a long time and he is agreeable to the divorce," Martha said. "It's just a question of locating him and getting the papers signed."[84] Once married, Martha and Nick hoped to honeymoon overseas, entertaining soldiers. By December, however, Louella O. Parsons reported that Martha believed Lang was intentionally stalling on signing the necessary papers.

In December 1943, Martha began a ten-week personal appearance tour, opening at the Roxy in New York City. Without notifying the press, she married Nick Condos in Newark, New Jersey, on February 22, 1944. Not until March did she publicly acknowledge published reports that she and Nick were married. "Sorry I can't reveal when or where [the marriage took place] until we return home," she telegraphed from Baltimore.[85] The likely reason for the vagueness became apparent less than a month after the wedding announcement was issued, when Martha and Nick announced that they were expecting their first child. On July 26, 1944, while *Pin-Up Girl* was in wide release, Martha's only child, daughter Melodye, was born. The new arrival, weighing six pounds, six ounces, was named in honor of Martha's late sister. Nick professed to the world that he and his wife were delighted by the new arrival.

Martha's daughter would experience a tumultuous upbringing. Many years later, journalist Raymond Strait quoted a bitter Melodye as saying, "I arrived at the height of my mother's film career. She never hesitated to let me know that my birth ruined it all for her."[86] Publicly, however, Martha doted on her new daughter, who was christened at a Greek Orthodox church in Los Angeles that fall.

Less happy news came in January 1945, when Martha and her new family were the victims of a burglary. The thief, cutting a screen at their home while they were away, relieved Mr. and Mrs. Condos of fur coats and jewelry with an estimated value of $10,000. Among the items stolen was a bracelet inscribed "To Martha Raye, a great artist, from Al Jolson."

On March 16, 1945, another loss came when Martha's brother Buddy, 26, died of tuberculosis. He had been admitted to a Los Angeles hospital shortly before his death. He, too, had had his share of difficulties, having been taken to court by ex-wife Ruth in 1941 for being delinquent on his alimony payments. Buddy told the judge he had been working only four nights a week at $3 a night, and could not raise the $20 monthly payment.[87]

In the summer of 1945, Louella O. Parsons reported that Martha's fourth marriage was "working out very well. Nick has become her manager and will abandon his dancing profession to devote time to the promotion of Martha's career."[88] In his new role, Nick told Parsons that Martha "has turned down dozens of offers for both stage and screen, she's so happy just being a mama."[89] Nick played his final engagement with the Condos Brothers in September, afterwards devoting himself fully to managing Martha as well as his brother, Steve, as a single act.

Martha signed with club owner Lou Walters to play a 15-day engagement at the Latin Quarter in New Orleans, opening in September 1945. However, according to *Variety*, the unexpected closing of war plants and resulting unemployment caused nightclub business to tank. The Ritz Brothers, who preceded her at the club, played to small audiences, leading club owners who had recently taken over the establishment to attempt to cancel Martha's expensive engagement. The William Morris Agency, representing Martha, vowed to collect on their client's behalf or take up the matter with the nightclub performers' union.

In late 1945, William Morris was pitching Martha to be the star of her own weekly radio variety show, written for her by radio veteran John P. Medbury. According to *Variety*, the agency was asking $10,000 per week for the series, her first since appearing opposite Al Jolson some years earlier. A radio show would have been an ideal gig for the mother of a youngster, as it would not require extensive travel or lengthy work hours. However, the project never came to fruition.

Already there were rumblings of trouble in Martha's marriage to Nick, a familiar pattern to those who had been following her private life. In December, Dorothy Kilgallen was among the first to report rumors of a trial separation, noting that Martha and her husband were being seen around town separately.

Nick's work as Martha's manager was also apparently complicating the relationship between her and her longtime agent Abe Lastfogel. In March 1946, informed that Martha might not be renewing her representation with William Morris, Lastfogel leaped into action. In a letter sent to Martha in Chicago, where she was fulfilling a nightclub engagement, he wrote, "We have been together since the time you started to grow up, and you have had a relationship with me that only a handful of people have had insofar as my affections and the handling of their careers are concerned." He concluded by advising Martha that he expected to hear her decision on the matter "from you and you alone," and commented, "Not that I don't have any regard or respect for Nick, but this is something between us and us only, and our relationship insofar as your career is concerned transcends Nick." Lastfogel copied Nick Condos on the letter, writing in a cover note, "I urge you not to interfere or use your influence in any way to disturb the relationship that has existed between Martha and myself since she has been thirteen years old."[90] Ultimately, Lastfogel prevailed, and would continue to represent Martha into the 1950s. However, Condos would continue to act as her manager.

What seemed to be a big career break came in April 1946, when columnists reported that Charlie Chaplin had chosen Martha for the main female role in an upcoming film, then titled *Comedy of Murders*. The film, Chaplin's first since *The Great Dictator*, was expected to be in production by the end of June. Pleased as she was to be offered a plum role, she was initially unnerved—"sick with fear," as she put it—at the prospect of working with the great Chaplin. "I asked myself, 'I'm going to try to be funny in front of this man, this *genius*?'"[91] She was delighted to find that Chaplin was completely supportive of her work, and readily accepted his direction as she enacted the character of Annabella, the wife whom the lead character could not seem to shake. By the time principal photography was completed on *Monsieur Verdoux,* as the film was ultimately titled, Martha had reason to be optimistic about its prospects and a possible upward surge in her movie popularity.

Shortly after wrapping *Verdoux,* Martha filed for divorce from Nick, citing mental cruelty. She requested no alimony, saying she was self-supporting, but wanted full custody of daughter Melodye. "The Martha-Nick quarrels have been no secret to Broadwayites for months and months," reported Dorothy Kilgallen that fall, "but whenever a columnist printed that they were tiffing, they always gave out with the 'But, honey, we've never had a cross word!' routine."[92] Noted Hollywood attorney Greg Bautzer was engaged to represent Martha in the action.

Then, within days of filing the paperwork, Martha apparently reconsidered and called off the divorce action. "I think we'll stay separated for a while," she told columnist Harrison Carroll, clarifying that her decision did not mean a full-out reunion. "Of course, we are friendly and may go out together. And Nick still is my manager, you know." Carroll predicted, "Martha is just being cautious. And the full reconciliation will take place any minute."[93] Together, they were developing new projects. "Martha Raye will play herself in her autobiography, to be filmed independently by herself and husband Nick Condos. Frank Tuttle will direct, from a script on which Miss Raye collaborated."[94]

Under Chaplin's guidance, Martha had delivered one of her best film performances. *Monsieur Verdoux* would prove to be a highlight of Martha's motion picture career, but the controversy that surrounded the star-director could not be overcome, and the picture was a box office disappointment upon its release in 1947. She was disappointed by the response but treasured the experience. "I learned so much from that man," she would say years later. "He taught me that, if a woman is going to play low comedy, the better she's dressed, the funnier she'll be. In other words, if a woman in a designer gown and diamonds falls on her face, it's funnier than when a woman in baggy clown pants does it."[95]

Another milestone in Martha's life came with the death of her mother on October 20, 1947. By then Peg Friedman, the former Peggy Reed, "had undergone an emergency appendectomy." Martha and Nick flew in from Boston, where she was playing an engagement, upon being notified.[96] Her father Peter Reed, who resurfaced occasionally in gossip column items that had him on the verge of marrying some pretty young woman, passed away in October 1959, leaving Martha as the last surviving member of the Reed-Hooper troupe.

The advent of television, among other factors, had the motion picture industry struggling by the late 1940s. The failure of *Verdoux* did nothing to encourage engaging Martha for other films, though she could still pack in audiences as a nightclub performer. In 1948, Martha accepted an offer to perform in England, with her appearance at the London Palladium the highlight of the trip. "I was afraid my type of comedy might be a bit too boisterous for staid English people," Martha said. "What a relief to find out I was wrong! I mugged and clowned all over the place and they came back for more."[97] Not even a torn ligament kept her out of action. While unable to be on her feet, Martha "worked in a sitting position on top of a piano, being carried on and off by her husband, Nick Condos."[98]

Wanting to bring some stability to their lives, Martha and Nick purchased an ownership interest in the Miami Beach Five O'Clock Club, a Florida nightclub where she had frequently performed. Their plan was to use Miami Beach as their home base, traveling elsewhere as film work or other bookings necessitated. When she wasn't headlining at the club, she was often present as emcee, while Nick managed the business details. In 1949, they sold their California home to Doris Day and her husband Marty Melcher, as Martha firmly believed her Hollywood career was over.

Actor and musical director Richard Wall—later to be known for his featured role in *Parting Glances*—met Martha in the late 1940s, when his parents took Richard, then five, along on an evening of nightclubbing in Miami Beach. "You don't normally have a five-year-old kid in a nightclub," he recalled, but in his case there was another child present—young Melodye Condos, who was there with Martha and Nick. The two youngsters danced together, and Richard had his photograph taken with Martha. Introduced to the star, Wall found her "not at all like her stage personality—very warm, very friendly." Visiting her backstage nearly 40 years later when Martha was performing in an Atlanta production of *Everybody Loves Opal*, Wall found that the star still remembered the incident well, and greeted him cordially.[99]

In clubs, of course, she could deliver material that would never be permitted on the radio or movie screens. Catching a New York performance in 1948, *Billboard* (March 13, 1948) remarked, "If there is any artistry in selling blue material, then Martha Raye is an artist. She's got that leer plus an innocent stare down to a fine art…. It's a combo of gags with blue snappers, really funny bits of biz, plus a delivery and salesmanship out of the top drawer."

Even when she tried to relax, things almost inevitably went awry for Martha. In November 1950, she was hospitalized at the St. Francis Hospital in Miami Beach, diagnosed with pneumonia. Martha eventually spent so much time at this particular hospital that she would show her gratitude by gifting the sisters who worked there with a large television set, and saying, "Good night, sisters," on her NBC television show.

III. Television Star

In the early 1950s, Martha and Nick were still living in Miami Beach. However, the newly emerging medium of television was ideally suited for visually oriented comics, as Milton Berle displayed with his popular NBC show *The Texaco Star Theater*. Martha became a favorite Berle guest, invited back for repeat appearances, and there was discussion of a regular series for her. She soon found herself traveling north more than she had anticipated.

"It was rugged," she recalled of that period, when they were dividing their time between TV engagements in New York and operating their Florida club. "Nick and I'd close the club in Florida at 3 a.m., hop a plane for the four-hour ride to New York. I'd sleep in a bed for three or four hours and then rush to my first rehearsal. After each telecast, we'd fly home and open the club again. The pace was killing."[1]

Not helping matters, according to one observer, was the amount of alcohol she consumed, combined with her dislike for flying. Betty Shain, an aspiring performer befriended by Mr. and Mrs. Condos, recalled an incident when Martha received a last-minute phone call from Nick, telling her to take the next plane for New York so that she could appear at a benefit. "We had about five drinks and Martha swallowed a couple of sleeping pills because she was very nervous about flying. By the time she boarded the plane, she was smashed and could hardly walk." Only moments after taxiing away from the landing strip, the plane made an about-face and one passenger was abruptly ejected. "The door opened and out staggered Martha. She did not sober up for three days.... Nick was furious."[2]

In the summer of 1951, Martha was on stage in Los Angeles, playing the lead role in a production of *Annie Get Your Gun*. "It's one of those things that come along once in a lifetime," Martha said of the opportunity to play Annie Oakley. "Every girl who has played Annie feels the same way."

Miami Beach was still her home base, though she had begun to make inroads into television. She explained,

We own the Five O'Clock Club there, Nick runs the business and I play hostess and entertain. You see, we save money that way. We have steady customers, something few clubs out here [in Hollywood] boast, and most of them are loaded—with money—which makes things real nice.... I can fly to New York in a very short time, and there's plenty of television work.[3]

Commuting between Miami, New York and wherever else engagements were booked, along with a regular schedule of nightclub, radio and television performances, left Martha little time to be a hands-on mother. In the early 1950s, according to Melodye, she was enrolled in a convent school at the insistence of the family doctor, who could see that she was not receiving proper care at home.

Martha's success with TV guest appearances led to an offer to be one of the rotating hosts of NBC's *All Star Revue* (formerly titled *Four Star Revue*), which aired on Saturday nights. She appeared in four segments of the show's 1951–52 season. Her segments attracted both critical acclaim and strong ratings. Though executives and sponsors aware of her freewheeling nightclub work—and fondness for risqué ad libs—had some hesitation in putting her on TV live, she adhered to the rules of the new medium.

Off-camera, however, her impetuous nature occasionally landed her in trouble. In February 1952, Five O'Clock Club patron Francis Serpico, an out-of-towner vacationing in Miami Beach, was arrested in the wee hours of the morning after Martha charged that he had assaulted her. Accounts of what happened varied. Some early reports indicated that she became angry when Serpico heckled her during a performance. However, according to later police reports, Serpico and his female companion had tried to gain access to Martha and Nick's club after it had closed for the evening. Martha went to the door and an argument developed. "He called me a dirty name, and I couldn't take that," she later explained. "I slapped him and he popped me right back in the mouth with his fist."[4] Serpico, a television salesman from Long Island, New York, charged in turn that several onlookers, including Nick Condos, had beaten him. The involved parties were ordered to appear before a magistrate the following Monday morning. However, after a wave of publicity, Martha and Nick apparently thought better of pursuing the matter, and she telephoned Miami Beach police asking that the charges against Serpico be dropped.

In the spring of 1952, Martha signed on for another season of live variety shows on NBC-TV. Columnist Erskine Johnson noted, "High brass is all smiles about her cleaned-up humor and willingness to listen to TV directors."[5] October found her once again hospitalized in Miami Beach. Looking forward to a relaxing vacation in Jamaica, she fell seriously ill shortly after arriving. "I went to bed dreaming of long days in the sun," Martha recalled. "By dawn, I crawled out of bed, a red-hot flame licking my insides." A local doctor diagnosed the problem as a kidney ailment. "They put me on a stretcher, stuffed me with pain-killers, and we flew to Miami."[6] She was diagnosed with an intestinal disorder, but soon went back to work.

With videotape not yet available, variety shows like Martha's were broadcast live, and there was plenty of room for mishaps when camera movements, use of props, or the strenuous physical comedy went awry. Seasoned performers like Raye, ready to deal with whatever might happen during a wild and woolly broadcast, were perfectly suited to the work. Looking back years later, she noted, "We never heard of cue cards. We learned the shows and did them. I don't see how any sketch comedians can work well with the cards. Personally, I couldn't read them because of my eyes."[7] Added Nick Condos, "Doing an hour TV variety show is like shooting a full-length movie in a week. Except when you do the show for real, you can't have any retakes."[8]

As Martha's film career had amply demonstrated, she could wring laughs out of second- or third-rate material, drawing on her repertoire of gestures, grimaces and pratfalls. However, she was not always the best judge of her own work—as many stars are not—and TV performers quickly learned that new material was needed much more often than it had been in nightclubs.

Early in the tenure of her NBC show, she was fortunate to be the beneficiary of a talented writer-director who would guide her show to both critical and ratings success. Nat Hiken (1914–1968) was assigned to her *All Star Revue* segments in 1951. Under Hiken's leadership, Martha's NBC variety shows differed from the norm. Rather than presenting a hodgepodge of unrelated sketches and musical numbers, Hiken developed a format that presented a storyline in each segment. In essence, each show was a musical comedy, with an original script punctuated by songs (mostly popular standards) that accentuated the action.

One of Hiken's best-remembered contributions to the show was his casting of retired prizefighter Rocky Graziano (1919–1990) as Martha's boyfriend. Active as a fighter since 1942, Graziano was winding down his boxing career. In no way a trained actor, he took the job with some hesitation, unsure he could meet the demands of learning and reciting lines. Hiken, however, had a fondness for using untrained actors, believing that he could draw on their natural personalities to bring laughs from the audience. With enough coaching, Graziano was able to read the lines written for him with a charmingly rough quality that made him seem a suitable on-screen love interest for Martha, who impulsively named him "Goombah."

Graziano made his debut on the September 1952 season opener, along with guest stars Cesar Romero and opera singer Risë Stevens. During rehearsal, he made the crew laugh pronouncing Miss Stevens' name as "Rise," rather than "Reesa," and even more so with his reaction to being told to toss a salad. As he later reported, "I pick up the whole bowl an [sic] fling the whole bowl and salad way across the stage against the wall. Took a good ten minutes to stop everybody from laughin [sic]. They all pissin [sic] in their pants."[9] Both gags made it into the finished show, and it was soon apparent that roughhousing Martha had a new leading man.

Publicly, he would say, "It took me a half hour to learn how to act."[10] Martha reportedly told him he'd be fired if he enrolled in dramatic training. What he lacked in training, however, Graziano made up for with effort, and his willingness to be coached. He recalled one scene in which all he had to say was, "But, Martha." During rehearsals, he realized that his reading of the line was unsatisfactory. "I found me an empty room near the rehearsal studio and went to work on the line because I knew I didn't give it the right kind of lift. So I stood in there and said the two words it must have been a thousand times to the wall. When the show went on, I got a good laugh."[11] The retired prizefighter earned a reported $50,000 per year once he settled in as a regular on Martha's show.

Raye and Graziano enjoyed each other's company off-screen as well, though not in a romantic sense (Graziano was a married man of some years). More than 25 years later, he remembered with appreciation her ability to think funny even without a script, as evidenced by her encounter with a drug-store perfume clerk. Listening doubtfully to the saleslady's enthusiastic pitch for the product's miraculous qualities, Martha said, "If it can do everything you say, how come you [sic] still working here?"[12]

Martha's television popularity had her agent, Abe Lastfogel, pitching her to movie studios. In the fall of 1952, Lastfogel wrote to Nick about "a plan for Martha and another girl to work on the order of Marie Dressler and Polly Moran, though of course on a much younger level" as a comedy team. The idea had been pitched to executives at Warner Brothers, Lastfogel reported, "and Jack Warner and Milton Sperling reacted very strongly to it."[13] Martha's agent continued to shop the idea around various studios, but didn't succeed in making a deal. Martha would not make another motion picture for almost ten years, and television would continue to occupy the lion's share of her professional time.

Martha and Nick made a good team professionally, but their marriage again showed signs of strain as her television success grew. As the season's work on *All Star Revue* wound down, their arguments grew more intense. Although columnist Hy Gardner reported that spring, "Friends believe that time will heal the Martha Raye-Nick Condos marital fracture,"[14] by July she was in a Miami courtroom, ready to eject her fourth husband from her life. Circuit Judge George E. Holt granted her a decree that "permanently enjoined Condos from molesting Miss Raye, entering her residence, place of employment or visiting her at any place whatsoever." She testified about an incident in early May when he was "so violent that she was forced to leave home and seek refuge at the home of a neighbor."[15]

But Martha and Nick would by no means live separate lives. Greatly respecting his ability to protect her professional interests, she continued to employ her ex-husband in that capacity. "Nicky is a better manager than a husband," she told columnist Gardner in 1954. "I'd rather be his client than his wife. He takes more than a ten percent interest in me that way!"[16] For his part, Nick would later recall Martha telling him, "I've had three husbands before you and none of them showed me such consideration." He concluded, "We just happened to click."[17]

With her marriage to Nick ending, Martha rented a 150-year-old house on the outskirts of Westport, Connecticut. Aside from a maid and a secretary, she was kept company by a dog, Maggie. "Maggie hasn't a feller either," Martha joked. "We've been thinking we ought to do something about it for all of us. Maybe set up a fruit stand across the way, or a diner, or sell canned beer. That way one of us might catch a live one."[18] From her home, it was an easy commute into New York City by train for daily rehearsals.

Writing about her 1953–54 *All Star Revue* season opener, syndicated columnist John Lester called her "the most thorough performer of all the comediennes on television at the moment," finding her outranking Lucille Ball, Imogene Coca (*Your Show of Shows*) and Joan Davis (*I Married Joan*).

> Her tremendous sentimental appeal and often amazing projection of warmth and heart, in addition to a seemingly rubberized face and a fine sense of comedy timing, certainly make her the greatest clown of that foursome…. A point by point comparison would prove, I think, that Martha does nearly everything the others do as well or better than they and then goes on to do many things most of them can't do at all.[19]

As *Life* magazine described it, Martha spent days at a stretch

> prancing violently … grimacing, shouting songs, never stopping for a breath until she has scarcely a pant left and never sitting down to rest until she is nearly prostrated. Cast as an addlepate who gets into impossible situations, she works herself out of them more by physical vehemence than by brain power.[20]

Asked by *TV Guide* where she got her prodigious energy, Martha said, "I don't know where it comes from. But I'm glad I've got it. Back in the war, when I was overseas singing for the GIs in the ETO [European Theater of Operations], I picked up a yellow fever bug and almost conked out for good. But the old vitality pulled me through somehow."[21]

By 1953, Martha was earning a reported $15,000 for each of her telecasts. Hers had become the most popular segments of *All Star Revue,* which had tried and dismissed several other rotating performers during the past couple of seasons. Overall, the show's ratings were not strong enough to be picked up as a weekly series for the new year. However, the network needed a monthly substitute for *Your Show of Shows,* which filled a Saturday night slot three weeks out of four. *All Star Revue* had become, for all practical purposes, *The Martha Raye Show,* and in early 1954 that became its official title. Observing rehearsals for an October 1953 telecast with Martha, Graziano and guest stars the Gabor sisters, columnist Hal Boyle said the star "bounces around the room like a tennis ball," laughing merrily when she missed a line. "She puts out as much in rehearsals as she does on the show itself," observed a bystander, "and when the show is over she always throws a big party for everybody in the cast. Everybody—not just the big shots."[22]

The results impressed columnist Jack Gould, who wrote, "If Martha Raye had a regular weekly television show this season the chances are good that she would be pressing Lucille Ball for top honors among TV's comediennes."[23] Others thought her monthly shows as good as or better than the critically acclaimed one for which they were filling in. Among her television fans was comedian Jack Benny. "Well-wishers gathered around after his show Sunday afternoon to congratulate him. He brushed them aside with the comment, 'Yes, but did you see Martha last night? Her show was the greatest.'"[24]

Having begun *All Star Revue* with four hour-long segments per season, she was now doing twice as many shows, for 90 minutes at each outing. At the height of its popularity, however, members of the company became aware of tension growing between Nat Hiken and his star. According to camera director Grey Lockwood, "The word was out that it's this guy behind those words and those ideas—she's a great performer but where would she would be without Nat? She apparently couldn't handle it too well. It bugged her."[25] Though insiders were well aware of Hiken's importance to the show, it was still Martha who had her picture plastered on the covers of national magazines, enjoyed the adulation of fans, and received the star treatment from NBC. In charge of the show's comedy, Hiken also had occasional clashes with the star and her manager, Nick, when they insisted on devoting more airtime to her musical gifts.

Despite the backstage drama, the show continued to receive accolades, notably Emmy nominations for Martha two years running. In 1953, she was nominated as Best Comedienne, competing with Eve Arden (*Our Miss Brooks*), Imogene Coca (*Your Show of Shows*), Joan Davis (*I Married Joan*) and Lucille Ball (*I Love Lucy*), the latter ultimately taking the prize. A year later, Martha was in the running for Most Outstanding Personality at the sixth annual awards show. The all-encompassing category found her competing with the likes of Bishop Fulton J. Sheen, journalist Edward R. Murrow and *Dragnet* creator-star Jack Webb. At the ceremony, not yet broadcast nationally, Murrow was the winner.

With Nick's help, Martha was inveigled into an appearance on Ralph Edwards' popular *This Is Your Life*. Each segment of Edwards' show represented the culmination of weeks of planning, tracking down and inviting guests from the subject's early life, and usually a ruse to get the star there on the night of the broadcast, unaware of the spectacle about to occur. Told she was needed at the NBC studio to record a promotional film, she acquiesced, but almost failed to arrive by showtime. "She wouldn't wait for Milton Berle to pick her up," Condos was heard fretting backstage. "She kept saying she knew where the Center Theatre was, she didn't need to wait for Milton."[26]

A *Life* magazine photographer was backstage during rehearsals for Martha's mid–April broadcast with Charlie Ruggles and captured two notable incidents. One was the mishap that befell Martha when simian guest star J. Fred Muggs (familiar to viewers of NBC's *The Today Show*) took a nip at Martha's arm. The chimp likewise bit Martha's stand-in, causing the scene to be reblocked to place the star at a safe distance from him.

More significantly, the photographer captured photos of Martha alongside the newest man in her life, 30-year-old Edward Thomas Begley (1924–2011), a member of the dancing troupe featured on her show. Once the show had been successfully beamed to the nation on April 17, 1954, Martha kicked into high gear with her plans to take her fifth trip down the matrimonial aisle.

Martha married Begley on April 21, 1954, in Arlington, Virginia. (They had originally made plans to be married in Maryland, but were stymied by the 48-hour waiting period required in that state for marriage licenses.) The couple borrowed a wedding band from friends in order to proceed with the ceremony. Dr. Arthur L. Maiden, a retired minister, officiated, with talent scout Carl Eastman and his wife in attendance. "This time it's for good," Martha was overheard to say.[27] Over the next few days, rather than honeymooning in seclusion, Martha and her new husband would be seen out and about frequently, celebrating in various New York nightspots.

Fans—some of them wrongly believing she'd married the actor Ed Begley—were eager to learn more about her new husband. A journalist described Martha's Begley as "good-looking, soft-voiced, with the rather shy manners of an Ivy League college senior." Of his relationship with Martha, Begley said, "We've known each other a long time, you know, two or three years, at least. And then, one evening … we decided we had to be married right away. You know, not in three days or even the next afternoon, but right *now*, before we could change our minds or get bogged down in red tape or new shows."[28]

Change was the order of the day that spring. The difficulties between Martha and Nat Hiken over creative control of her TV show became a moot point, when he accepted a lucrative offer from rival network CBS to develop new comedy shows. Though at least one columnist reported that the network hoped to lure Hiken *and* Martha away from NBC, ultimately she stayed put.

The Martha Raye Show returned for another season in the fall of 1954, now airing on Tuesday nights, and still using the basic format Hiken created. Her new head writers were Norman Lear and Ed Simmons, previously in the employ of Dean Martin and Jerry Lewis, with Dickson Ward now the show's producer-director. The cosmetics manufacturer Hazel Bishop sponsored Martha's show. Not long into the season, however, Lear took over as director in addition to his writing chores. Like his predecessor, Lear sometimes clashed with Nick Condos, whom he would describe some years later as "a great guy, but a pain in the ass." Lear quickly realized that Martha came across best when her most extreme instincts were tempered, but found that Condos gave her contradictory advice. Much as he grew to dislike Condos' input, though, Lear would say of Raye, "I adored her."[29]

"We had been in rehearsal just one day at Martha's first show when we got into this directing business," Simmons later explained. "Martha phoned us that night and said she couldn't stand the way things were going and would we take over? Norman had done some Little Theater directing and we both had absorbed a lot of TV technique, so we gave it a try." Of their concept for the show, Lear commented, "We take a believable premise and stretch it as far as it will go. To be funny, a thing has to be real."[30]

The change in writers didn't escape critics' notice, and her 1954–55 season opener, with Wally Cox, drew mixed reviews. *Billboard*'s Jane Bundy (October 9, 1954) thought the script, which cast the milquetoast Cox against type as a serial killer, in dubious taste, but added, "Martha Raye personally gave a wonderful performance that finally established her right to be called the funniest and most versatile lady clown on video today."

In September 1954, Martha filed suit against a Florida man after a nightclub brawl in which she claimed he hit her over the head with a whiskey bottle. The results, according to the legal papers, were "blurring eyesight, fainting spells and insomnia." Newspaper accounts reported that Begley was present, but did not take part in the row.[31] Mr. and Mrs. Begley tried to present a more dignified image when they appeared as Edward R. Murrow's guests on an October installment of CBS's popular interview show *Person to Person.*

An anxious Nick telegraphed Martha in November after she failed to appear for a scheduled television rehearsal, writing, "Darling you must come in today where is the trouper that we talked about last night." In the event of a no-show, he warned her, "NBC refuses to pay for all the people who are waiting for overtime etc. and you will be libel [sic] for this huge amount of money.... Your personal life has never had anything to do with your career before, don't let it start now at this late stage."[32]

That same month, Nick wed 22-year-old fashion designer Barbara Caplin in South Carolina. Nick's second wife, 17 years his junior, was the daughter of renowned boxing manager Hymie Kaplan. The wedding took place at the Aiken home of probate judge E. Glenn Willis, with only a few friends in attendance. Apparently Nick still harbored some resentment about being displaced in Martha's personal life. Publicly, he'd said, "I know Ed and like him. He's a fine boy. If he can make Martha happy, that's all that matters."[33] However, in private, according to Barbara, he referred derisively to Begley as "her faggot husband."[34]

Unexpectedly, her new stepmother proved to be a good friend to Melodye Condos, understanding better than her parents the attention that a growing young woman needed. While the young bride's first meeting with Martha nearly took a wrong turn when a bystander innocently mistook Barbara for teenaged Melodye, the new Mrs. Condos realized that her predecessor was trying to be supportive of the relationship. "If he gives you any trouble," Martha told Barbara Condos, "come to me. I can keep Nick in line."[35]

Continuing with another hectic season of 90-minute shows, as well as adjusting to her new marriage, proved stressful for Martha. December found her hospitalized in Miami Beach shortly before a club date there. She was ordered by her doctor to spend a few weeks in a Cincinnati rest home, and Milton Berle stepped into her booking. "The object of placing her there was to assure absolute quiet," said Dr. Ralph Robbins. "She was on the verge of a nervous breakdown."[36]

According to her friend Berle, it wasn't surprising that many of TV's top comedians wore themselves to a frazzle, given the demands of live performances. Berle, who himself had once suffered a collapse that prevented him making a scheduled appearance on Martha's show, claimed, "[T]he grueling ordeal of tickling 30,000,000-odd funny bones per week—and waiting to see if you've launched a guffaw or laid an egg—gives us all the screaming meemies."[37]

Around the first anniversary of Martha's marriage to Ed Begley, columnist Earl Wilson reported that Martha and her fifth husband were "now living more apart than together. He's mostly living with Westport friends."[38] Called for comment, Nick Condos refused to confirm the reports, but Martha herself told a journalist who tracked her down at home, "Oh, he lives with neighbors. Do I expect him back? Oh, sure, I hope it will be soon."[39]

Martha's show was lucrative for NBC, and executives watching the prevailing TV trends wanted her to relocate to the West Coast, where she could do it on film, as many others were now doing. "They asked me to film mine and move it out to Hollywood, but not me. I like my New York and my Connecticut."[40] Fifteen years later, she had not forgotten how quickly she became persona non grata in Hollywood once her Paramount contract was dropped, and found it difficult to shake her distaste for the way the business operated on the West Coast.

Network executives placed her under long-term exclusive contract in 1955. As one fan magazine noted, "All the big stars are angling for long-term deals, eager for some

Martha does a little math to see how much her new NBC-TV contract is worth to her.

security and knowing that TV popularity can't last forever." According to that account, the deal "guarantees her at least $25,000 per program. And if she doesn't work after ten years, she gets retirement money."[41] Welcome as the money would be, she appreciated the gesture just as much. "Can you imagine what this 15-year contract means to me—the security of it after all those years of struggling, wondering what the next club date would be and how long this radio show would last? If there would be another movie? I'm just afraid I'll wake up."[42] In truth, Martha was about to be rudely awakened from that dream of lifelong security.

The Martha Raye Show was renewed for another year, scheduled for 13 shows during the 1955–56 season, up from ten she'd done the year before. Poised for her greatest success yet on TV, she instead found everything she had worked to achieve slipping away. For some of this she herself could be held accountable; however, factors beyond her control also came into play.

The season opener in September 1955 featured young African-American spelling champion Gloria Lockerman, who had received widespread publicity for winning $16,000 on the popular game show *The $64,000 Question*. The show went smoothly, and attracted some nice critical notice. However, according to Norman Lear, Martha and Tallulah Bankhead's spontaneous displays of affection for the girl during the show's closing moments resulted in letters of complaint to the sponsors, and marked the beginning of the show's downfall. Though Lear noted that sponsors, then and later, were inclined to overreact to a small amount of mail, he recalled Charles Revson's admonition, "I'm sure [Martha] can be entertaining without being so physical and unwomanly."[43]

Not much better received was the telecast with guest Douglas Fairbanks, Jr., as reviewers continued to complain about mediocre scripts. The *New York Times*' Jack Gould wrote, "Miss Raye's show was not in very good taste. The comedienne was led astray by a prolonged sketch. Its writers sought to find humor in pouring whipped cream over an extra's head, in inundating Miss Raye with endless streams of soda water, in throwing left-over food around the stage and in using an electric chair for a blackout. The proceedings were most unamusing."[44] Once again, according to Lear, his attempt to direct Martha into a more subtle approach was undermined by Nick Condos' back-seat driving, and the sponsor who wanted his star to be more "womanly" saw her being something else altogether.

The sponsors' fretting was amplified as the ratings race began to play out that fall. Competing with *The Martha Raye Show* was a new CBS situation comedy created for Phil Silvers by Martha's former head writer Nat Hiken. Originally titled *You'll Never Get Rich*, it found Silvers playing his wily Sergeant Bilko character on a peacetime military base. It took a little time to be found by viewers, but soon showed signs of becoming a popular hit. Silvers was initially handicapped by his 8:30 p.m. time slot, following a quite different type of military show, *Navy Log*, which forced comedy fans to switch channels at the half-hour to sample his show. But a few weeks into the season, Silvers' show moved to 8 p.m., and the tide began to turn. Those who had predicted Silvers' quick demise against the opposition of Berle and Raye began to see that *The Phil Silvers Show* (as it was soon renamed) was winning new viewers every week. By early 1956, it was a bona fide hit that hurt the ratings of everything that played against it.

It certainly didn't escape the notice of those in Martha's camp that it was Hiken who had engineered this popular new show, endangering her popularity. Nick Condos said resentfully, "Phil Silvers got our writer, that's what Phil Silvers got. He got Nat Hiken. Phil Silvers got the drum-beaters pounding their tambourines all over town for his show. We got nothing."[45] In March, Dorothy Kilgallen reported that there might be a thaw in the "feud" between Raye and Hiken. "Along Broadway, insiders are saying the talented script writer has come up with a sizzling new format for Martha—an idea so appealing she's in a mood to forget the differences that caused their bitter parting."[46] But Hiken's Phil Silvers show soon went on to even greater success, and Martha's television reputation was hung out to dry.

Martha's marriage to Edward Begley was over except for the legal paperwork. By late 1955 rumors were flying that Martha was romantically involved with Bob O'Shea, a local policeman. She had reportedly been receiving threats, which she believed came from her estranged husband, and had engaged O'Shea as a bodyguard after being dissatisfied with the level of protection local law enforcement could offer. Her new employee happened to be wed to his high school sweetheart.

In the early months of 1956, Martha was facing not only falling ratings, but personal publicity that could hardly have been less favorable. Press reports indicated that Begley was attempting to serve her with a divorce summons, while in the meantime she had been slapped with a $50,000 alienation of affections lawsuit from O'Shea's wife Barbara. Mrs. O'Shea's suit charged that Martha had presented her husband with expensive gifts and enticed him with the prospect of being involved with a famous TV performer. Adding to the tension of the situation, and the negative publicity for Martha, was the fact that Barbara was a new mother. O'Shea's father-in-law William Farr told a reporter for the Westport newspaper, "He's just a mixed-up kid—a good, clean-cut American boy." Added Barbara's mother, "We all tried to talk to him, but it didn't do any good. The day Barbara came home from the hospital, he packed his clothes and left, saying he was in love with Martha Raye."[47]

Martha's attorney Shirley Woolf characterized her client as "completely shocked" by Mrs. O'Shea's allegations, saying, "She has never had any romantic alliance with Mr. O'Shea." As to Mrs. O'Shea's claims that Martha had plied her husband with gifts, Woolf said, "On or around Christmas time Miss Raye had a big party for family and friends and, being the nice person that she is, she invited all people that worked for her, with their wives, and gave everybody gifts."[48]

The controversy resulted in O'Shea being placed on unpaid leave from his job with the Westport police. In a letter he wrote to the town selectmen, asking to be reinstated, he said, "The alienation suit is based upon a misrepresentation of all the supposed facts gotten together by families involved.... This is strictly a domestic situation, and there is nothing whatsoever about it concerning Martha Raye."[49] O'Shea claimed that he had been estranged from his wife for some time. He told a reporter that he had tried to make an explanation to Mrs. O'Shea, but that family members prevented him from reaching her by phone.[50]

Newspapers published a photo of Martha seemingly out on a date with O'Shea at the Stork Club. As published, Martha claimed, the picture was misleading. O'Shea, by her account, was on duty as her bodyguard. Cropped out was her "real boy friend, Al Riddle," from Las Vegas, seated on the other side of her. "I met him out there when I was playing in one of the gambling joints. Al's a dealer at one of the tables. We liked each other right off, and he came to New York several times to visit me." Proffering a copy of the unaltered photograph, Martha said, "See—I wasn't sitting alone in the Stork Club with O'Shea, as you can plainly see."[51] In fact, a relationship between Martha and Al Riddle had been reported in gossip columns at least a few times. Hedda Hopper had written a few months earlier that Martha would be divorcing Begley "to pave the way to her wedding of Al Riddle of the Las Vegas set."[52]

Ultimately, lawyers—and Martha's checkbook settled the differences between her and Mrs. O'Shea, though Raye's Westport lawyer, Leo Nevas, said the $20,000 figure cited in newspaper accounts was an exaggeration: "The purpose of the settlement was to enable the plaintiff to obtain court costs, counsel fees and other expenses."[53]

The tumult caused NBC to advise Martha's management that she was in violation of the morals clause in her contract. Although the bad publicity stemming from Martha's private life was blamed for the cancellation of her NBC show that spring, its falling ratings would have been reason enough for the sponsor to withdraw.

In May 1956, Begley filed for divorce. A process server presented her with the papers at the Brooklyn hotel where she was staying, and according to Nick Condos she accepted them willingly. But Begley's attorney Walter Pick said that he had been trying to deliver the papers for some time. "I wouldn't say she was trying to evade it," Pick commented, "but the process server showed up at several of her TV shows and only got as far as backstage."[54] Pick said his client and Martha had been living apart for about a year. According to Dorothy Kilgallen, Begley had been seen around town in the company of an old girlfriend, a singer, since his marriage fell apart. As columnists gleefully noted, the only legal reason for divorce under New York law was adultery. Pick declined to say whether O'Shea or anyone else would be cited as co-respondent in Begley's suit against Martha.

Martha finally responded publicly by issuing a statement read to reporters by Shirley Woolf: "Begley left me a year and a half ago, and I haven't filed for divorce because I have no desire to be free. I have no new romance, nor do

I intend to get married again."[55] In October 1956 the onetime Mr. and Mrs. Begley obtained a divorce in Juarez, Mexico, on grounds of incompatibility. Although initial reports stated that neither she nor Begley was present at the proceedings, Dorothy Kilgallen later wrote, "Ed was there all right, but when he checked into the Hilton Hotel he used a *nom de guerre*."[56] In mid–June, O'Shea was restored to his position as patrolman with the Westport police. Ironically, on his first shift, he was dispatched to respond to a fire alarm call at Martha's residence, after she fell asleep in bed with a lighted cigarette.

That same month, with her TV show kaput, Martha announced plans to give up her Westport home. "I've got nothing against the state or the people of Connecticut," she said, "but in the two years I've lived there there's been nothing but trouble. I've had three fires in my home and I face an alienation of affection suit."[57]

Though she was eager to put Westport behind her, that did not mean that she would cut Bob O'Shea out of her life. In July, O'Shea, at Martha's urging, resigned from the police force in order to accept a full-time position as her bodyguard. He would later testify that he had been promised an annual salary of $12,000 for the work, which consisted of "services rendered as a personal bodyguard ... on a 24-hour, seven-day a week basis. I also performed certain secretarial duties ... answering correspondence, keeping some of the accounts ... chauffeuring and miscellaneous other things."[58]

In Las Vegas that summer, Martha was again seen in the company of Al Riddle, as reported in Louella O. Parsons' widely syndicated column. However, asked a few days later if she was on the verge of marrying Riddle, she said flatly, "I'm not going to marry anyone. I've been married three times [sic] and that's plenty! Al left the day after I arrived here to go east to see his mother who has been very sick, and when he returns I suppose I'll see him."[59]

The travails in Martha's personal life, combined with the loss of her TV series, sent her plunging into despair that summer. *Variety* (August 15, 1956) had the star "reported near death in St. Francis Hospital [in Miami Beach] after swallowing 20 sleeping pills." Her physician Ralph Robbins told the press Martha "was in very poor condition" and "had been despondent for the past week."[60] Nick Condos' life was also not serene. His 24-year-old wife Barbara was admitted to a Miami hospital in December 1956, reportedly in a coma after an overdose of sleeping pills. She had consumed, according to her doctors, "40 to 50 barbiturate capsules," in what was described as a "suicide attempt, her second in the last two years."[61]

With the television door closed to Martha at the moment, her agent and manager pursued work for her elsewhere while she recuperated. *Variety* (August 22, 1956) reported that she would "star in *Boffola*, new revue scheduled for Broadway production this season by Harry Rigby and Harry Jacoby." Plans called for rehearsals to get underway in November, followed by a six-week road tour that would prepare the show for a February 1957 New York opening. The show failed to come together. Producer Rigby would make a second attempt in July 1957, announcing Martha as the star of *For Amusement Only,* an adaptation and Americanization of a London hit show. Ultimately, however, it would be another ten years before Martha set foot on a Broadway stage.

Although Martha would not have a regular television series in the 1956–57 season, it was widely assumed that her prized NBC contract entitled her to hefty paychecks regardless of whether or not she actually worked. *Variety,* however, declared that the contract would pay out at its full amount only if the star was on the air in a sponsored show. Martha's salary, as reported publicly, was said to be exaggerated for publicity purposes. "There will, of course, be some deferred payments, per contractual agreement, but an NBC spokesman was inclined to think that if she earned $50,000 from the web this season it would be a lot."[62] However, she continued to be in demand as a TV guest star, offered $7500 that fall for an appearance on columnist Walter Winchell's new show.

Insiders continued to speculate that Martha was not well. Syndicated columnist Marie Torre quoted an anonymous "colleague" as saying,

[Raye] spends hours in front of her television set, and when she does go out it's usually to a nightclub. Once in a while, she makes a trip to Florida, where her friends aren't exactly members of the elite. She likes to be with them because she knows she's a little above those people, and that makes her feel like a lady.

Another observer claimed Martha "consumed a bucket of sleeping pills" to cope with her life as it was at the age of 40.[63]

While Martha had initially resisted the idea of relocating to Hollywood and working in a filmed series, the cancellation of her New York-based variety show, as well as her many unhappy experiences while living in Connecticut, caused her to reconsider. In the spring of 1957, she was signed to play the lead in producer Jess Oppenheimer's revival of *Baby Snooks* as an NBC-TV filmed sitcom. Oppenheimer, signed to a lucrative pact with the network after five years as writer-producer of *I Love Lucy,* had written for the radio Snooks, Fanny Brice, in the 1940s. According to preliminary reports, "The format of the situation comedy series concerns a television performer who creates a 'Baby Snooks' character. She draws upon the imagination and activities of her sister's daughter for material, and in return the child imitates her aunt."[64]

The pilot script was written by Oppenheimer and comedy writer Henry Garson. Actor Hanley Stafford, the radio "Daddy," was set to reprise his role, with child actress Ruthie Robinson cast as the niece. "I am very thrilled about *Snooks*," Martha said that spring. "I only hope people aren't prejudiced and get the idea that I'm trying to steal Fanny Brice's stuff. I guess I sound like her every now and then, but I'm really playing it my way, not hers."[65] Filming the pilot in California, Martha took along Bob O'Shea in his capacity as bodyguard, though she continued to deny that they were personally involved.

Although Dorothy Kilgallen reported in May that early viewers of the *Snooks* pilot had called it "sensational" and a "sure winner," the series failed to find a place on the 1957–58 NBC schedule. According to syndicated columnist Hal Humphrey, "a series of mishaps plagued Martha Raye right afterwards, and apparently NBC was afraid to try to sell the series with the star in what could be called a shaky status."[66]

One such incident took place in mid–May, when she was rushed by ambulance to New York's Doctors' Hospital. Nick, as her manager, tried to downplay the importance of the incident. Condos told the press his ex-wife was merely run-down, and having a checkup, though skeptics pointed out she had been rushed to the emergency room from her hotel in the wee hours of the morning. Said Condos, "I was with her all evening and the reason we hired an ambulance instead of calling a cab is that the doc had given her a sedative earlier and she was half asleep and we didn't want to get her too wide-awake again."[67] Martha's manager noted that she had upcoming bookings on Steve Allen's TV show and at the Sahara Hotel in Las Vegas, and anticipated that she would be able to honor the engagements after a suitable rest.

As her private problems became public knowledge, Martha was angered by CBS's plans to stage a live drama called "The Mother Bit," which to her ears (and Nick's) sounded too much like an unsympathetic and exploitative retelling of her life. The story centered around a songstress-comedienne whose ex-husband dies, leaving her to inherit custody of their teenage daughter. Sensitive to the implication that she had neglected her daughter, Martha lashed out when she learned of the TV drama. Reacting somewhat defensively to the complaints, "Mother Bit" star June Havoc said, "This amounts to rather a pathetic admission. I'm sorry she sees herself as that type of a woman…. I'm surprised Miss Raye would stand up and say, in effect, she is the insensitive, unattractive person in the play."[68]

When the drama aired in June 1957 on *Studio One Summer Theatre*, critical reaction suggested Martha needn't have worried about its impact. According to *Daily Variety*'s June 12 review, "Had Miss Raye and Condos kept quiet, odds are none would have associated her with the characterization." *Variety* (June 12) added, "The hullaballoo was more interesting than the play itself."

In August, Dorothy Kilgallen reported that final preparations for Raye's stage vehicle *For Amusement Only* hinged on a star who was hesitating. "Although they've raised more than $150,000 from angels who are enthusiastic about Martha's talent, she hasn't actually signed the contract—and at last reports she was refusing to inscribe the precious autograph until every last one of her terms was met."[69] Although her TV career was running at less than top speed, the deal to star her on Broadway never came to pass.

On the whole, Martha was working less than she might have preferred in the latter part of 1957. With neither the Broadway show nor the proposed TV sitcom having coalesced, she was depicted by columnist Marie Torre as having little more to do than putter around the house and watch TV. "Ironically," Torre noted, "Miss Raye cannot talk about her place in television today because the industry has no place for her." Putting the best face on it, Martha chatted with the columnist about the "relatively easy winter" she expected to spend decorating her new house.[70]

Though Martha continued to insist that there was no romantic relationship between her and Bob O'Shea, they did not lose contact. O'Shea was among the entourage accompanying Martha on a trip to Europe in the summer of 1958. Asked by reporters if the two of them were romantically involved, she gave a shrug and said, "Yes and no."[71] Not until October 1958 did Martha confirm that she would marry O'Shea. According to Raymond Strait's interview some years later with daughter Melodye, Martha did not go into the marriage blindly. She had supposedly retained the well-known private investigator Fred Otash, who frequently provided dirt to the notorious 1950s gossip magazine *Confidential,* to check into O'Shea's background. What came back, according to Melodye, was "a full and damning report" of the man she described as "a junkie."[72] It apparently did nothing to dissuade Martha from going forward with her matrimonial plans.

Martha married O'Shea on November 7, 1958, in Teaneck, New Jersey, at the home of Mayor August Hannibal. Her friend Joan Crawford served as matron of honor, with Crawford's fourth husband, Alfred Steele, as best man. What was intended to be a small ceremony was soon disrupted: "A battery of nearly two-score cameramen who found a chink in Mayor Hannibal's front door and marched in fired away all during the ceremony.... When the lensmen invaded, Mayor Hannibal shrugged his shoulders and went on with the business anyway."[73] After the wedding, Martha set up her new husband in business with a detective agency. The business venture drained a considerable amount from Martha's bank account, but did not ultimately achieve success.

As the 1950s came to an end, television work for Martha continued to be sporadic. Steve Allen's show was one of the few booking her during 1958 and 1959, and she would make a dozen appearances. His writers knew how to present her effectively, and she trusted their judgment. In February 1959, Dorothy Kilgallen reported that Martha was finalizing a deal to portray the late movie actress Marie Dressler in a television "spectacular," but the project never came to pass. That same month, a scheduled guest appearance on *The Garry Moore Show* unexpectedly turned into a substantial career break for a young performer named Carol Burnett. After Martha left a Friday rehearsal complaining of a sore throat, Nick called the producers on Sunday to say she was seriously ill, and unable to appear in the live broadcast on Tuesday evening.

With the clock ticking, and no time to secure a big-name replacement for Martha, Burnett, who'd previously appeared on Moore's CBS daytime show, was rushed in to take Martha's place. Given just two days to learn the sketches and songs, Burnett made such a strong impression on the Moore company and on viewers that she was hired later that year to be a series regular. After the show went off the air, an exhausted Burnett received a bouquet of roses sent by Martha and a telephone call pledging to never be sick again, saying, "You were too good."[74] Several years later, her own stardom firmly established, Burnett would return the favor when she welcomed Martha for multiple guest appearances on *The Carol Burnett Show*. The two would also record an album together in the 1960s.

In August 1959, the *New York Post* broke the story that Martha's sixth marriage was coming to an unhappy end after only nine months. Ironically, it was once again Martha's ex-husband, Nick, in his capacity as her manager, who was left to explain to the press, "It's all over between them. They have separated with the intention of divorcing."[75] Acting on Martha's behalf, Shirley Woolf instructed O'Shea to vacate the couple's home. In the aftermath of the split, both claimed to be the victim, Martha reporting that O'Shea had stolen a substantial amount of furniture from her home upon his departure. O'Shea, in turn, reported that she had never paid him the salary promised to him as a bodyguard in 1956, and owed him more than $20,000 for his work prior to their marriage. The failure of her sixth marriage seems to have left Martha uninterested, at least for some time, in future matrimonial efforts. Her divorce from O'Shea was not finalized until well into the 1960s.

In September, she was once again hospitalized for a supposed rest cure, after dropping out of a Boston production of the musical comedy *Bells Are Ringing*. Officially, the diagnosis was a kidney ailment; said columnist Dorothy Kilgallen, "But those who know her best fear that she's suffering from one of her periods of deep depression; only a few weeks ago she was acting like the gayest woman in Florida, staying out long after daybreak and making brief brush-off jokes about her most recent marital failure."[76]

The October 1, 1959, death of her father, Peter Reed, out of the limelight for many years, attracted little public attention. His passing in Miami rated a brief mention in *Variety* (October 7, 1959), noting his "ex-vaude" status, and that he had lived in Florida for the past ten years. An even shorter item circulated by the Associated Press appeared in some newspapers around the country. Neither published item carried any comment by his famous daughter.

IV. Moving Target

Martha took to the road as the 1960s dawned, accepting well-paid engagements across the country, usually in musical comedies. Her assignments often found her stepping into roles other actresses had originated on Broadway, in shows like *Anything Goes*, *Goodbye Charlie*, and *Wildcat*. Her television fame insured that audiences eagerly bought tickets to see her in person.

In December 1960, Martha was the victim of a robbery in Chicago, where she was playing an engagement of *The Solid Gold Cadillac* at the Drury Lane Theatre. Her apartment, which the theater provided to visiting stars, was robbed of furs and jewelry valued at $43,500. It was not the first time such a break-in had taken place; Paulette Goddard and Gypsy Rose Lee were victims in similar incidents earlier in the year. In a surprising twist, FBI agents recovered her lost furs, and one belonging to a guest of hers, while watching the shop of local furrier David Kaufman. "Agents said that Kaufman was seen entering his place of business … carrying a suitcase resembling one taken in the Raye burglary and learned that it contained the three coats." Since the alleged thief was not believed to have broken any federal laws, the case was turned over to the local police.[1]

Doing *Separate Rooms* in Massachusetts in the summer of 1961, Martha told an interviewer that she had largely given up nightclub work, which she now found dull. She was dividing her energies between live theater and TV guest spots. A bundle of energy onstage every night, she said she did "absolutely nothing" during the day to compensate.[2] As always, Martha deviated from the script when inspiration struck—or when the unexpected happened. During one performance, when a scene was punctuated by the sound of Martha's pet poodle barking, she called out, "Quit padding your part!"[3]

That fall, however, after a nearly 15-year hiatus, an unexpected opportunity arose to put Martha back on movie screens. In the upcoming light musical comedy *Billy Rose's Jumbo*, which would star Doris Day, Jimmy Durante, and Stephen Boyd, she was offered the role of Madame Lulu, Durante's longtime girlfriend, with the script affording her chances to display both her comic and melodic gifts. Production was expected to be underway by January 1962, with former choreographer Charles Walters chosen to direct.

She was also said to be in discussions with Broadway producers about playing the lead in a musical comedy adaptation of well-known madam Polly Adler's 1953 book *A House Is Not a Home,* aimed for the fall 1962 season. (That project ultimately morphed into a 1964 film with Shelley Winters assuming the role of Adler.)

During production of *Jumbo* that spring, Martha was once again hospitalized, this time in Hollywood. After failing to return from what she told her daughter was an evening stroll, she was found unconscious on a lonely stretch of Malibu beach. Although her stomach was pumped upon arrival at Malibu Emergency Hospital, her physician Morris Katz "denied she had taken an overdose of pills," and the treatment was said to be a "precaution."[4]

Dr. Katz said Martha had taken "a couple of sleeping pills," which he had prescribed to help her sleep after suffering a painful fall on the *Jumbo* set.[5] As was usually the case when Martha suffered a collapse while working, the diagnosis, at least for public consumption, was exhaustion. After a couple of days under observation in the hospital, she was permitted to rest at home.

Though many saw Martha as loud, boisterous and indefatigable, some observers looked deeper and recognized the contradictions that existed within her. Observing her in action on the *Jumbo* set, journalist Lloyd Shearer wrote, "Essentially she is a small, shy, quiet, tender, sincere, gullible, middle-aged woman. She is sweet, gracious, unknowledgeable, a trusting sucker for any sob story ... frequently victimized by hustlers quick to recognize her omnipresent hunger for love and companionship, and to capitalize on it."[6] Shearer reported that she had become friendly with actor Joe Waring during production of *Jumbo,* and some thought he was a candidate to become Martha's seventh husband. But she would not remarry for many years to come. In fact, she had not yet taken the trouble to finish the process of divorcing her previous spouse.

Though she was long divorced from Nick, they still remained part of each other's lives, and in the life of their daughter, now nearly 18. In early 1962, Dorothy Kilgallen reported "an unexpected tug-of-war" involving Melodye and her parents. The teenager, who had shown signs of inheriting her mother's singing talent, wanted to pursue a show biz career. Her father preferred that she get more education in Europe, while Martha wanted her back in school in California.[7] A few weeks later, Kilgallen reported that Melodye "seems to have won her fight for parental permission to go into show business," noting that she was on the verge of recording an album for Decca. "Subconsciously, Martha must have known her daughter would wind up in a glamorous profession; good night, she gave her a mink coat when she was about five years old."[8]

Studio executives had high hopes that *Billy Rose's Jumbo* would be a popular hit with family audiences of the 1962 holiday season. However, while it drew some nice notices upon its December release, with Martha often singled out for praise, movie patrons failed to flock to it as expected, and its considerable production costs were not offset by ticket sales. She would not make another film until the close of the decade.

In the meantime, theater engagements and television guest star stints took up the slack. Publicly, she professed herself satisfied with her bookings. "Once a month is enough on television," she said. "You wear out your welcome. I don't care how good you are. You can't bat 1000 every week in an hour show. Maybe you can do it in a half hour situation comedy. That's what I want to do."[9] NBC executives noted what an effective guest star she was on the shows of Perry Como, Andy Williams, Red Skelton and others, and were said to be looking at a sitcom format for Raye, but she would not make it back on the air with a weekly series role for some years to come.

One TV guest shot turned into a family affair: Martha and her daughter were booked for a joint appearance on Red Skelton's highly rated CBS show. Was the daughter expecting to have a career trading on her famous mother? "I don't think I have to," Melodye told columnist Joseph Finnigan in 1963. "It's the same old story. I would rather that an audience liked me for myself, not because I'm somebody's offspring. My mother is a great talent and a good mother. But I think I have enough to make it on my own. My mother feels that way."[10] Melodye held down a job as a secretary at the William Morris Agency while pursuing her professional ambitions. That same year, she married Edmund L. Lancaster. The marriage, which would produce Martha's only grandchild, would last until 1972, when the couple divorced.

Despite her success, Martha hadn't forgotten her own humble show biz beginnings. Asked in 1963 what would make her angry, she replied, "People who mistreat waiters, bartenders, busboys…. I was a waitress myself, in Chicago, and I could tell you some stories about mistakes I made. I see a waitress being mistreated and I burn."[11]

In the spring of 1964, it appeared that Martha would be returning to weekly television when CBS gave the green light to *Bill and Martha*, a sitcom in which she would co-star with actor William Bendix (*The Life of Riley*). Though the show was said to be headed for the network's fall schedule, and was presented to potential sponsors, CBS decided against going forward a few weeks later. The reason apparently had little to do with Martha, but rather (according to several columnists) the network's concern over Bendix's health. The actor, who would pass away in late 1964, filed a lawsuit over the cancellation, while Martha was left to seek work elsewhere.

With her series comeback tabled, Martha made plans to embark upon a tour of *Wildcat*, the musical comedy that had starred Lucille Ball on Broadway. She would star as Wildcat Jackson, with Melodye as her sister. When Melodye learned she was pregnant, she had to drop out. In Atlanta, *Wildcat* played an outdoor amphitheater designed to hold an audience of 2000. Audience member Richard Wall remembered that it was disrupted in mid-scene by a noisy airplane flying overhead. "She would stop the show and shake her hands at the clouds.... She never missed an opportunity to get a laugh, ever."[12]

Columnist Dorothy Kilgallen spotted an interesting duo out on the town in New York one night that spring: Barbara Condos and Neal Lang. As Kilgallen noted, there was "nothing unusual in that, except for the fact that Barbara used to be married to Nick Condos, who used to be married to Martha Raye, who at various times was married to Nick and Neal."[13] Although Lang was part of Martha's past, Nick was still very much involved in her life, both professionally and personally. Periodically, gossip columnists would report that the couple might reunite, since they seemed to spend so much time together. But on paper, at least, she was still Mrs. Robert O'Shea.

As spring gave way to summer, Louella O. Parsons reported that Martha was eagerly anticipating the birth of her grandchild. "I can hardly wait to start spoiling it," she told the columnist.[14] She was delighted with grandson Nick when he arrived in January 1965. Still, her relationship with Melodye remained less than ideal. An unidentified "friend" told an interviewer, "Melodye had her own career for a while. Maggie wanted to run it. She was like a child who never wanted to grow up. Melodye made her constantly face the fact that she had grown up."[15]

In early 1965, Raye was headlining a Los Angeles stage production of *The Solid Gold Cadillac*. The *Los Angeles Times'* reviewer acknowledged her talent, but decried her approach to the script.

> Miss Raye, whose flexible face is one of nature's antic triumphs, upsets the whole structure of the Howard Teichmann–George S. Kaufman comedy in roughly five seconds. It takes her just about that long to start ad-libbing. The rowdy actress has incorporated her nightclub act into this Broadway fable.... Don't expect to see *The Solid Gold Cadillac*.... Not the real thing, anyway.[16]

The lingering issue of Martha's sixth marriage was still in limbo. In the summer of 1965, a letter from a law firm in Germany advised that O'Shea wished to dissolve the union. "Mr. O'Shea has recently received his discharge from the U.S. Army and has established residence in the Frankfurt area where he intends to remain indefinitely," said the correspondence from O'Haire, O'Connor & Jones. A response from Shirley Woolf advised that her client had "no objection" to proceeding with the divorce, provided that O'Shea assumed the cost of the legal fees, and eventually Martha was once again a single woman.[17]

Martha continued to be a popular guest on musical variety shows of the 1960s. Readily able to perform sketch comedy, appear in song-and-dance numbers, and exchange banter with the host, she was repeatedly booked on *The Carol Burnett Show*, *The Red Skelton Hour*, *The Andy Williams Show* and *The Hollywood Palace*. She also appeared on the shows of Judy Garland, Jerry Lewis and Milton Berle.

On stage, one of her most frequently performed shows was a favorite called *Everybody Loves Opal* by John Patrick (1905–1995), better known for the successes *The Hasty Heart* and *The Teahouse of the August Moon*. Although the show, starring Eileen Heckart, had flopped on Broadway in 1961, closing after only 21 performances, it was an ideal piece of lightweight entertainment on the dinner theater circuit. Martha played the title role of Opal Kronkie, a middle-aged woman living in a junk-filled mansion at the edge of the city dump. Three young crooks find their way to her home, plot to insure her heavily and then arrange for—and profit by—her speedy demise. Good-hearted, cheerful Opal, described in Patrick's script as "a birdlike little woman in her late fifties," not unlike Martha's *Monsieur Verdoux* character, somehow thwarts all attempts to bump her off.

By this point, Martha was a veteran trouper who took almost anything that happened on stage in stride. At a 1965 summer stock performance of *Everybody Loves Opal* in Massachusetts, a blown transformer unexpectedly threw the theater into darkness on opening night. "Martha dashed out from behind the curtain before the audience could panic and sang out in her inimitable style 'Hello Dolly.' Her cheery notes put the audience at ease and was the beginning of a 30-minute impromptu show…. 'If anyone has gold teeth, smile wide and it will light our way,'" she called out merrily. When it became clear that the lights could not be restored quickly, Martha offered to continue nonetheless, and with the audience's approval the remainder of the play was done via candlelight and other temporary measures.[18]

At a New York stop with *Opal*, reviewer Paul Aaron noted,

> She is zany in the finest sense of the word, exuding a genuine warmth that draws the audience to her the moment she appears on stage. There are not many actors with her ability for instant communication, and it's a pleasure to watch the ease and the enjoyment with which she accomplishes it.[19]

Nineteen sixty-five also marked the year in which the American military established a significant presence in Vietnam. The developing conflict would continue for the next decade. While many civilians disapproved of American involvement in the fight for control of South Vietnam, Martha knew and cared only that troops were once again being deployed overseas. She still felt a strong pull to support military men and women, as she had done during World War II. As syndicated columnist Inez Robb—a war correspondent during 1942–43—wrote in 1965 of Martha's earlier tour of duty (with Carole Landis, Kay Francis and Mitzi Mayfair),

> Within a few weeks the going got too tough and the air raids too personal for the other three women. They quit, came back to the United States, wrote a book about their adventures, and sold it to the movies. They were the darlings of the public and picked up all the applause. In the meantime, back at the battlefronts of North Africa, Martha by herself was fulfilling the obligations of the quartet.

Though acknowledging that Martha was not motivated by awards, or recognition, Robb added, "For some inexplicable reason, Martha always seems to be behind the door when the medals and the kudos are handed out."[20]

For the remainder of the 1960s, and into the early 1970s, Martha's show business commitments would once again have to be arranged to accommodate the war work she found so fulfilling. She typically spent at least a few months per year outside the U.S., taking part in USO-arranged activities, and eventually continuing or extending tours at her own expense. Not wishing to profit personally from her work in Vietnam, Martha shied away from posing for publicity photographs, though she would happily pose for informal snapshots with individual soldiers. At no time did she attempt to exploit her work for a television program, and she bridled at other entertainers who wouldn't put themselves out. "I had a popular female vocalist all lined up to come over, but at the last moment she got her doctor to say she was allergic to shots. These Hollywood people are allergic to shots all right. They found out they're using live bullets."[21]

Stars and Stripes reported that, at one stop at a naval station during her fall 1965 tour, she "in a four-hour visit gave three unscheduled performances, shook every hand in sight and was made an honorary citizen of the base." From there, she "climbed aboard a plane at 3 p.m. and flew to Subic Bay Naval Station where she performed at the base hospital."[22] She also made occasional appearances on *Magic Mansion*, a comedy program produced by the Armed Forces Radio and Television Services, and broadcast live to military personnel overseas.

Back home in early 1966 after spending four months in Vietnam, she was asked by a *Variety* reporter about anti-war demonstrators in the U.S. Martha minced no words: "At the end of each program I told [the soldiers] two things: The demonstrators are just a bunch of illiterate kooks, and remember they aren't good enough to shine your shoes."[23] In January 1967, she was presented with a certificate of appreciation by Army General William

C. Westmoreland, for her "outstanding contributions to the morale and welfare of the United States and other Free World military assistance forces in the Republic of Vietnam while touring the command, entertaining personnel of all military services."

Martha made her first return to Broadway in more than 25 years when she accepted an offer from producer David Merrick to become the third actress to star in the Broadway smash *Hello, Dolly!*, following in the footsteps of Carol Channing and Ginger Rogers. The show was already three years into its very successful run, and Channing had won a Tony Award for her interpretation of the role. Merrick had met up with Martha in Saigon almost two years earlier, where a performance of *Dolly* was being staged for a military audience. He offered her the chance to take on the role, and she was happy to agree. In 1966, while in Vietnam, she received the formal offer and signed the contract with Merrick's organization.

The *New York Times* reported that she would play her first performance with the company on February 27, 1967. She was unavailable to rehearse with the full company when she was offered the role, but worked with director Gower Champion in Los Angeles while fulfilling a television commitment there. "I just hope I can do half as well as the last two ladies," she said modestly of her predecessors Channing and Rogers.[24]

While some reviewers thought her slightly miscast as Dolly Levi, a reviewer in *Variety* (March 8, 1967) commented that Martha's interpretation of the character "illustrates the old show business adage that when a role and a show are good enough there are countless ways of playing it and personalities suitable for

In 1967, Martha stepped into the lead role of the Broadway hit *Hello, Dolly!*

it…. [Raye] mugs and plays frankly to the audience, giving a considerably bigger performance than Miss Rogers did and adding a touch of buffoonery that neither of her predecessors had."

Columnist Whitney Bolton was also favorably impressed:

> I found myself, sitting there after two other Dolly portraits, wanting Miss Raye to score all on her own, and she does. She couldn't be another exact Channing if rifles were pointed at her, she couldn't be another Rogers if threatened with death…. She has her own ample gifts and they have served her well. She has, additionally, an acute and immediate, most personal appeal. She smiles at you and you melt.[25]

Following a May performance, Martha was presented with the USO's "Woman of the Year" award, with previous winner Joan Crawford serving as honorary chairman of the event. A supper and dance at New York's Rainbow Room in Martha's honor served as a fundraiser for USO activities overseas. After she completed her six-month engagement, she was succeeded in the role by her longtime friend Betty Grable in June 1967. *Hello, Dolly!* would run on Broadway until 1970, surpassing *My Fair Lady*'s record as Broadway's longest-running musical, and would be occasionally revived by regional theaters in the 1970s with Martha in the lead.

Even high-profile work as a Broadway star ran second to her interest in being on the scene in Vietnam. Interviewed by Earl Wilson that spring, she said she had already committed to return to her war duties by early fall. Asked why this was such a priority in her life, Martha said, "I guess it's from feeling needed. It's one of the most rewarding things you can do. You receive so much more than you give. It gives you a richer life."[26] To another reporter, she explained, "The response you get from an audience on Broadway is beautiful to hear, but there's just no comparison with what it is like when entertaining troops. It isn't just the performing, but of being under fire with them, sharing and being close to them."[27]

That fall, with permission from Merrick's organization, Martha took a stripped-down version of *Hello, Dolly!* to Vietnam. "I had 19 people with me," she later recalled, "and there were a few places we had to do the show in our fatigues. Walking on boxes and trying to sing 'Hello, Dolly' is really something."[28] The effort caught up with her in Saigon in early October, when she fainted during the finale. She was carried off stage for treatment. USO representatives told the press that Martha had been overcome while giving an energetic performance, wearing heavy costume and wig, in temperatures exceeding 90 degrees. "Her first thought was that someone should go out and reassure the GIs," said the USO spokesman. "She said the troops have enough to worry about without worrying about her."[29] In late November, Martha had to be rescued by helicopter after the Green Beret camp in which she was entertaining came under enemy fire. Diverted from a mission nearby, the pilots were able to land on a small mountaintop to rescue Martha and four other entertainers.

In early 1968, she embarked on another tour with *Wildcat*. Reviewer Martha Ann Hemphill called a Houston Music Theater performance "a delightful evening to watch a real 'star' perform." Hemphill noted that, during her times offstage, Martha "was usually perched behind the orchestra seats watching the action and leading the laughter."[30] A few weeks later, the show was at the Carousel Theatre in West Covina, California. Reviewer Brent Howell called Raye "360 degrees of charm. No scene-stealer she, Martha has the scene from the beginning and never lets go of it."[31] At some performances she drew standing ovations.

Cast as her sister in the West Covina company was singer-actress Carole Wells, a veteran of the CBS television series *Pistols 'n' Petticoats*. Though Wells, still in her twenties, had been warned that Raye was "a tough cookie," she formed a different opinion over the course of several weeks rehearsing and performing side by side, remembering her many years later as "one of the nicest women I've ever known. I watched how she worked; she never missed a line. She always was on time. A real professional, the way I was trained to work."

Over the course of her career, Wells would work with several stars, including Ethel Merman, Groucho Marx and Barbra Streisand, giving her an opportunity to see how different actors used their power in a professional setting. Although Raye "wanted to have things done right," she was able to achieve that goal without "being a prima donna and abusing people. Martha Raye was not like that…. You could do it and be kind. You don't just have to be a bulldozer." Said Wells, "All the gypsies really liked her."

After a week of rehearsals, the *Wildcat* company began several weeks of performances. "Martha Raye gave at every performance 100 percent, even to the last show," Wells noted. When Martha, a few minutes into one performance, spotted her old friend Jimmy Durante in the audience, she abruptly left the stage, according to Wells, "walked down to shake his hand," and announced to playgoers, "Ladies and gentlemen, Jimmy Durante is here!" After the production closed, Raye and Wells never worked together again, but would remain in friendly contact for some years.[32]

From there, Raye went to the Mill Run Playhouse in Illinois, where she appeared in a revival of George Axelrod's *Goodbye Charlie,* playing the lead role of a man reincarnated as a woman. According to critic James Betchkal, Axelrod's comedy "comes off a lot like those TV shows in the Fifties when Martha Raye cavorted with Milton Berle and Rocky Graziano." He wasn't complaining, however. Nor were paying customers. "She peppers a pretty bland script into something kind of special, all tied up with torn sneakers, drooping sox and a dirty raincoat."[33]

She continued her television performances as well. Martha would return frequently to *The Carol Burnett Show* in its early years, ultimately making eight guest appearances. Of Burnett, Martha said, "She's the best. Carol is the most unselfish, delightful human being. She gives a lot to her guests and never worries about herself. I do three or four shows a year with her, and I've never heard her holler."[34] In 1968, Carol and Martha teamed for the album *Together Again for the First Time,* released on the Tetragrammaton label.

In October 1968, she boarded another flight for Vietnam, spending nearly 20 hours in the air to reach her destination. She was greeted upon arrival by the sound of Army Band musicians playing "Hello, Dolly!" An emotional Martha said, "It was marvelous to see all my Green Berets out there and to see the band. We saw the band as we were coming in for touchdown and all the men were saying it was for me, but I didn't believe it."[35] In December, she was briefly hospitalized for exhaustion in Vietnam.

Her labors on behalf of the military were acknowledged in 1969 when she became the tenth recipient (and the first *female* recipient) of the Jean Hersholt Humanitarian Award, presented by the Academy of Motion Picture Arts and Sciences for her "devoted and often dangerous work in entertaining troops in combat areas almost continuously since World War II."[36] Bob Hope presented the award during the show's live broadcast, saying, "But even more important, she's earned the love and respect and the undying admiration of every homesick kid in uniform who so desperately seeks to touch and feel a moment of home." An emotional Martha, visibly nervous and fighting back tears, described it as "the most beautiful, honorable, wonderful, exciting day of my life—stateside."[37]

That spring and summer, Martha was touring in a new musical, *Hello, Sucker,* based on the life of actress Texas Guinan, proprietress of a well-known New York speakeasy during the Depression. "I think this is harder than facing the VC [Viet Cong]," she told a Baltimore reporter of the tour. With script revisions being made almost daily as audience reactions were gauged, she said, "[E]very show is like opening night."[38] A critic who attended an August 1969 performance in Cleveland reported that Martha received a lengthy standing ovation on her first entrance, which he attributed to her personal reputation as "one of the nicest ladies in the theater" as well as audience awareness of her work in Vietnam. Of the show itself, he reported, "Few of the songs are memorable or even singable" and "the show isn't that funny," and then he added, "But when Martha Raye performs in person, the vehicle really doesn't matter. You enjoy her and all that she means to the world of comedy and the theater."[39] The *Washington Post*'s Richard L. Coe said that Raye "contributes her unique blend of plebeian cheer and guilty courage to her Texas Guinan…. [She] can dance and prance on slim, trim pins but coaxes you into the false idea that she is hopelessly awkward. To do what she does requires enviable grace and control."[40]

At the conclusion of a late August performance in Massachusetts, Martha was reduced to tears when the Westover Air Force Band surprised her, parading into the theater to play "Happy Birthday" in honor of her turning 53. Unfortunately, as several critics had predicted along the tour, *Hello, Sucker* would not make the grade as a Broadway attraction.

Nineteen-seventy also found Martha's film career reactivated, although her two movie roles weren't everything she might have wished. She was one of many guest stars booked to appear in *The Phynx*, an ill-conceived film that was shelved after a few preview engagements. She received wider exposure playing a comic witch in *Pufnstuf*, an adaptation of Sid and Marty Krofft's popular TV children's show. She was also interviewed for the 1970 documentary *No Substitute for Victory*, in which Martha said, "Nobody wants a war. God knows that, and especially our troops that are fighting one over there. But as long as we are fighting a war over there, the least we can do back home here is just to give them the support, the love, the dignity and the respect that they, our flag, and our country deserve. And that's all they ask of you."

Having impressed producers Sid and Marty Krofft with her work in *Pufnstuf,* Martha was offered the role of Benita Bizarre in their new NBC Saturday morning live-action series, *The Bugaloos*, which debuted in September 1970. Benita would be the comic villainess of the musically oriented series, much as actress Billie Hayes was on *H.R. Pufnstuf.* "Yes, I'm really looking forward to this new series," she said in the summer of 1970. "Anything that's new is a challenge to me and don't forget, my whole life is entertaining."[41] Her look for the role included a long, sharp nose and feather-laden costumes in bright primary colors, resulting in a look some compared to Phyllis Diller. "I play a vicious witch but not really," she explained. "I live in a juke box, wear a turkey-feather boa, and want to make a record even though I can't sing. What more could a girl ask?"[42]

The show would attempt to make four young, little-known British performers into a popular music group, much as had been done with the Monkees a few years earlier. Filming continued through the fall of 1970 at Paramount, on a stage adjoining the one where *Here's Lucy* was being shot. Said director Tony Charmoli, "What she brought to this series, too, is really that note of professionalism that the other, inexperienced actors needed."

Charmoli said Raye studied her lines every morning while undergoing the lengthy makeup session needed to bring Benita Bizarre to life. Once on the set, she knew her dialogue cold, and taught her co-stars by example. "She gave those kids a lot of energy," he said.[43] Young co-star John Philpott, who played Courage, agreed: "It was such a joy to watch her perform.... She was just so professional."[44]

"Once I got to know her, I fell in love with her," concurred John McIndoe (I.Q.).[45] Shooting for the first season was complete by December 1970, leaving Martha free to embark on another Vietnam trip. Although *The Bugaloos* was well-received, budget-minded NBC executives declined to finance new episodes after the initial season, and a planned movie version fell through.

Martha was pleased to see that there were opportunities opening up for younger women interested in pursuing comedy. "Up to six or ten years ago," she said in a 1971 interview, "there were only me and Joan Davis and Imogene Coca. But now there are many and I think some of the young ones, like Lily Tomlin and Ruth Buzzi, are very good."[46]

Martha went back on the road. In the fall of 1971, she revived *Hello, Dolly!* at the Long Beach Civic Light Opera. (The road had its own hazards; late in 1971, Nick was forced to take legal action on Martha's behalf when a Pennsylvania nightclub's $12,000 paycheck to her bounced.) Her professional bookings, however, continued to be arranged to allow her to make yearly visits to Vietnam.

Because Martha was willing to roll up her sleeves and do whatever needed doing when she volunteered in military hospitals, it was sometimes mistakenly said that she was a qualified nurse. Though she had some training as a nurse's aide, and volunteered in hospitals as far back as the early 1940s, she had never actually completed the relevant coursework. She said,

> If I hadn't become an entertainer, I would like to have been a doctor or a nurse. I feel that the American nurse has never been sufficiently honored or even acknowledged for her service overseas. And I have known too many who lost limbs or were killed. I'll be happy when I see a ticker-tape parade honoring the American nurses. Even the military brass and the government have never given these women the recognition they deserve.[47]

When she came home from a Vietnam tour, Martha often spent time over the following weeks telephoning family members of servicemen she had met. She would relay messages given to her by the men, and try to bolster the spirits of family members awaiting their safe return.

Not everyone viewed her war work in a positive light, given that the war itself was extremely controversial. In the years immediately following the Vietnam War, Martha came to believe that she was paying the price in Hollywood for what she had viewed as a patriotic, rather than a political, act. "It took three years after the war to get my first TV guest shot," Martha said in 1979. "It was an unpopular war and anyone connected with it still is unpopular in this country today…. Some people still call me a warmonger. That's the reason I haven't been able to get work in this town."[48] Another factor may have been the changes that had taken place in television by the early 1970s. By and large, the variety shows that had booked her in the 1960s had wound down, and the performers who knew her best were themselves seen much less frequently on TV. Although some new variety shows did crop up during the 1970s, none of them proved to be ones on which she was welcomed as she had been by Red Skelton, Andy Williams and the like.

Demographics were becoming increasingly important to TV executives and the advertisers, not a boon to the careers of stars over 40. Even *The Carol Burnett Show,* on which she had appeared twice yearly since 1967, stopped booking her after 1971, though it seems unlikely that this was in response to her military service. In its fifth year, the show moved from a ten p.m. time slot to an early evening one where it was under more pressure to attract young viewers, which may explain why Martha was passed over in favor of talent such as the Carpenters, Burt Reynolds and Cass Elliot.

With TV work scarce, Martha and Nick pursued opportunities for her in New York. In the fall of 1972, Martha joined the cast of the Broadway revival *No, No, Nanette,* stepping into the featured role of Pauline for which actress Patsy Kelly had won a Tony Award. The role was somewhat rewritten to accommodate Martha's gifts, and allowed her to perform a tap dance number that had previously been assigned to Ruby Keeler. A new song, "Don't Turn Your Back on a Bluebird," was added for her.

Interviewed in Baltimore shortly before she joined the *Nanette* company, Martha expressed her gratitude to be cast, though she thought her predecessor Patsy Kelly "silly" to have relinquished the role: "You don't back away from a winner." She told her interviewer, "At 56, I'm just lucky that nostalgia is in. I intend to stay on the boards as long as I can. I'm staying because I love it."[49] Although critic Clive Barnes, reviewing the show shortly after she joined the cast, praised her "manic gusto," the engagement proved to be a relatively brief one for Martha. The long-running show posted its closing notice in February 1973, having played more than 800 performances since opening in 1971.

When television and Broadway work was not available, Martha would accept bookings in theaters around the country, where her fame still sold tickets, and where she would frequently encounter veterans and family members who regarded her quite differently from the TV executives who seemingly saw her as passé and/or hawkish. Though there were occasional

For much of the 1970s, Martha earned her living on the road, starring in *Everybody Loves Opal*. Here she's pictured with featured actor Sidney Breese, playing a medico.

opportunities to broaden her horizons—she was once offered the lead in a production of the serious drama *Come Back, Little Sheba*—Martha opted for what felt the most comfortable for her, which was comedy.

Though she played various shows during the 1970s, she returned often to her old standby *Everybody Loves Opal*. As a reviewer attending a summer 1973 performance in Florida noted, the show occasionally "becomes a Martha Raye revue, and the audience loves it. The best seats in the house are up front. She plays to the laughers in the front row, delivering asides and broadsides, breaking out of character time and again and again, and scoring laughs just about as often."[50] *Variety* (January 29, 1975) caught a performance on Long Island and noted, "Raye is an inventive comedienne willing to do anything for a laugh and generally does…. She makes it virtually a one-woman comedy."

Describing the phenomenon of dinner theater as it existed in the 1970s, writer W.L. Taitte said, "Because the star is crucial, he has most of the power connected with the production. He chooses the script (subject to the provision that it has to be a light comedy and that it not have played the area within the last year), and has a say about the other elements of the package." Shows were typically headlined by a performer who enjoyed name recognition with a middle-class, often middle-aged (or older) audience that usually knew the star from television work. Said one cynical theater owner of the performers who frequented dinner theater, "They're so damned lazy they won't bother to learn the lines for a new show."[51]

Actor Joseph Culliton, who appeared with Raye in a 1973 production of *Opal*, likened the freewheeling atmosphere to *Hellzapoppin'*: "*Everybody Loves Opal* was used as a mere framework for her skilled clowning." When Martha wasn't in a scene, she could sometimes be found in the audience, "heckling the actors who were onstage." Still, when the time came for her to perform a sad scene in the play, Culliton noted, "tears *poured* out of Maggie's eyes at every performance."[52]

Literary merits aside, *Opal* had attraction for Martha: "There's a part in it for a cat and in every town we went to I insisted that they get a cat from the animal shelter, one that was due to be put to sleep. It was in my contract. After the show closed, the cat would be up for adoption. Everybody wanted a famous cat." She estimated that some 200 cats had been successfully homed over the years by this plan.[53]

Wherever she stepped onstage, Martha increasingly found herself welcomed by Vietnam veterans and their families. "[I]nstead of stage-door Johnnies, Martha Raye's stateside dressing rooms are usually crowded with ramrod-straight, crew-cut men awkwardly holding flowers," said one observer.[54] When she was home in Bel Air, she frequently played host to veterans who had copied down the address and telephone number she posted on bulletin boards in countless camps. "I had no idea so many of them would take me up on it," she said in 1973. "But I'm delighted. These men fought under worse conditions than men in both World War II and Korea.... The veterans of other wars came home to warm welcomes. These poor guys are treated like murderers. It isn't right."[55] Also frequently found at Martha's home was Nick Condos. Although long divorced from her, he continued to maintain a close relationship with his ex-wife.

While theater work paid the bills in the 1970s, she was eager to find steadier work in television, which would allow her to do less traveling. In late 1975, Martha received her highest-profile TV role in several years when she guest-starred on NBC's *McMillan & Wife*. In its fifth year as one of the rotating elements of NBC's *Sunday Mystery Movie*, the series starred Rock Hudson as San Francisco Police Commissioner Stewart "Mac" McMillan and Susan Saint James as his wife Sally. The February 1976 episode "Greed," written by Virginia Aldridge, focused on the demise of wealthy Aunt Wilhelmina, whose family included nieces Mildred (series regular Nancy Walker) and her sister Agatha (Martha). The nearly million-dollar inheritance initially benefits the dowager's great-niece Jenny, but other family members are set to inherit if Jenny should be unable to do so. When Jenny is seemingly murdered, Agatha, visiting with the McMillans, quickly becomes dissatisfied with Mac's methodical approach to solving the case, taking it upon herself to become what he dryly describes as "our Miss Marple."

Martha's scenes found screwball Agatha staring down the nose of a pistol when she's caught breaking into a suspect's office, giggling coyly when a gold-digging playboy tells her she's "physically entrancing," and ultimately having to be rescued by the Coast Guard when she makes an unexpected jump off a burning boat. "Don't you worry, commissioner, we'll solve this," she cheerfully assures Mac, who says, "You have a fascinating mind, Agatha."

Though it was for all intents and purposes a ready-made showcase for Martha, her *McMillan* role wasn't a shoo-in for her. "Everybody had a lot of doubts," said producer Jon Epstein. "Martha hadn't worked in Hollywood in years. People wondered whether she could remember her lines, whether she was physically up to it. And let's face it, some thought she was a political nut."[56]

Martha received Special Guest Star billing over her fellow players, including Slim Pickens, Tab Hunter and Alejandro Rey, in the two-hour episode. Given substantial screen time and comic possibilities, her work paid off when she was nominated for an Emmy Award as Best Supporting Actress that spring. Though she didn't win, the exposure provided a boost to her career.

At the time Martha filmed her first *McMillan & Wife* appearance, the series was thought to be winding down. But in the summer of 1976, Universal publicists announced that Martha would join the cast of *McMillan* as a regular for the coming season. The series was undergoing big changes; virtually the entirety of Rock Hudson's original supporting cast was absent as the show went into its sixth season. With both Hudson and Saint James' original five-year contracts at an end, it appeared that the series would fade to black. However, while fulfilling a stage engagement, Hudson accepted an offer from Universal to star in six more 90-minute segments, which would be titled *McMillan*. In order to accommodate Hudson's schedule, filming would not begin until September 1976, meaning that the first segment would not air until well into the fall. Not only had leading lady Susan Saint James left the series, leaving Hudson's character a widower, but so had Nancy Walker (as his housekeeper), who was starring in her own ABC-TV sitcom that season. John Schuck, signed to a starring role in ABC's *Holmes and Yoyo,* was expected to make infrequent appearances.

Signing Martha as a regular was reportedly done to please Hudson who, according to at least one syndicated columnist, intervened when producers thought her asking price too high. Executive producer Leonard Stern said NBC executives balked. "They said, 'Nah, you don't want to use her. She's too old. Nobody knows who she is.' They were stupid reasons." Hudson offered to make a phone call to clear the way, and Martha was cast.[57] "Rock adored Martha," said director Bob Finkel. "When she came on the show, it was a whole new Rock."[58]

Though the cast changes energized the star, *Variety* (December 8, 1976) gave the *McMillan* season opener a lukewarm review: They said it was "something of a relief to get rid of those cute husband-wife scenes," but then proclaimed that Hudson "seemed surprisingly ill at ease in the role of swain." The trade paper found Martha's Agatha to be one of the better additions: "Raye fit in at once."

Martha appeared in all six Season 6 episodes. Back in the limelight at age 60, she was spotlighted in a *TV Guide* feature the following spring. Her success on *McMillan* seemed to have broken the dam in terms of TV casting, and she was once again in demand. She happily accepted an engagement to perform during NBC's telecast of the Macy's Thanksgiving Day Parade that fall. In early 1979, she made the first of two guest appearances on *The Love Boat*, opposite Ray Bolger.

Later that year, she guested on the popular CBS sitcom *Alice* starring Linda Lavin. Her role as Carrie Sharples, mother to Vic Tayback's Mel, whom she lovingly addressed as "Fatso," became a recurring feature of *Alice* over the next few seasons, with Raye ultimately playing the role in 12 segments. The series used many celebrity guests over the years, not all of whom endeared themselves to cast and crew. However, *Alice* associate producer Douglas West remembered Martha as "a hoot to work with. She pretty much had everybody around the craft service table in tears of laughter."[59]

Her resurgence in television popularity led to a lucrative endorsement deal in 1980, when she was signed by Polident to do commercials and advertisements for the denture cleanser. Anticipating possible complaints about truth in advertising, company executives wanted a celebrity willing to personally attest to using the product. After eyeing Dorothy Lamour, who coolly informed them that her teeth were her own, they turned their attention to Martha, but "asked for some proof that she actually wore dentures. The proof came when Raye slipped out the choppers and dropped them in the exec's hand."[60]

When Martha's commercials began to appear, *Variety* columnist Carroll Carroll termed it "a clever hunk of casting," given that many of her fans from the movies "are by now candidates for some sort of denture cleanser." However, he decried the use of the "take it from the big mouth" slogan, suggesting that the company instead "allow their potential customer to recall her a funny lady with a rather remarkable singing voice."[61]

Between scenes on the TV movie *The Gossip Columnist,* she told an interviewer, "At this point my personal life is much calmer than my professional life.... I very seldom go out. I enjoy my home, my family, my four dogs." A fan of daytime soap operas, she added, "Nobody in the world can suffer as much as those poor people I tune in on! ... Watch a soap and your own worries are nothing."[62]

Much as her career required her to be on the road, Martha always had the house in Bel Air to come back to. "I'm such a gypsy, but I'll never give up my home," she said in 1979. "I need roots." Her idea of enjoyable entertaining, she said, was to "invite five or six friends over for dinner. We play games or watch my old TV show or get movies from a studio.... I've never given a big party in my life!"[63]

In 1981, Martha was invited to join the ensemble company touring the country as 4 Girls 4. Launched in 1977, the quartet had originally included singers Rosemary Clooney, Barbara McNair and Margaret Whiting, teamed with singer-comedienne Rose Marie. McNair dropped out early, to be replaced by big band singer Helen O'Connell. Now Rose Marie had withdrawn from the production; she would later write that she "was slowly having a nervous breakdown because of all the bickering going on with the show."[64] Both she and Clooney attributed many of the problems to Helen O'Connell's mercurial nature and outspokenness. In Miami, Martha reportedly received standing ovations from audiences. *Variety,* catching the show in Albany, New York, commented on September 16, 1981, "Martha Raye wowed the audience with her vaudeville antics, frenetic perambulation, her skill at balancing on the fine line between comedy and vulgarity. Every now and then she would allow a listen of her true vocal ability, but would puncture the effect with a sight gag." Martha played a few dates with 4 Girls 4, but her time with the company was limited. "She couldn't take the bickering either," Rose Marie claimed.[65]

She was still touring with *Everybody Loves Opal.* Mort Sertner, who appeared in the Chicago company, said,

> It all looks pretty chaotic, but people should appreciate the precise timing somebody as experienced as Maggie brings to a show like this. We break a lot of rules of acting out there, but if we played this straight, we'd die. The script isn't strong enough. In the end, people love the way we do it.[66]

Not everyone, however, viewed her working methods so benignly. Actor Allen Hall, who appeared with Martha in a 1983 dinner theater production of *Everybody Loves Opal* in Jacksonville, Florida, described her as "a phenomenal talent,"[67] but nonetheless found working with her disconcerting. Originally cast in a minor role, Hall was asked to step into the male lead only a few days after the show opened, to replace an actor who'd dropped out due to a family emergency. He furiously studied his new role, but the single day of rehearsal he got before going on didn't include the star.

"She would not come to rehearsal," he said. "She did not ever work with me. She would have nothing to do with anyone during the daytime," which she typically spent holed up in her hotel room watching television. Left to work with the star's stand-in, he learned his lines and blocking well enough to go on that night (not carrying a script as he'd been told he could do if necessary), and well enough to subsequently earn a flattering write-up in the local newspaper.

At curtain calls that night, Hall was surprised to be congratulated onstage by Martha, who told the audience "what this young man has accomplished today." As he basked in her praise, and the audience's enthusiastic applause, he was startled to hear the star turn upstage and say quietly to him, "Now get the fuck off the stage. This is my show."

Over the course of the next few weeks, Hall had time to admire Martha's gifts as a performer, and to be impressed by how functional she was despite being what he described as "pretty much drunk all the time." He recalled that the stage manager stood in the wings at every performance, ready to press a substantial glass of vodka into her waiting hands as soon as she finished performing. "I thought she'd die of cirrhosis for sure," Hall said. After a performance, she often wanted to gather a group for a late-night card game, from which Hall chose to excuse himself.

Knowing the play inside and out after years of taking it on the road, Martha felt free to improvise occasionally from night to night, expanding on a moment or ad-libbing a laugh line if the audience seemed particularly responsive. Her freewheeling approach meant that a fellow actor might not hear a cue quite when he expected, but as Hall recalled, "She could go outside the walls, but she'd always come back in to give you the line. You might stand there longer than you were comfortable, but she always came back."

Attending to her needs throughout the show's multi-week run was Nick, by then silver-haired; Hall played a round of golf with Condos during the show's run and found him an engaging and amiable man. Hall saw little warmth in Martha's attitude toward Condos: "She treated him like a piece of dog crap. She verbally berated him around others. It was embarrassing." Melodye, as quoted by Raymond Strait, characterized her parents' relationship as "a classic sadomasochistic relationship," with her mother repeatedly haranguing Nick over his use of alcohol.[68]

In the summer of 1983, Martha was on the Kenley theater circuit, playing the comic villainess Miss Hannigan in the hit musical *Annie*. Critic Ande Yakstis called Martha a "real show stopper" and noted that she "drew applause and laughs from the crowd for her antics as the mean old Miss Hannigan."[69] She did the show again the following summer.

Although Hollywood could be less than kind to performers over 60, Martha was open about the aging process. While performing in an Illinois production of *Opal,* the 68-year-old star said, "Too many people, especially in our business, are afraid of growing older. That's stupid! People dye their hair, using that boot black stuff. It looks so phony. Who do they think they're kidding? You have to accept age. Why not? We earned it!"[70] In 1985, she was singing in a New York cabaret, enjoying a rare opportunity to perform some of the jazz standards she loved, without couching them in her usual comedic style, and playing a guest role on an early episode of *Murder, She Wrote,* one of her last television performances. That fall, she was cast in a Broadway-bound musical, *The Prince of Central Park,* adapted from the book by Evan H. Rhodes. Production proved troublesome, and by the time the show finally made it to Broadway more than four years later, Martha was no longer attached to the project.

After more than 60 years, Martha's career was finally winding down.

V. Civilian

By the 1980s, the days were long gone when the private lives and personal peccadilloes of Hollywood stars were verboten subjects. Not long after her adoptive mother Joan Crawford's death in 1977, Christina Crawford published the scathing memoir *Mommie Dearest*, alleging that the star had been a child abuser. That hugely popular book paved the way for a multitude of others, such as Gary Crosby's *Going My Own Way*, which impugned the parenting skills of his father Bing Crosby, and *My Mother's Keeper*, written by Bette Davis' daughter, B.D. Hyman.

Though she could likely have peddled her own tell-all, Melodye chose to remain largely out of the spotlight, living quietly in Burbank. However, in the mid–1980s, she consented to an interview with author Raymond Strait, who wrote several books such as *Hollywood's Children* and *Star Babies*. Strait spent several hours getting Melodye's story, which made one of the saddest chapters in his book *Hollywood's Star Children*.

According to Strait, Melodye said, "My mother never wanted me. All my life I've been told the only reason she didn't abort me was fear of what my father might do to her."[1] Unable to sustain a successful singing career, Melodye firmly believed that her mother had blackballed her with Hollywood friends and associates. Though she well understood why people outside the family admired Martha's gifts, and her work with the military, she said that being her daughter was quite a different proposition.

While her work as a performer had slowed, Martha continued to be an avid TV viewer. She was angered by a joke made at her expense on NBC's *Late Night with David Letterman*. Riffing on her Polident commercials, and their "take it from the big mouth" tagline, the talk-show host cracked on his March 5, 1987, broadcast that he had seen a "terrifying" new commercial in which the comedienne endorsed condoms. After a complaint was filed with the network, a retraction was aired on April 1, "but Raye claims it was broadcast much later in the show and was done in a sarcastic and arrogant manner."[2] Her case, filed in Superior Court, sought $10 million in punitive damages. Within a few months, the complaint was dismissed by a judge who found it without merit.

An important chapter in Martha's life closed when her ex-husband and longtime manager Nick Condos died on July 8, 1988, at the UCLA Medical Center in Los Angeles. "There goes a fine person," Martha told *Variety* columnist Army Archerd.[3] Another loss came in May 1990 when her onetime TV leading man, Rocky Graziano, died of a heart ailment in a New York hospital at the age of 71.

Martha's own health deteriorated significantly in the late 1980s, and without Nick's guidance and attention she allowed her career to wind down. Her Polident endorsement deal was not renewed. She suffered her first of several strokes in 1990, as well as enduring a hospital stay after breaking several ribs in a fall at home. In May 1991, Martha's well-being received wide attention after a letter from a World War II veteran appeared in Ann Landers' nationally syndicated column. The writer had seen Martha using a wheelchair in a television appearance, and asked the columnist to find out the state of her health. A few weeks later, another veteran, Ramon Rodriguez, who was in Martha's employ, wrote, "About 18 months ago Martha had a stroke that left her partially paralyzed.... She is in a wheelchair, taking physical therapy three times a week and making remarkable progress. This great trooper [sic] is anxious to get back to work."[4]

After being single for more than 25 years, Martha's life took a surprising turn when she embarked on a whirlwind romance with a much younger man, one that quickly led to the altar. She married Mark Steven Harris in Las Vegas on September 25, 1991. The pair had been introduced by Martha's friend, comedian Bernie Allen. At the age of 42, Harris was more than 30 years Martha's junior. Initially, Harris was said to be just an ardent fan and aspiring performer who was eager to meet a star he'd long admired, and arrangements were made for him to visit her at her home. Martha, inclined toward loneliness, readily agreed. Within days they had established a relationship, one that puzzled many observers. On short acquaintance, they announced their plans to marry, which immediately opened her up to ridicule.

"Big-Mouth Martha Raye, 75, Weds Toyboy Lover," crowed a *Globe* headline (October 15, 1991). "He makes me feel very young and womanly," she told journalist Bob Thomas. "I'm really in love this time."[5] Martha credited Harris with helping her recover from the debilitating effects of her strokes and giving her a reason to live. "My physical therapist says, 'I can work on you, but you have to work on yourself. I can do so much but you have to do it for yourself—your wanting to'—and he's right."[6]

They reaffirmed their vows at a ceremony in Beverly Hills in December 1991, with around 100 guests in attendance, among them actors Cesar Romero and Anne Jeffreys. "It's our own business if we want to get married, so long as *we're* happy," Martha said resentfully. "It's not easy to find happiness today.... He's proven himself to me, or I wouldn't take a chance again."[7]

Journalist Stephanie Mansfield scornfully characterized the relationship between Martha and her seventh husband as one of a type recognizable to Hollywood insiders: the aging star wooed by a much younger admirer. Mansfield wrote,

> For a monthly allowance, they blow-dry what's left of the diva's hair, do the shopping and cooking, remind the diva on a daily basis what a fabulous *star* she still is, and every so often are invited to share the diva's bed, although sexual performance is secondary to slavish attention and the will to gossip.... In return, the young men—usually frustrated performers—bask in the fading glow of the spotlight, desperately cranking up the publicity machine like a teenager trying to push-start a '57 Chevy.[8]

Some noted a similarity to the controversial 1970s relationship between Groucho Marx and his secretary Erin Fleming, which erupted into a court battle over his estate after the comedian's death.

It quickly became apparent that Harris was involving himself in his new wife's business affairs. Martha signed paperwork that authorized Harris to sell a movie adaptation of her life story, with his participation to be lucrative for him. He was angered by the release of 20th Century-Fox's *For the Boys,* starring Bette Midler and James Caan, which seemed to undercut an authorized biographical film about Martha, and which he believed was a thinly veiled version of her story.

As far back as 1983, Midler acknowledged that she and Raye had met, and that the younger star had some awareness of Martha's wartime service. "Martha Raye once said she had had some offers to do her life story," Midler noted, "and she said the only person she wanted to do it was me."[9]

Harris told *Entertainment Weekly* in late 1991 that he and his wife were "shopping for the best high-profile lawyer we can find" after attending a matinee performance of *For the Boys.* Though Midler was purportedly playing a fictitious character, representing an amalgam of performers who entertained troops overseas, Harris said he and his wife did not believe the disclaimer. "What other performer was dismissed from her television show in the '50s and had her own nightclub?"[10] The resulting lawsuit targeted Midler, director Mark Rydell and 20th Century-Fox.

Alarmed by this new marriage, Melodye filed suit late that year in Los Angeles Superior Court, asking that a conservator be appointed to oversee her mother's finances. Judge Edward Ross approved the appointment of a temporary conservator, pending a January hearing at which the issue of a permanent conservator would be considered. The conservator's responsibilities would be limited to managing Raye's finances, but did not extend to decisions pertaining to her health care needs. In response to the suit, Martha's attorney Valerie Byer said the star "has suffered a series of strokes. She is physically not ambulatory. But that has had no impact on her ability to function mentally."[11]

Melodye was not the only one to fear that her mother was slipping mentally, questioning her judgment in marrying a man she had known for only a short time, and one widely viewed as a fortune hunter. In a 1992 interview with *People* magazine, Martha said, "Before Mark I was very lonely. Life was very puny then. Now my life has some class and intelligence to it."[12] Bernie Allen, who'd brought Raye and Harris together, would later say, "My personal feeling is that he rushed Martha into marriage for his own gain and to further his career. I don't want him to hurt her."[13] But those who knew Martha knew that she had long had a habit of impetuous marriages.

As far back as the 1980s, Melodye had said that she did not expect to inherit much from her mother's estate, claiming she had been shown a will that bequeathed her one dollar. According to Raymond Strait, Melodye said, "She'll probably leave her money to my father if he outlives her, or whatever bum happens to be hanging around at the time."[14]

That fall, Judge Edward Ross approved a plan that placed Martha's finances under the watch of a certified public accountant, who would pay her routine bills. The plan called for her to receive $3000 per month for incidental expenses, a generous amount for someone who now rarely ventured far from home.

In October 1993, Martha's circulatory problems forced doctors to amputate her left leg just below the knee. Though she was said to be in critical condition at Cedars-Sinai Medical Center, hospital spokesman Ron Wise announced that this was primarily an indication of the severity of the procedure she'd undergone, and added, "She tolerated the surgery pretty well."[15] Still, her ailments, which included gangrene, continued to worsen, and eventually part of her right leg was removed as well.

While Martha struggled with illness and incapacitation, efforts were underway to recognize her longtime devotion to the U.S. military, and the time and effort she had given to entertaining troops. Former Army nurse Noonie Fortin, in conjunction with Belle Pellegrino, had for some time been spearheading an effort to see Martha's war work recognized with the Presidential Medal of Freedom, the nation's highest award for civilians. Explained Fortin,

> She went places that no other women would go. She did more than entertain. She nursed wounds, worked with surgeons and in emergency rooms in field hospitals. She was in the actual war zones. And when a photographer would come by for a publicity picture, she would turn her back.[16]

For even an obviously deserving candidate, the process of getting a name on the Medal of Freedom honors list was long and arduous, and the women devoted many hours to letters, phone calls and interviews. Now, with Raye in fragile health, the project took on a new urgency.

Finally, in November 1993, Martha was presented with the Presidential Medal of Freedom on behalf of President Bill Clinton. "The American people honor Martha Raye, a woman who has tirelessly used her gifts to benefit the lives of her fellow Americans," Clinton said in the official White House news release.[17] Given Martha's health, arrangements were made to present the medal in a ceremony held at her Bel Air home.

Serving as the event's master of ceremonies was Army Reserve Lt. Col. Michael R.S. Teilmann, who had known Martha during her Vietnam USO tours. Explaining that she was recently back from the hospital, and not up to speaking, Teilmann read a statement from Martha, saying that she was "ever so grateful to President Bill Clinton for this honor, and she accepts it on behalf of the tens of thousands of American fighting men and women who she has worked with, nursed and entertained in more than two decades of military service to our men and women." Cesar Romero and Anne Jeffreys were among the guests in Martha's home.

In early 1994, Mark Harris was reported to be circulating a book proposal to New York publishers, with the working title *Take It from the Big Mouth*. Among the juicier tidbits promised: the inside scoop on Martha's alleged lesbian relationship with Joan Crawford. The proposal would likely have been snapped up by some enterprising publisher a few years later, but it attracted no serious interest in 1994.

Around the same time, a judge dismissed the lawsuit against Bette Midler and her colleagues, finding too little ground for the belief that *For the Boys* was based on Martha's life. Midler said, "The stories have no resemblance except for one thing—they both were entertainers during wartime."[18] In any event, the main remuneration Martha's attorneys had originally sought—a percentage of the film's profits—would have amounted to relatively little since it had not been a box office success, falling well short of recouping its estimated $40 million budget. In a press release issued by Fox publicists, Midler said, "While I am delighted this frivolous lawsuit is over, and I had no doubt that justice would prevail, I am extremely angry at the tremendous waste of time and taxpayer money resulting from this baseless action."[19]

By that time, the outcome of the lawsuit was something of which Martha was scarcely aware, given her illness. Martha died on October 19, 1994, at Cedars-Sinai Medical Center, where she had been readmitted as a patient a few days earlier. According to hospital spokesman Ron Wise, the cause of death was "an aggregate of [circulatory failure] and other health difficulties."[20]

In the days following her death, tributes poured in from friends and colleagues. Said comedian Sid Caesar, "She represented the kind of talent that is rare today—the all-around entertainment pro, equally at home in movies, on TV, radio and recording."[21] Bob Hope was quoted as saying, "She was more popular with the GIs than a weekend pass. They loved her in Vietnam. She was a Florence Nightingale, Dear Abby and the only singer who could be heard over the artillery fire."[22]

A memorial service was held at Fort Bragg, North Carolina, where she was granted the honor of being the first civilian buried in its military cemetery. Said Jimmy Dean, executive secretary of the Special Forces Association, "How many entertainers in this world would go to a country called Vietnam, where a war was going on, for nine straight years, four months a year, and spend three of those months out with isolated Special Forces detachments in camps all over the country?"[23] Members of the Green Berets served as pallbearers at the ceremony, attended by approximately 300 mourners.

The will favored Mark Harris, who received approximately 75 percent of the estate, with a reported bequest of $50,000 to Melodye. The terms stipulated that Melodye would be disinherited altogether if she filed a legal challenge to the will. Other beneficiaries included several charities, including People for the Ethical Treatment of Animals and an AIDS service organization. Both Mark and Melodye were present at the memorial service. Martha's gravestone was marked with her dates of birth and death, and a note: "Civilian." According to her friend, veteran film producer A.C. Lyles, the box at Paramount Studios where her fan mail was collected had been updated to read "Martha Raye—Heaven."[24]

Asked in 1984 about her trailblazing career in comedy, Martha said, "I was lucky enough to work with Charlie Chaplin, W.C. Fields, Abbott and Costello, Red Skelton and Olsen and Johnson. They were the geniuses. To be a comedian, one must be born with talent. There are no schools to learn that. You learn only by watching the pros."[25] Likewise, during her lifetime and beyond, there have been many up-and-coming performers, comediennes especially, who looked upon Martha's work with admiration, and were inspired by her accomplishments in a field then dominated by men. Actress-singer Kaye Ballard, who described Martha as "one of my idols,"[26] perhaps put it best when she said, on behalf of herself and peers like Carol Burnett, "If it hadn't been for Lucy (and Martha Raye) leading the way, our careers, along with those of so many other comediennes, would have been a lot more difficult."[27]

Filmography

Rhythm on the Range *(Paramount)*

Release: July 31, 1936

Running time: 87 minutes

Cast: Bing Crosby (*Jeff Larabee*), Frances Farmer (*Doris Halloway*), Bob Burns (*Buck*), Martha Raye (*Emma*), Samuel S. Hinds (*Robert Halloway*), Warren Hymer (*Big Brain*), Lucille Webster Gleason (*Penny Ryland*), George E. Stone (*Shorty*), James Burke (*Wabash*), Martha Sleeper (*Constance Hyde*), Clem Bevans (*Gila Bend*), Leonid Kinskey (*Mischa*), Charles Williams (*Gopher*), Sons of the Pioneers (*Ranch Hands*), Sam McDaniel (*Porter*), Oscar Smith (*Waiter*), Dorothy Tennant (*Dowager*), Ellen Drew (*Party Guest*), Harry C. Bradley (*Minister*), Otto Yamaoka (*Houseboy*), Frank Sully (*Rodeo Cowboy*), Ella Ethridge (*Seamstress*), Irving Bacon (*Rodeo Announcer*), Frank Dawson (*Butler*), Herbert Ashley (*Brakeman*)

Crew: Norman Taurog (*Director*), Benjamin Glazer (*Producer*), John C. Moffitt, Sidney Salkow, Walter DeLeon, Francis Martin (*Screenplay*), Mervin J. Houser (*Story*), Edith Head (*Costume Designer*), Ellsworth Hoagland (*Editor*), Boris Morros (*Musical Director*), Hans Dreier, Robert Usher (*Art Directors*), Gene Merritt, Don Johnson (*Sound Recording*)

Synopsis: Rough-hewn, middle-aged Penny Ryland, owner of an Arizona ranch, visits New York City in conjunction with a rodeo. She's none too pleased to see that her pretty niece, Doris Halloway, who lives with her wealthy father Robert on Park Avenue, is on the verge of marrying a stuffy stockbroker, whom she clearly does not love. Accompanying Penny on her trip are two of her ranch hands, Jeff and Buck, who hope to earn enough rodeo prize money to buy their favorite bull, Cuddles.

Deciding at the last minute that her Aunt Penny's advice is correct, Doris flees from her imminent wedding, stowing away on the train car where Aunt Penny and her ranch hands plan to return to Arizona. Doris' father, who doesn't receive the telegram she sent advising him that she is safe and well, reports his daughter missing and offers a sizable reward for her return.

Another train passenger is Emma, a boisterous young woman on her way to the dude ranch to visit her brother. Complications ensue, among them a trio of varmints itching to hold the heiress for ransom. Thrown together by circumstances, Doris and Jeff find a mutual attraction, as do Buck and Emma. However, arriving at the ranch prior to her aunt's return, Doris still hasn't disclosed her true identity to Jeff, and accepts Buck's advice to await the proper moment. Before that can happen, Penny and Doris' father show up, both intent on breaking up the burgeoning romance.

Notes: Martha Raye makes an auspicious feature film debut, both as comedienne and singer, in this popular feature that earned her a long-term Paramount contract and introduced her to nationwide audiences. A late addition to the film's cast, fourth-billed Raye makes her first entrance nearly halfway through the film, as a passenger on the westbound train. Raye demands audience attention the moment she arrives. She's given substantial footage in the last half-hour, and makes the most of it. While one character labels her Emma "the most annoying person I've ever met," viewers mostly begged to differ.

Clearly interested in landing herself a man, Emma watches with fascination as another female passenger disembarks and kisses a waiting man, pausing to tip the train porter and thank him for all his help. Pressing a coin of her own into the porter's hand, Emma says eagerly, "See what you can do for me!" When she spots Buck, she likes what she sees and immediately plants a kiss on him. Noticing that Buck is departing on the same train a few moments later, she says, "I just wanted to rent him! I didn't want to buy him!" Thanks to a few unexpected jolts from the moving train, however, Emma and Buck find themselves much better acquainted after a breakfast together.

Plopped down in the desert some 30 miles away from the Frying Pan Ranch, city girl Emma promptly calls loudly for a taxi. "The nearest taxi's in Tucson," Buck advises her laconically. "They could probably hear you all right, but it would take them two days to get here."

Raye's official film debut features several elements that will become trademarks in her screen career, and incorporates some of the best material from her nightclub act. In her first few moments on camera, she introduces what will become her catchphrase, "Oh, boy!" She also takes an unexpected plunge into water for the first time, when she falls into a newly dug well on the ranch. Musically, she performs "Mr. Paganini," perhaps the song most associated with her over the course of her lengthy career, and takes part in an ensemble performance of "I'm an Old Cowhand." Her mugging, though far from subtle, generates laughs.

Romantically, she's teamed with musical comedian Bob Burns (1890–1956), some 25 years her senior, with whom she shared the screen four more times during her first two years at Paramount. Having been friends in vaudeville some years earlier, when she was still a child working with her parents, they enjoyed the chance to work together on her first feature film. In real life, Burns was the husband of another film comedienne, Judy Canova. At the time of filming, he was known to radio audiences for his regular spot on *The Kraft Music Hall*. He later hosted his own show, *The Arkansas Traveler*.

Leading lady Frances Farmer (1913–1970) was a relatively new Paramount contract player. Stuck with a rather stock character, the runaway heiress so often seen in 1930s screwball comedies, Farmer's performance doesn't do much to perk up the proceedings, nor is her chemistry with Crosby especially potent.

Principal photography for *Rhythm on the Range* wrapped in June 1936, with some retakes done later that month in preparation for the film's release only a few weeks later. After filming was completed, director Norman Taurog, who had recently ended his seven-year stint with Paramount, took out an ad in *Daily Variety* (July

21, 1936) thanking Martha and "all those who cooperated to make this engagement one of the most enjoyable and worthwhile of my picture career ... and one of the happiest recollections of my life."

Raye was accompanied by her mother to a preview of *Rhythm on the Range*. She later told an interviewer, "That preview—I'll never have another night like that! You can't imagine the thrill of it.... I scarcely saw the picture; bawled all the way through it, and ruined the nicest dress I ever had. Mama nudged me and said, 'Don't cry, you idiot!—they like you.'"[1]

Said syndicated columnist Jimmie Fidler, "She is an awkward, ungainly girl (and well aware of it), but her face, save for its Joe E. Brown mouth, is not far from pretty.... When she grins, teeth seem to fly into her mouth from all angles. Keep your eyes peeled for her future exploits; it is my guess that she is headed for the heights."[2]

Reviews: "[Raye] gets in her drunk bit and has an opportunity to show off all of her tricks, particularly her mugging.... There are some flaws in Miss Raye's performance, which is to be expected, but at first sight she impresses as a very promising picture comedienne." *Variety*, August 5, 1936

"Miss Raye stops the show, both as a singer and an impersonator.... Audiences will regard her as either a priceless heritage or an unmitigated nuisance." Philip K. Scheuer, *Los Angeles Times*, July 31, 1936

"Martha Raye, the funny girl, will razz your nerves terrifically until you begin to get used to her and decide that she really is funny as the dickens! And how Miss Raye can 'swing' after a couple of shots of vodka!" *Washington Post*, August 22, 1936

The Big Broadcast of 1937 (Paramount)

Release: October 6, 1936

Running Time: 100 minutes

Cast: Jack Benny (*Jack Carson*), George Burns (*Mr. Platt*), Gracie Allen (*Mrs. Platt*), Bob Burns (*Bob Black*), Martha Raye (*Patsy*), Shirley Ross (*Gwen Holmes*), Ray Milland (*Bob Miller*), Frank Forest (*Frank Rossman*), Larry Adler, Benny Fields, Eleanore Whitney (*Specialties*), Irving Bacon (*Property Man*), Sam Hearn (*Schlepperman*), Virginia Weidler (*Flower Girl*), David Holt, Billie Lee (*Train Bearers*), Don Hulbert (*Page Boy*), Stan Kavanaugh (*Kavvy*), Billie Bellport (*Mrs. Peters*), Frank Jenks (*Trombone Player*), Ernest Cossart (*"Uncle" Actor*), Helen Ainsworth (*Penelope*), Murray Alper (*Taxi Driver*), Nora Cecil (*Radio Hostess*), William Arnold (*Jones*), Edward LeSaint (*Minister*), Pat West (*Stage Manager*), Jack Mulhall (*Clerk*), Harry Depp (*Assistant Property Man*), Ellen Drew (*Telephone Girl*), Leonid Kinskey (*Russian Man*), Leopold Stokowski and His Symphonic Orchestra, Benny Goodman and His Band

Crew: Mitchell Leisen (*Director*), Lewis E. Gensler (*Producer*), Walter DeLeon, Francis Martin (*Screenplay*), Erwin Gelsey, Arthur Kober, Barry Trivers (*Story*), Gordon Jennings, Paul Lerpae (*Special Photographic Effects*), Hans Dreier, Robert Usher (*Art Directors*), Stuart Gilmore (*Editor*), Harold Lewis, Louis Mesenkop, Charles Althouse (*Sound Recorders*), Theodor Sparkuhl (*Photography*), Ralph

Rainger, Leo Robin (*Music and Lyrics*), Boris Morros (*Musical Director*), LeRoy Prinz (*Choreographer*), A.E. Freudeman (*Interior Decorator*)

Synopsis: Jack Carson, manager of National Network Radio, sells wealthy Mr. and Mrs. Platt on sponsoring a new program, *The Platt Golf Ball Hour*. The program's host, popular singer Frank Rossman, takes offense when he hears a local broadcaster, Gwen Holmes, billed as "Your Village Nightingale," lampooning his performances. Rossman's agent, Bob Miller, suggests to Carson that they squelch Miss Holmes' mockery by giving her a radio contract in New York at a modest salary, and then leaving her "in cold storage." The plan goes awry when eccentric Mrs. Platt insists that Gwen be featured on the Platt program. Bob, who's falling for Gwen, takes her out on the town, but before she can go on the air, she catches a glimpse of a newspaper gossip column that reveals the real reason she was brought to New York. Angry, she nonetheless goes forward with her guest appearance on *The Platt Golf Ball Hour*, after coolly negotiating a higher fee.

Thinking that Bob was only using her, Gwen takes the suggestion of her pal Patsy and launches a strictly-for-publicity romance with the egotistical Frank Rossman. The scheme works only too well, winning Gwen a regular spot on Rossman's program, and culminating in plans for an on-air wedding to be heard by 50 million listeners.

Also turning up in New York is homespun musician Bob Black, seeking an audition for conductor Leopold Stokowski's program. Thwarted in his efforts to see the great maestro, Black wanders the halls of the studio, occasionally interrupting science programs, advice-to-the-lovelorn shows and other broadcasts in progress. Two days before the wedding broadcast, Gwen goes missing, giving Patsy an opportunity to make her radio singing debut.

Notes: Although she speaks the film's first line of dialogue, and gets things off to a rolling start with her tumble down some stairs, Martha's second Paramount picture doesn't stack up to *Rhythm on the Range* as a showcase for her talent, despite some effective moments. Cast as manager Jack Carson's secretary Patsy, she turns up only intermittently in the first hour, giving romantic advice to the heroine (while bemoaning her own unattached state), pitching a weak joke to her boss in hopes of landing a $15 prize offered by the station, and unwittingly joining Gracie Allen in a game of leapfrog.

Her standout scene comes near the end, when she takes center stage for a production number featuring her rendition of the song "Vote for Mr. Rhythm." A few minutes later, she provides a spirited vocal for a jazzy rendition of "Here Comes the Bride" as the film's happy ending looms. Though she would be paired romantically with Bob Burns several times during her Paramount stint, they have no interaction here. Nor is her singing talent in evidence until her last-minute opportunity to fill in.

During production, Martha met Jerry Hopper, assistant to Paramount musical director Boris Morros, and romance bloomed—briefly. She happily announced their engagement, but they soon parted.

Reviews: "Both in general entertainment appeal and in box office potentialities, it is tune-film property that hits the bull's eye." *Variety,* October 28, 1936

"All the players score, leaving no one disappointed. While it is unfair to single out one above the others, there is no mistaking the stronger audience reaction evoked by Bob Burns and Martha Raye." *Los Angeles Times,* November 1, 1936

"Martha Raye [is] a heap funnier and more likable in this piece than she was in *Rhythm on the Range.*" Mae Tinée, *Chicago Tribune,* November 10, 1936

"Martha Raye, who seems to have been teamed, more or less, with the Bazooka Burns lately, is held in a state of mild repression until the film has almost run its length, when she is turned loose with all of the fervor of her explosive nature to knock the customers flat on their backs…. Her modernized vocal version of 'The Wedding March' in the picture's finale is a comedy gem that must be heard to be appreciated." *Washington Post,* October 24, 1936

Hideaway Girl *(Paramount)*

Release: November 20, 1936

Running Time: 71 minutes

Cast: Shirley Ross (*Toni Ainsworth*), Robert Cummings (*Mike Winslow*), Martha Raye (*Helen Flint*), Monroe Owsley (*Count de Montaigne*), Elizabeth Russell (*Cellette*), Louis Da Pron (*Tom Flint*), Ray Walker (*Freddie*), Wilma Francis (*Muriel Courtney*), Robert Middlemass (*Captain Dixon*), Edward Brophy (*Bugs Murphy*), James Eagles (*Birdie Arnold*), Bob Murphy (*Captain MacArthur*), Lee Phelps (*Sgt. Davis*), Jimmie Dundee (*Detective*), Marten Lamont, Frank Losee, Jr. (*Sailors*), James Barton (*Motorcycle Cop*), Chester Gan (*Cook*), Donald Kerr, Bert Moorhouse (*Cameramen*), Harry Jordan, Allen Pomeroy (*Chauffeurs*), Kenneth Harlan (*Lead Steward*), The Avalon Boys (*Themselves*)

Crew: George Archainbaud (*Director*), A.M. Botsford (*Producer*), Joseph Moncure March, Eddie Welch (*Screenplay*), David Garth (*Story*), Arthur P. Schmidt (*Editor*), Hans Dreier, Robert Odell (*Art Directors*), A.E. Freudeman (*Interior Decorator*), Boris Morros (*Musical Director*), Al Siegel (*Vocal Arrangements*), Earl Hayman, Don Johnson (*Sound Recorders*), Hal Walker (*Assistant Director*)

Synopsis: Seen fleeing from a society wedding, Toni Ainsworth is suspected of using the alias Lady Jane and stealing a count's jewels. Toni assumes the alias Belinda Hipplewaite and hides out on the yacht of Mike Winslow, whom she met at a gas station after being mistaken for his wife by reporters. What begins as a phony romance gradually changes as Toni and Mike get to know each other while maintaining the pretense of being married. Complications ensue when it is revealed that Mike already has a fiancée, Muriel Courtney. Muriel threatens to sue him for breach of promise after finding him with Toni.

Notes: "The twin stars of *The Big Broadcast* [Shirley Ross and Martha] are here again!" crowed newspaper advertisements for this film. *Hideaway Girl* was adapted from a short story, "Cabin Cruiser" by David Garth, published in the May 1936 issue of *Redbook.* Studio publicity described the picture as "a mystery story "garnished with excellent music and dancing."[3] According to *Daily Variety* (November 14, 1936), Martha was a late addition to the cast. "Pic was turned out on short money schedule and Raye sequences were written in as an afterthought, with Eddie Welch credited with the winning script additions." Sam Coslow composed an original song, "Beethoven, Mendelssohn and Brahms," for Martha.

Director George Archainbaud (1890–1959) had a career that extended back to the silent film days, and would continue into television. He was often associated with Westerns.

The film was originally announced under the title *Hideaway*. Its production was said to be fraught with problems. "Since shooting started, several weeks ago, photographers Teddy Tetzlaff and Charles Lang have been put on the hospital list with minor ailments, Martha Raye was out for several days with laryngitis; Elizabeth Russell was stricken with ptomaine poisoning."[4]

An Indiana exhibitor who played *Hideaway Girl* to good box office at his theater reported in *Motion Picture Herald* (January 16, 1937), "Martha Raye is so near tops, there is no doubt about it, and it looks like from where I stand that the very next picture she is in will be biggest box office of all of them. If the next one she is in is equally as good as this one, everyone will be more than satisfied."

Prints of *Hideaway Girl* were all but unknown by the 21st century, making it Martha's most difficult feature film to see.

Reviews: "Perhaps patrons will go to see *Hideaway Girl* because of Miss Raye's presence; maybe not. They'll see her, and little else. This feature starts out like a society crook meller [melodrama], turns slightly musical, then goes rowdy comedy, next a big romantic and staggers off as hokum melodrama…. Without Martha Raye this would have been a dismal affair. Her comedy goes far towards warding off vacuum in the story and stumbling moments in the direction." *Variety,* January 20, 1937

"Miss Raye again skips, dances, sings, and shouts with a great deal of abandon, and the result is good entertainment without subtlety or sophistication, enjoyable if one is in the mood, and just noise if one is not." Hayden Hickok, *Syracuse* (NY) *Herald,* December 4, 1936

"Given careful direction, Miss Raye is one of the best low comedians on the screen, but without such direction she overdoes her act so far that many in the audience are not amused. A little more direction would have helped her in this picture." *Atlanta* (GA) *Constitution,* November 29, 1936

College Holiday (Paramount)

Release: December 19, 1936
Running Time: 86 minutes
Cast: Jack Benny (*J. Davis Bowster*), George Burns (*George Hymen*), Gracie Allen (*Calliope Dove*), Mary Boland (*Carola P. Gaye*), Martha Raye (*Daisy Schloggenheimer*), Ben Blue (*Stagehand*), Marsha Hunt (*Sylvia Smith*), Leif Erickson (*Dick Winters*), Eleanore Whitney (*Eleanore Wayne*), Johnny Downs (*Johnny Jones*), Etienne Girardot (*Prof. Hercules Dove*), Olympe Bradna (*Felice L'Hommedieu*), Louis DaPron (*Barry Taylor*), Jed Prouty (*Sheriff John J. Trimble*), Margaret Seddon (*Mrs. Schloggenheimer*), Nick Lukats (*Wisconsin*), Richard Carle (*Judge Bent*), Charles Arnt (*Ticket Clerk*), Harry Hayden (*Mr. Smith*), Priscilla Lawson (*Telephone Operator*), Charles R. Moore (*Redcap*), Fred "Snowflake" Toones (*Porter*), Edward LeSaint (*Dr. Channing*), Alexander Cross, Harold Webster (*Creditors*), Nora Cecil (*Miss Elkins*), Edward Peil, Sr. (*Cop in Park*), Mark Strong (*Conductor*), Lal Chand

Mehra (*Rahma*), Howard M. Mitchell (*Deputy*), Philip Hurlic (*Baby Cupid*), Willie Fung (*Man in Junk*)

Crew: Frank Tuttle (*Director*), Harlan Thompson (*Producer*), J.P. McEvoy, Harlan Ware, Henry Myers, Jay Gorney (*Screenplay*), Ralph Rainger, Leo Robin, Burton Lane, Ralph Freed (*Songs*), LeRoy Prinz (*Dance Director*), Hans Dreier, Robert Usher (*Art Directors*), Theodor Sparkhul, William C. Mellor (*Photography*), Edith Head (*Costume Designer*), LeRoy Stone (*Editor*), Farciot Edouart (*Special Photographic Effects*), Boris Morros (*Musical Director*), Harold Lewis, John Cope (*Sound Recorders*), A.E. Freudeman (*Interior Decorator*)

Synopsis: Sylvia Smith is called home from college to help her ailing father save his investment in the Hotel Casa Del Mar. Fellow investor J. Davis Bowster persuades its mortgage holder, chewing gum heiress Carola P. Gaye, to use it as the site for her new project, a eugenics experiment. Promising to deliver a healthy number of attractive young participants, Bowster recruits a passel of college students on summer break, all of them aspiring entertainers. Among them are handsome Dick Winters, who's been trying to locate Sylvia ever since he impulsively kissed her at a college dance, and naïve but boisterous Daisy Schloggenheimer, who lived a very sheltered life in a farming community.

Miss Gaye calls upon eugenics professor Hercules Dove, who believes his daughter Calliope is perfectly equipped to select ideal partners for each student. Calliope's choices don't sit well with the students, who spoil Miss Gaye's arrangements by pairing off of their own accord. Angry, she makes plans to foreclose on the current owners, leaving Sylvia, Dick, and their friends to save the place by putting on their own show.

Notes: An interesting cultural artifact as well as a modestly entertaining musical comedy, *College Holiday* offers a strong cast of 1930s movie and radio favorites as well as some dated racial and ethnic attitudes perhaps best exemplified by the finale, in which the leading characters raise money by putting on "an inter-collegiate minstrel show." That said, this is a whimsical, if not always riotously funny, film that offers a zany premise and a game cast of experienced laugh-getters giving it their all.

Martha plays Daisy, student at Cornucopia College in Corn City, who according to her mother "never has been outside Corn City, or outdoors after dark." Trained in a self-defense method involving a punch in the breadbasket for any boy who gets fresh, she employs it freely, including on Jack Benny's Bowster, whom she knocks out cold within moments of meeting him. She's given two effectively mounted musical numbers, "So What?" and "Who's That Knocking at My Heart?," the latter performed in blackface.

Top-billed Jack Benny (1902–1974) hadn't yet fully developed his comic persona, but has some amusing moments here. Avoiding his creditors, he takes refuge in the piano kept in his office, where he also has at hand a miniature keyboard, snacks and a tiny guard dog.

Martha is one of three very accomplished comediennes given screen time. Gracie Allen (1895–1964) plays a character whose professor father calls her "the perfect mind in the perfect body," and insists she can only be matched with her ideal male counterpart. In search of the physically impeccable Adonis, she has fun taking the measurements of most of the male cast, as partner George Burns (playing an unspecified sidekick named George) looks on in mild annoyance. Spotting one bare-chested specimen, she coos, "George, isn't he pretty? Get the tape measure." Strangely, most of her victims seem to measure 32 inches, left, right, backwards, or forwards, but all of them fall short of her ideal. Mary Boland (1880–1965), as Carola P. Gaye, has some funny scenes as the flighty, middle-aged heiress who thinks Calliope's mate selection process is working just *fine* when it pairs her with handsome, blond Dick Winters.

The last of the comic players to arrive on the scene is Ben Blue (1901–1975), cast as an electrician who provides sets and props for the Hotel Casa Del Mar stage show, as well as a spark of inspiration for Calliope's matchmaking. Among the young newcomers unbilled in smallish roles are Dorothy Lamour, Ellen Drew and Marjorie Reynolds. In short order, Lamour be would playing lead roles at Paramount, with Martha in support.

At the time of *College Holiday*, the study of eugenics was at or near its peak, having been incorporated into the academic program of many universities, both in the U.S. and abroad. The film doesn't make a strong argument one way or the other for its validity, although it's implied that this is just the latest in a long string of Miss Gaye's faddish interests, most of which quickly fade. Certainly the film itself shows obvious signs of its age, in terms of its approach to non-white, non–Eurocentric characters and beliefs.

Studio publicity quoted director Frank Tuttle as saying, "I'd like to suggest that Miss Raye's success springs from the fact that she is a combination of Miss [Marie] Dressler and Miss [Clara] Bow. She has Marie's slapstick spontaneity and the almost boundless energy of Clara in her heyday."[5]

Reviews: "The names will probably get it by for fair business, yet it's too bad that with such an assemblage of good and well known talent that the picture rates above average neither as entertainment nor as a potential big grosser.... Miss Raye is okay again, through her own efforts and ability, but her songs this time are not so hot." *Variety*, December 30, 1936

"*College Holiday* is just the sort of frivolous amusement the excitement-jaded film fan craves at the moment.... The picture is sumptuously staged and costumed, smartly directed and moves at fast tempo." Mae Tinée, *Chicago Tribune*, December 29, 1936

"A very merry show.... Martha Raye has some very funny scenes and rings the bill [sic] with her song and dance in blackface." *Washington Post*, January 1, 1937

Waikiki Wedding (Paramount)
Release: March 23, 1937
Running Time: 89 minutes
Cast: Bing Crosby (*Tony Marvin*), Bob Burns (*Shad Buggle*), Martha Raye (*Myrtle Finch*), Shirley Ross (*Georgia Smith*), George Barbier (*J.P. Todhunter*), Leif Erikson [Erickson] (*Dr. Victor Quimby*), Grady Sutton (*Everett Todhunter*), Granville Bates (*Uncle Herman*), Anthony Quinn (*Kimo*), Mitchell Lewis (*Koalani*), George Regas

(*Muamua*), Nick Lukats (*Assistant Purser*), Prince Leilani (*Priest*), Maurice Liu (*Kaiaka*), Raquel Echeverria (*Mahina*), Iris Yamaoka (*Tony's Secretary*), Emma Dunn (*Mrs. Marvin*), David Newell (*Radio Operator*), Harry J. Vejar (*Desk Sergeant*), Pierre Watkin (*John Durkin*), Ralph Remley (*Tomlin*), Harry Stubbs (*Keith*), Alfonso Pedroza (*Doorman*), Gloria Williams (*Tourist*), Alexander Leftwich (*Harrison*), Spencer Charters (*Frame*)

Crew: Frank Tuttle (*Director*), Arthur Hornblow, Jr. (*Producer*), Frank Butler, Don Hartman, Walter DeLeon, Francis Martin (*Screenplay*), Frank Butler, Don Hartman (*Story*), Boris Morros (*Musical Director*), Leo Robin, Ralph Rainger (*Words and Music*), Victor Young (*Orchestrator*), Al Siegel, Arthur Franklin (*Arrangements*), Karl Struss (*Photography*), Farciot Edouart (*Special Photographic Effects*), Robert E. Bruce (*Hawaiian Exteriors*), Hans Dreier, Robert Usher (*Art Directors*), Paul Weatherwax (*Editor*), Edith Head (*Costume Design*), Gene Merritt, Louis Mesenkop (*Sound Recorders*), A.E. Freudeman (*Interior Decorator*)

Synopsis: Tony Marvin of Imperial Pineapples, Ltd., dreams up a promotional stunt in which a young woman will be named the company's "Pineapple Girl" and win a three-week romantic trip to Hawaii. His boss J.P. Todhunter thinks it's a brilliant idea, until contest winner Georgia Smith spends a few days on the islands,

Waikiki Wedding reunited Martha with Bing Crosby (center), star of her first Paramount film, and was her third film with Shirley Ross (right).

says she's not having any fun and wants to go home early. With arrangements already made for national syndication of the winner's dispatches from the islands, Tony takes matters into his own hands by pitching woo to her. At first he unwittingly charms the wrong young lady, Georgia's stenographer pal Myrtle Finch, while his relationship with Georgia gets off to a rocky start. Determined to show her Hawaii's romantic side, Tony arranges for Georgia to be transported to a nearby island, where he begins to win her interest. Meanwhile, Myrtle takes a shine to Tony's farm-bred sidekick Shad, though she seems to be in competition for his affections with his pet pig. Complications ensue when Georgia's erstwhile boyfriend from home, Dr. Victor Quimby, comes to her rescue after she falls out of touch. Georgia begins to suspect Tony's motives in romancing her.

Notes: Martha is reteamed with two of her co-stars from her first movie success *Rhythm on the Range,* Bing Crosby and Bob Burns, with limited success in this serviceable musical comedy/travelogue. Although her screen time is substantial, the *Waikiki Wedding* script doesn't provide her with solid laugh lines or situations, depending on her to liven up the proceedings with pratfalls, gawks and grimaces. Once again, comedian Bob Burns serves as her would-be swain. She's directed here for the second time by Frank Tuttle, who previously worked with her in *College Holiday.* In one of his first significant screen roles, 21-year-old Anthony Quinn (1915–2001) plays Kimo, a bare-chested "native" who proves not to be what he first seems. According to Paramount publicity, the film boasted "a supporting cast of two hundred and fifty dancers, musicians and specialty performers" and gave Martha "her best role to date," a sentiment with which few reviewers would agree.

Once again, Martha's alleged homeliness is a target for gags, as when Shad asks her how she earned the money to pay his bail. "I won first place in a dog show," she says brightly. In another scene, Shad mistakes a monkey for Martha's character, saying, "Myrtle, how'd you get your face so dirty?" Musically, the emphasis here is on Bing Crosby and Shirley Ross, though Martha does get one bright number.

Exhibitors reporting to the *Motion Picture Herald* (August 14, 1937) said business was strong. A small-town Texas theater manager said the picture "broke all house records for us. Martha Raye will fill my house any day in the week." In Nebraska, "an excellent box office gross" was noted but "many of our patrons said it was not as good as they expected."

Reviews: "Story is along the old mistaken identity lines, and would not have stood up without that Hawaiian color. It could have been shortened considerably. Comedy isn't strong, but here again something is saved, this time through Miss Raye's mugging." *Variety,* March 31, 1937

"It is a honey for Martha Raye. She gets howls with her distinctive style and really sells her [musical] number." *Hollywood Reporter,* March 20, 1937

"Considered as a vehicle for the Crosby warbling and the Raye–Burns brand of fun, *Waikiki Wedding* holds up pretty well." *Washington Post,* April 17, 1937

Mountain Music (Paramount)
Release: June 18, 1937
Running Time: 76 minutes

Cast: Bob Burns (*Bob Burnside*), Martha Raye (*Mary Beamish*), John Howard (*Ardinger Burnside*), Terry Walker (*Lobelia Sheppard*), Rufe Davis (*Ham Sheppard*), George Hayes (*Grandpappy*), Spencer Charters (*Justice Sharody*), Charles Timblin (*Shep*), Jan Duggan (*Ma*), Olin Howland (*Pappy*), Fuzzy Knight (*Amos Burnside*), Wally Vernon (*Odette Potts*), Goodee Montgomery (*Alice*), Rita La Roy (*Mrs. Hamilton Lovelace*), Ward Bond, Wally Maher (*G-Men*), Miranda Giles (*Aunt Effie*),

Woebegone Mary (Martha Raye) is consoled by her Aunt Effie (Miranda Giles) in *Mountain Music.*

Arthur Hohl (*Prosecutor*), Lew Kelly (*Mailman*), Louis Natheaux (*Hamilton B. Lovelace*), Georgia Simmons (*Ma Sheppard*), Eddie Tamblyn (*Bellboy*)

Crew: Robert Florey (*Director*), Benjamin Glazer (*Producer*), John C. Moffitt, Duke Atteberry, Russel Crouse, Charles Lederer (*Screenplay*), MacKinlay Kantor (*Story*), Karl Struss (*Photography*), Boris Morros (*Musical Director*), Sam Coslow (*Words and Music*), Victor Young (*Orchestrator*), Al Siegel (*Vocal Supervisor*), Hans Dreier, John Goodman (*Art Directors*), Eda Warren (*Editor*), Le Roy Prinz (*Dance Director*), Philip Wisdom, Don Johnson (*Sound Recorders*)

Synopsis: In rural Arkansas, the Sheppards and the Burnsides have been feuding for generations, but an arranged wedding between Bob Burnside and Lobelia Sheppard is supposed to seal the deal for a ceasefire. Bob, knowing that Lobelia really loves his brother Ardinger, goes on the lam. After his abrupt disappearance, his hat is found by the river, pierced by a hole from a stray bullet. With Bob presumed dead, Ardinger is charged with his murder. Bob winds up in the town of Monotony, Arkansas, where he meets singer-dancer Mary Beamish. Unhappily single, Mary invents a mysterious beau from out of town to impress the other girls in the show, but is put on the spot when they want to meet him. Along comes an amnesiac Bob Burnside (when he's hit on the head, Bob doesn't know who he is) He is immediately attracted to Mary. But any time he's doused with water, he regains his memory and no longer finds Mary appealing. Sensing that her man is needed back at home to save his brother's life, Mary prepares to make a sacrifice—"a far, far greater thing I do."

Notes: Raye is teamed once again with comedian Bob Burns—and in this outing, they're the top-billed stars. "In accordance with Hollywood custom," screen publicists noted, "two comic players who have helped add life to many a feature are rewarded with starring roles.... [Burns and Raye] grab the lion's share of the film footage in this nonsensical bit about life in the Ozarks."[6]

That this isn't going to be an especially dignified outing for Burns is apparent from his first entrance, when the audience is confronted with his backside stuck out toward the camera before his face is seen. Over the course of the proceedings, he's doused with water multiple times.

The film's chief running gag concerns Bob Burnside, who when he's of sound mind has little use for Mary Beamish. First spotting her visage on a poster outside Odette Potts' entertainment emporium, he's unimpressed.

> POTTS: She's on the road to fame and beauty.
> BURNSIDE: Brother, she may be on the road to beauty, but her face is off on a terrible detour.

A whack on the head turns him into a fervent admirer of her charms, much to her delight:

> BURNSIDE: Mary, all I know is I love you so hard it makes my head hurt.
> MARY: There's something wrong with you, honey, but whatever it is, I wish every man had it.

The high point of Raye's clowning comes in a sequence where she fills in for another dancer in a raucous musical act, letting loose with an "Oh, boy!" when she finds herself hanging upside down from a chandelier. Later, in a courtroom, she wreaks havoc with a fire hose.

Sam Coslow, who gave Martha her signature song "Mr. Paganini," composed new songs for this outing, notably "Good Morning," heard twice in the film.

Visiting the film set during production, columnist May Mann wrote of Martha, "[A] more chirpy songful youngster never graced a picture lot…. She twisted her braids, handed Bob Burns a phoney [sic] cigar that exploded with a bang and played pranks on her director. In the middle of a take she remembered she was starving and that it was time for lunch, grabbed the megaphone of the assistant director and called 'one hour for lunch' and the company dismissed."[7]

Reviews: "[This is] an honest though only mildly successful effort to fit Bob Burns and Martha Raye to a feature in which they top the cast…. Both … struggle valiantly, but if they are to move up from support roles in features that star others, they'll need something better than *Mountain Music*…. The big-mouthed comedienne works too hard and is continually forcing her comedy…. She should tone down, for a little of it goes a long way." *Variety,* June 30, 1937

"Miss Raye clowns and sings to her heart's content. Story is pretty silly but Burns and Raye may put it over." John Scott, *Los Angeles Times,* June 25, 1937

"Here's an elegant dish of broad travesty and robustious [sic] slapstick, served with songs and played with a gusto that puts it over for a rollicking funfest…. Martha is demure and riotous in turn but most of her comedy and singing is acceptably toned down from previous outbursts, and is genuinely and acceptably comic." *Hollywood Reporter,* June 9, 1937

"Bob Burns is kinda sweet and Martha Raye is kinda likable and their picture is kinda lousy." Mae Tinée, *Chicago Tribune,* June 22, 1937

Artists and Models (Paramount)
Release: August 13, 1937
Running Time: 97 minutes
Cast: Jack Benny (*Mac Brewster*), Ida Lupino (*Paula Sewell*), Richard Arlen (*Alan Townsend*), Gail Patrick (*Cynthia Wentworth*), Ben Blue (*Jupiter Pluvius*), Judy Canova (*Toots*), The Yacht Club Boys, Cecil Cunningham (*Stella*), Donald Meek (*Dr. Zimmer*), Hedda Hopper (*Mrs. Townsend*), Martha Raye, Andre Kostelanetz and His Orchestra, Russell Patterson and his "Personettes," Judy, Anne and Zeke, Connie Boswell (*Specialties*), Peter Arno, McClelland Barclay, Arthur William Brown, Rube Goldberg, John LaGatta (*Artists*), Sandra Storme, Don Wilson (*Themselves*), Virginia Brissac (*Seamstress*), Howard C. Hickman (*Mr. Currie*), Jane Weir (*Miss Gordon*), David Newell (*Romeo*), Nick Lukats (*Photographer*), Kathryn Kay (*Lois Townsend*), Alan Birmingham (*Craig Sheldon*), Jerry Bergen (*Bartender*), Elsa Connor (*Stenographer*), Dell Henderson (*Early*), Harry Hayden (*Lord*), Alphonse Martell, Alexander Pollard (*Waiters*), Rex Moore (*Attendant*), Bernie Lamont, Reginald Simpson (*G-Men*), John Graham Spacey (*Englishman*)
Crew: Raoul Walsh (*Director*), William LeBaron (*Executive Producer*), Lewis E. Gensler (*Producer*), Walter DeLeon, Francis Martin (*Screenplay*), Eve Greene, Harlan Ware (*Adaptation*), Sig Herzig, Gene Thackrey (*Story*), Boris Morros (*Musical*

Director), Phil Boutelje (*Musical Adviser*), Victor Milner (*Photography*), Gordon Jennings (*Special Photographic Effects*), Alma Ruth Macrorie (*Editor*), Hans Dreier, Robert Usher (*Art Directors*), Harold Lewis, Louis Mesenkop (*Sound Recorders*), A.E. Freudeman (*Interior Decorator*), LeRoy Prinz (*Choreographer*), Travis Banton (*Costumes*)

Synopsis: Advertising agency owner Mac Brewster, serving as chairman of the annual Artists and Models Ball, persuades client Alan Townsend to finance a publicity campaign spotlighting a beautiful model as the queen of the ball. Mac plans to elect his girlfriend, up-and-coming model Paula Sewell, as the Townsend Girl, but the client insists the winner must not be a professional model, but instead a young woman who can be found in the Social Register. Knowing she is disheartened about the state of her career, Mac proposes marriage to Paula, but she is determined to make something of herself professionally first.

Learning that Mr. Townsend is spending a few days in Miami, Paula follows him there in order to pose as socialite "Paula Monterey" and win the modeling contract. She succeeds in making the acquaintance of Alan and his family members, who think she looks familiar (from her magazine ads) but can't place her. Alan not only thinks she's perfect for the modeling job, but also falls in love with her. When Mac arrives in Miami with his own potential Townsend Girl, socially prominent Cynthia Wentworth, Paula's masquerade is exposed, threatening to cost her Alan's affection.

Notes: Considering that Martha doesn't even appear onscreen until nearly 90 minutes into the 97-minute *Artists and Models*, her brief role attracted quite a bit of attention, not all of it welcome. Like so many Paramount pictures of the period, this is primarily a variety show, stitched together with the most perfunctory elements of plot. Seen as a performer at the Artists and Models Ball, Martha dons blackface for a Harlem-set musical sketch with Louis Armstrong, centered around the song "Public Melody #1."

Though Martha told reporters she'd jumped at the chance to work with the talented Armstrong, *Variety*'s reviewer correctly predicted that her blackface sequence would prove controversial with some Southern theater managers and moviegoers. Columnist Franklyn Frank, whose column was syndicated to African-American newspapers, thought this a tempest in a teapot: "Miss Raye is a comedienne and therefore has no Greta Garbo reputation to maintain; it is therefore difficult to see how she can be harmed by appearing in blackface.... She does not kiss Louis Armstrong or associates, nor does she embrace them. What, then, can the objection be?"[8]

But reviewer Dudley Glass, writing for the Hearst chain's Atlanta newspaper, responded much as *Variety*'s article had predicted. "It is coarse to the point of vulgarity," Glass wrote of the sequence. "I have no objections to Negroes on the screen. I like them from Bill Robinson down the line. Their stuff usually is good. But I don't like mixing white folk—and especially a white girl—in their acts."[9]

Though *Artists and Models* has a respectable share of laughs, songs and glitter, it all too often resembles a movie assembled from the leftovers found on Paramount's cutting room floor. Judy Canova, as Paula's roommate Toots, is paired comedically with Ben Blue, cast as a professional rainmaker who pitches woo at her.

Top-billed Jack Benny, effectively presented, earns his share of laughs. In one scene, Benny's character listens as announcer Don Wilson introduces the Jack Benny program on a nearby radio, and comments, "Very clever fellow. I've always liked him." Ida Lupino (1918–1995), cast in the type of unimportant ingénue role that marked much of her early career, is adequate as Paula, though her speech is so impeccably correct and high-toned from the get-go that there's no noticeable difference when she decides to assume the role of a socialite.

A few other interesting names help fill out the cast. Among the real-life cartoonists seen sketching beautiful models at the ball are Peter Arno and Rube Goldberg. Goldberg, who's given a dialogue scene with Jack Benny, creates a typical cartoon that, not surprisingly, doesn't much resemble the pretty young lady who posed for it. Character actress Cecil Cunningham (1888–1959) has some amusing moments as Mac Brewster's dry-witted, sardonic secretary. Seen to no great advantage as Alan Townsend's socialite mother is actress Hedda Hopper (1885–1966), who would soon launch her far more successful career as a syndicated gossip columnist.

Raoul Walsh (1887–1980) would work with Martha again a year later in *College Swing*. He ultimately enjoyed far more success as a director of rough-and-tumble action pictures than musical comedies, though he had the dubious distinction of directing Benny's much-mocked *The Horn Blows at Midnight* (1945).

Artists and Models was successful enough to result in a sequel of sorts, *Artists and Models Abroad* (1938). Of the original cast, only Jack Benny and the Yacht Club Boys were invited back for it, and the connection between the two films didn't extend much beyond the names. The later Martin and Lewis comedy *Artists and Models* (1955) borrowed nothing but the title.

Reviews: "It holds enough variety, comedy, color, spec[tacle], flash, dash and novelty for a couple of pictures … a fetching mélange and quite skillfully held together." *Variety,* August 4, 1937

"[A] suave, witty and polished show, one of the sprightliest of the season's musical comedies…. We could have done with less of the Martha Raye–Louis Armstrong sequence, but that's a minor fault." Frank Nugent, *New York Times,* August 5, 1937

"Martha Raye has a rowdily exciting specialty to do with Harlem setting, scarcely one of her best…. Raoul Walsh … welded the ingredients in pretty satisfying style." Edwin Schallert, *Los Angeles Times,* August 12, 1937

Double or Nothing *(Paramount)*

Release: September 17, 1937
Running Time: 90 minutes
Cast: Bing Crosby (*"Lefty" Boylan*), Martha Raye (*Liza Lou Lane*), Andy Devine (*Half Pint*), Mary Carlisle (*Vicki Clark*), William Frawley (*John Pederson*), Benny Baker (*Sailor*), Samuel S. Hinds (*Jonathan Clark*), William Henry (*Egbert Clark*), Fay Holden (*Martha Sewell Clark*), Bert Hanlon (*Nick Praxiteles*), Gilbert Emery (*Mr. Mitchell*), Walter Kingsford (*Mr. Dobson*), John Gallaudet (*Johnny Rutherford*), Alphonse Berg, Tex Morrissey, Frances Faye, Ames and Arno, Ed Rickard, Steve and Andre Calgary (*Specialties*), Harry Barris (*Orchestra Conductor*), Jimmy Notaro (*Dancing Cop*), Arthur Housman, Charles Irwin (*Drunks*), Jack Pennick (*Taxi*

Driver), Rolfe Sedan (*Headwaiter*), Michael Pecarovich (*Papouras*), George Burton (*Ticket Taker*), Alexandria Dean (*Secretary*), David Newell (*Nick's Lawyer*), Garry Owen, Charles Sherlock (*Process Servers*)

Crew: Theodore Reed (*Director*), Benjamin Glazer (*Producer*), Charles Lederer, Erwin Gelsey, John C. Moffitt, Duke Atteberry (*Screenplay*), M. Coates Webster (*Story*), Boris Morros (*Musical Director*), Al Siegel (*Vocal Supervisor*), Max Terr (*Sing Band Arrangements*), Victor Young (*Orchestral Arrangements*), Arthur Franklin (*Musical Adviser*), Karl Struss (*Photography*), Hans Dreier, Roland Anderson (*Art Directors*), Edward Dmytryk (*Editor*), Charles Hisserich, Don Johnson (*Sound Recorders*), Edith Head (*Costume Design*), LeRoy Prinz (*Choreographer*), A.E. Freudeman (*Interior Decorator*)

Synopsis: Eccentric millionaire Axel Clark's will gives his surviving family only token bequests, while using the remainder of his fortune to settle a "lifelong difference of opinion" with his brother Jonathan. Unlike Axel, who believes people are fundamentally "honest and intelligent," Jonathan declares them "rogues and fools." To that end, Clark's lawyers Dobson and Mitchell are instructed to drop 25 purses in public places, each containing a $100 bill. Of the 25, four are returned by honest people: singer-musician "Lefty" Boylan, small-time businessman John Pederson, dimwitted Half-Pint and burlesque performer-turned-actress Liza Lou Lane. Each of the four is given $5000 from the Clark estate, with the rest of the money to be awarded to the first person to double his or her $5000 by "honest endeavor" within 30 days. If none of them manages to do so, then brother Jonathan will inherit the family fortune.

Pederson persuades his fellow contestants to pool their resources; if any one of them wins the competition, they will all share in the proceeds. However, greedy Jonathan enlists his wife, son and daughter to befriend the contestants, egging them on to make bad investments that will prevent them from winning. Stuffy son Egbert is dismayed to be assigned to "that vulgar young woman," Liza Lou. Pretty Vicki Clark, who finds Lefty charming despite herself, declines to help in the plot, until Jonathan leads her to believe winning the money will save him from an impending charge of embezzlement.

One by one, with the connivance of the Clarks, the contestants fall victim to failed schemes. John Pederson soon loses his money investing in a phony gold mine, while Half-Pint opens a golf range that attracts business but awards cash prizes that drain his capital. While Lefty opens his own nightclub, the Four Wind Club, Liza Lou purchases the rowboat concession in a nearby park, staffed by some of the lovely young ladies with whom she worked onstage ("the lake propelled solely by girl power"). Unfortunately, with the combination of a leaky boat, a sabotaged musical cue, and a timely summons to the police, Liza Lou's plan falls apart. With the 30-day deadline at hand, only Lefty's nightclub stands a chance of success.

Notes: If not one of Martha's best roles at Paramount, this is nonetheless a slick, fast-paced, entertaining film that gives her select moments in the spotlight. One of its running gags finds former burlesque queen Liza Lou overcome with the uncontrollable urge to strip any time she hears the song "It's On, It's Off," which featured in her act. Though there's little romantic interest for her character here, it's refreshing to see her as a woman attractive enough to earn a living in burlesque, as opposed to earlier films that depicted her as horrifically homely.

Brassier than she is bright, Liza Lou's first idea for spending the money involves her mother:

> LIZA LOU: Gee, now if I would, I could get my mother that operation.
> HALF-PINT: What's the matter with your mother?
> LIZA LOU: Oh, nothing. She just likes operations.

Most of the film's last half-hour is taken up with the opening night performance at Lefty's club, which involves his unique "Sing Band" (with human voices taking the place of musical instruments), several specialty acts and a rousing number centered on Martha and specialty performer Frances Faye as "The Lane Sisters," accompanied by Bing Crosby.

Martha works here for the first time with comic actor Andy Devine, who teamed with her again for her comedy *Never Say Die*. According to *Life* magazine (July 18, 1938), the sight gag that finds Liza Lou's zippered dress armed with padlocks (to prevent unexpected stripteases) was found vulgar by censors in Australia, who had the scene cut.

Box office reports from neighborhood theaters varied, as reported in the *Motion Picture Herald* (November 20, 1937). "This one is very good, the kind that will get them in and please about as near as 100 percent as possible," reported an exhibitor in Oklahoma. "Better than average business." However, an Indiana theater owner found that the film "dragged so much that we had a number of walkouts halfway through…. The first three reels had all the pep that was in the picture."

Reviews: "Stage is set for the public to go for Raye in a big way right now, but the studio muffs the chance, as she has little to do beyond an exaggerated and noisy broad comedy part. Her song numbers have been built up with elaborate production backgrounds, but they contain nothing she hasn't done before, and the edge is dulled by repetition." *Variety*, August 18, 1937

"A lightweight musical comedy with a bare plot and plenty of singing." Nash and Ross, *The Motion Picture Guide*

"This piece is a pleasing comedy with music. Nothing to get het-up about, but brain-resting entertainment." Mae Tinée, *Chicago Tribune*, September 13, 1937

The Big Broadcast of 1938 (Paramount)

Release: February 11, 1938
Running Time: 91 minutes
Cast: W.C. Fields (*T. Frothingill Bellows/S.B. Bellows*), Martha Raye (*Martha Bellows*), Dorothy Lamour (*Dorothy Wyndham*), Shirley Ross (*Cleo Fielding*), Lynne Overman (*Scoop McPhail*), Bob Hope (*Buzz Fielding*), Ben Blue (*Mike*), Leif Erikson [Erickson] (*Bob Hayes*), Patricia Wilder (*Honey Chile*), Grace Bradley (*Grace Fielding*), Rufe Davis (*Turnkey*), Lionel Pape (*Lord Droopy*), Dorothy Howe [Virginia Vale] (*Joan Fielding*), Russell Hicks (*Captain Stafford*), Kirsten Flagstad, Tito Guizar, Shep Fields and His Rippling Rhythm Orchestra (*Specialties*), Don Brodie (*Radio Operator*), James Craig (*Steward*), Robert Allen, Jerry Fletcher (*Gas Station Atten-*

dants), Wally Maher (*Court Clerk*), Edgar Norton (*Bellows' Secretary*), Leonid Kinsky (*Ivan*), Ray Hanford (*Pilot*), Irving Bacon (*Prisoner*), Mae Busch (*Chaperone*), Billy Daniel (*Page Boy*), Rex Moore (*Caddy*)

Crew: Mitchell Leisen (*Director*), Harlan Thompson (*Producer*), Walter DeLeon, Francis Martin, Ken Englund (*Screenplay*), Howard Lindsay, Russel Crouse (*Adaptation*), Frederick Hazlitt Brennan (*Story*), Ralph Rainger, Leo Robin (*Music and Lyrics*), Harry Fischbeck (*Photography*), Gordon Jennings (*Special Photographic Effects*), Hans Dreier, Ernest Fegté (*Art Directors*), Chandler House, Eda Warren (*Editors*), Boris Morros (*Musical Director*), Arthur Franklin (*Musical Adviser*), Gene Merritt, Don Johnson, Charles Althouse (*Sound Recorders*), Edith Head (*Costumes*), A.E. Freudeman (*Interior Decorator*), Leon Schlesinger (*Cartoon Sequence*)

Synopsis: Two ocean liners, the S.S. *Gigantic* and the S.S. *Colossal,* embark on a trans–Atlantic race from New York to Cherbourg, France, attempting to set a new speed record. T. Frothingill Bellows, owner of the *Gigantic,* books passage on the *Colossal* for his trouble-prone brother S.B., in hopes of slowing down the rival ship. Arriving by mistake on the *Gigantic,* S.B. proceeds to muck things up on the wrong ship, refusing to allow young inventor Bob Hayes to increase the *Gigantic's* speed with his radio-powered equipment.

Acting as emcee for a radio broadcast of the race is thrice-divorced Buzz Fielding, who placed a $50,000 bet on the *Gigantic* to win in hopes of paying off the back alimony he owes his ex-wives. Seeing that Buzz has a new lady friend, Dorothy Wyndham, his exes decide to come along on the voyage, not happy at the prospect of their alimony being shared down the road with a fourth spouse. Dorothy seems to be the object of Buzz's latest romantic attention, but she also catches the eye of Bob Hayes.

With the *Gigantic* falling behind in the race, Bob, Dorothy and Buzz scheme to distract S.B. Bellows with the attentions of a woman, so that Bob's new invention can be used to speed things up. Meanwhile, a distress signal from a lifeboat finds the *Gigantic* rescuing S.B.'s daughter Martha, of whom he says, "My daughter cannot be described as human. Wherever she goes, disaster follows." True to her reputation as a jinx, things indeed seem to go wrong whenever she's nearby.

Notes: *The Big Broadcast of 1938* is yet another all-star musical variety show that finds Martha in support of top-billed comedian W.C. Fields (1880–1946). "Easily the most lavish potpourri of music and mirth, fun and beautiful girls of the current season," promised studio publicists. According to the *New York Times, Big Broadcast of 1938* production began on September 13, 1937, with Fields in front of a movie camera for the first time in more than a year. Nowhere in sight during the film's first half, Martha is heard before she's seen, when her inimitable voice comes over the ship's radio.

Her strongest contribution comes in a lengthy show-stopping production number centered on Rainger and Robin's "Mama, That Moon Is Here Again." It finds her being tossed hither and yon by a team of dancers clad in sailor suits, showcasing both her foghorn singing voice and her amazing physical agility. Her other comedy scenes are few, though her trademark "Oh, boy!" is heard a couple of times, notably when she takes an unexpected detour down the ship's garbage chute. Her supersized mouth is once again the object of jokes, as Martha demonstrates her ability to steer the lifeboat with the power of her breath, while her status as a jinx is shown by the tendency of mirrors to shatter spontaneously when she comes into view.

The scene with Fields at the wheel of the *Gigantic,* nonchalantly steering the ship through multiple icebergs, is a bit surprising in light of the associations with the ill-fated *Titanic* it inevitably evokes.

Much of the cast was familiar to Martha from previous films, as she'd already shared the screen with Leif Erickson, Shirley Ross, Ben Blue and Rufe Davis, to name a few. *The Big Broadcast of 1938* marked the feature film debut of comedian Bob Hope (1903–2003). He introduces his signature song "Thanks for the Memory" in a duet with Shirley Ross. Hope would work with Martha again during the next few years, until his fame and box office pull surpassed hers. Richard Denning, who would become a fixture of B movies in the 1940s and 1950s, is noticeable in a bit part as a ship's officer near the film's finale.

This was the last of the *Big Broadcast* films, though it was a box office success.

Reviews: "It is pictorially original and alluring, upholding the showmanship traditions of Param[ount]'s annual parade of radio and screen talent.... Picture should prove satisfactory for all types of audiences." *Variety,* February 9, 1938

"Martha Raye, large-mouthed comedienne, is scarcely at her best in the picture, but she has one excellent song.... Her comedy, however, is a trifle wearying." *Boston Globe*, February 18, 1938

"Miss Raye gets the roughest treatment. She is tossed all over the place, shot down refuse chutes, thrown through ship's ventilators and otherwise manhandled, all in the name of good clean fun." *Washington Post,* February 26, 1938

College Swing (Paramount)

Release: April 29, 1938

Running Time: 86 minutes

Cast: George Burns (*George Jonas*), Gracie Allen (*Gracie Alden*), Martha Raye (*Mabel Grady*), Bob Hope (*Bud Brady*), Edward Everett Horton (*Hubert Dash*), Florence George (*Ginna Ashburn*), Ben Blue (*Ben Volt*), Betty Grable (*Betty*), Jackie Coogan (*Jackie*), John Payne (*Martin Bates*), Cecil Cunningham (*Dean Sleet*), Robert Cummings (*Radio Announcer*), Skinnay Ennis (*Skinnay*), The Slate Brothers (*Waiters*), Bob Mitchell and St. Brendan's Choristers (*1738 Choir*), Jerry Colonna (*Professor Koloski*), Edward LeSaint (*Dr. Storm*), Charles Trowbridge (*Dr. Ashburn*), Jerry Bergen (*Professor Jasper Chinn*), Tully Marshall (*Grandpa Alden*), Nelson McDowall (*School Magistrate*), Alphonse Martell (*Headwaiter*), James Craig, Richard Denning, John Hubbard, June Ray (*Students*), Charles K. French, Edmund Mortimer, Broderick O'Farrell, Harry Stafford (*Professors*), Barlowe Borland (*Dean*)

Crew: Raoul Walsh (*Director*), Lewis E. Gensler (*Producer*), Walter DeLeon, Francis Martin (*Screenplay*), Frederick Hazlitt Brennan (*Adaptation*), Ted Lesser (*Idea*), Frank Loesser, Hoagy Carmichael, Manning Sherwin, Burton Lane (*Original Songs*), Victor Milner (*Photography*), Hans Dreier, Ernest Fegté (*Art Directors*), LeRoy Stone (*Editor*), Harold Lewis, Howard Wilson (*Sound Recorders*), Edith Head (*Costumes*), A.E. Freudeman (*Interior Decorator*), Boris Morros (*Musical Director*), Arthur Franklin (*Musical Adviser*), LeRoy Prinz (*Choreographer*)

Synopsis: In 1738, Grandpa Alden is frustrated when his granddaughter is unable to graduate from school after trying for nine years. He bequeaths the family fortune to the school, unless at least one female Alden can obtain a degree within 200 years. In 1938, when Gracie Alden surprises everyone by passing her final examination, she inherits Alden College. With the help of her tutor Bud Brady, Gracie proceeds to turn the world of higher education upside down, abolishing entrance exams and engaging a motley crew of faculty to mold the minds of Alden College's student body.

A mysterious, French-accented and veiled woman who appears in Bud's office one day to announce, "I teach love," turns out to be Mabel Grady from Oklahoma, who explains, "You were hiring so many screwballs for this faculty I thought I could get a job." Engaged as Professor of Practical Romance, with Bud as her all-too-willing pupil, she joins the faculty to teach the younger generation a few things. But when the results of Gracie's examination are challenged by wealthy alumnus Hubert Dash, who composed her test, the prospect of a follow-up examination not only puts the jobs of Mabel and her friends into jeopardy, but threatens the romance between fraternity boy Martin Bates and a faculty member's daughter.

Notes: Martha and comic Ben Blue are cast as dubious additions to the faculty of zany Alden College in this fun musical comedy (with a reported $1 million budget) that showcases much of the Paramount contract roster. Though Gracie Allen dominates the comic scenes, Martha holds her own with some funny vignettes.

Her best scene finds her paired with Bob Hope (in a role originally earmarked for Jack Oakie) for a musical comedy routine, "How'dja Like to Love Me," indulging her appetites for singing, seduction and a square meal. Paramount executives took note of how well they worked together. Her second major production number, in the film's finale, finds her teamed again with loose-limbed Ben Blue and singing "What a Rumba Does to Romance." This film provides one of the better showcases for Martha's musical comedy skills.

Another comedy sequence finds Mabel recruited to conduct a hopefully compromising late-night raid on the bedroom of notorious woman-hater Hubert Dash. A last-minute change in room assignments finds her instead surprising John Payne's Martin Bates with her nocturnal visit, and ultimately uttering a heartfelt "Oh, boy!" as she makes a hasty exit, falling from a roof parapet into an swimming pool.

Also on hand are Betty Grable and Jackie Coogan, in the midst of their brief real-life marriage, film newcomer Robert Cummings in a small role as a radio announcer, and promising young singing leading man John Payne. Martha was directed here for the second time by Raoul Walsh.

Page one of *Daily Variety*'s November 27, 1937, edition reported that both Martha and John Payne were injured during shooting of a scene, "as rail of stairway gave way while Payne carried Miss Raye, kicking up steps. Miss Raye was cut about the legs and bruised. Payne slashed his foot on a nail." They were reported to be back at work two days later. In early December, Martha was out ill with an attack of laryngitis. According to *Daily Variety* (December 3, 1937), she tried to come back too early, against her doctor's advice, but was unable to sing satisfactorily: "Physician stated that only complete rest will restore her voice. Director Raoul Walsh is continuing pic, shooting around Miss Raye."

Reviews: "[A] poor musical…. Miss Raye's familiar "o-boy" style of clowning is intermittently effective." *Variety,* April 27, 1938

"Though occasionally funny, the material for this latest campus fling squawks along in the rut of unoriginality." *Christian Science Monitor,* April 30, 1938

"There's a moth-riddled old statement to the effect that women are never really funny. This fool idea is stood on its head and has its ears boxed by Gracie Allen and Martha Raye in *College Swing.*" *Washington Post,* April 30, 1938

Tropic Holiday (Paramount)

Release: July 1, 1938

Running Time: 78 minutes

Cast: Bob Burns (*Breck Jones*), Dorothy Lamour (*Manuela*), Ray Milland (*Ken Warren*), Martha Raye (*Midge Miller*), Binnie Barnes (*Marilyn Joyce*), Tito Guízar (*Ramon*), Elvira Rios (*Rosa*), Roberto Soto (*Roberto*), Michael Visaroff (*Felipe*), Fortunio Bonanova (*Barrera*), Matt McHugh (*Joe*), Bobbie Moya (*Pepito*), Pepito (*Chico*), Irving Bacon (*Sol Grunnion*), Chris-Pin Martin (*Pancho*), Nell Craig (*Grunnion's Secretary*), Anna Demetrio (*Shopkeeper*), Blanca Vischer (*Josette*), Robert O'Conor (*Enrique*), Frank Puglia (*Co-Pilot*), The San Cristobal Marimba Band, Trio Ascensio del Rio (*Themselves*)

Crew: Theodore Reed (*Director*), Arthur Hornblow, Jr. (*Producer*), Don Hartman, Frank Butler, John C. Moffitt, Duke Atteberry (*Screenplay*), Don Hartman, Frank Butler (*Story*), Ted Tetzlaff (*Photography*), Farciot Edouart (*Special Photographic Effects*), A. Manuel Reachi (*Production Consultant*), Hans Dreier, Robert Usher (*Art Directors*), Archie Marshek (*Editor*), Boris Morros (*Musical Director*), LeRoy Prinz (*Choreographer*), Edith Head (*Costumes*), Agustin Lara (*Songs*), Ned Washington (*English Lyrics*), A.E. Freudeman (*Interior Decorator*), Earl Hayman, John Cope (*Sound Recorders*)

Synopsis: Hollywood screenwriter Ken Warren is visiting Mexico, instructed by his boss, producer Sol Grunnion, to "write me a great love story." Staying in the village of Rosario, and accompanied by his secretary Midge Miller, Ken meets pretty Manuela, daughter of the local tavern owner, who tells him his view of her country and her people is stereotypical. Although Ken is engaged to be married to movie star Marilyn Joyce, and expects to set a wedding date as soon as she finishes her current picture, he finds himself falling in love with Manuela.

Meanwhile, Midge is followed to Mexico by her childhood sweetheart Breck Jones, who has kept her waiting for a marriage proposal for ten years. Now that he is running for a Senate seat in Oklahoma, Breck is ready to settle down, but Midge has taken a shine to handsome Ramon, who serenaded her, and isn't sure she wants Breck any more. Because Ramon is impressed by the bravery of lady bullfighter Estrelita, Midge takes lessons in the art of bullfighting, and unexpectedly finds herself in the ring as a substitute for the injured Estrelita. In Hollywood, Marilyn gets wind of her fiancé's fling with another woman in Mexico and heads south of the border to stake her claim to Ken once and for all.

Notes: Martha is paired one last time with Bob Burns in this musical comedy that's stronger on the former than the latter. Otherwise, this is mostly a movie for viewers who enjoy hearing Dorothy Lamour sing—often. This script doesn't call for Martha's musical abilities at all, leaving the songs to Lamour, and there's only a limited amount of fun to be had in Martha's bumpy road to romance with Burns for the fifth time in two years.

Paramount publicists played up the casting of "some of Mexico's most popular entertainers, many of whom are now seen on the American screen for the first time."[10] Lamour, in her memoirs, would remember Martha as a fun colleague, albeit one who burned the candle at both ends. She was impressed by Martha's ability to stay out until the wee hours at a nightclub, living it up, and then report to work a few hours later none the worse for wear.

Martha's big comedy scene is her stint in the bullfighting ring, a natural arena for her rambunctious comic style. According to a *Los Angeles Times* story, director Theodore Reed had difficulty casting the role of the bull. "Finding American cattle centers notably lacking in Mexican ring bulls, Reed decided to send his searching crew into Mexico. And then, somewhat to his chagrin, a bullfighting expert volunteered the information that one bull simply wouldn't be enough. Fighting bulls, it seems, quickly learn that the matador's waving cape is a sham and they start charging the matador himself.... [S]ince a single bull is good for only a few charges, and a great many will be needed in the course of filming the sequence, six or more bulls are required."[11] According to studio publicists, "Martha trained under one of Mexico's foremost bullfighters, imported from his native country to teach the star all the tricks of the trade."[12]

Reviews: "Without Burns, Miss Lamour, Miss Raye and others, plus the song numbers, there'd be little to *Tropic Holiday* but a shell.... A bullfight in which Miss Raye and Burns both figure winds up the picture. Action in which they and the bull do their stuff has been well handled and photographed. Miss Raye is at her comedy best here as a femme matador." *Variety,* July 6, 1938

"Aside from the hilarious bullfight sequence ..., action in the picture is confined to moving from a patio to a hotel room to a beach and back again." John Scott, *Los Angeles Times,* July 15, 1938

"Paramount has accomplished that unaccustomed feat in Hollywood of producing a musical comedy that is rich in both music and comedy.... Martha Raye ... gives a completely convincing demonstration of what a lady matador should not do in the ring." Nelson B. Bell, *Washington Post,* July 16, 1938

Give Me a Sailor (Paramount)

Release: August 19, 1938
Running Time: 82 minutes
Cast: Martha Raye (*Letty Larkin*), Bob Hope (*Jim Brewster*), Betty Grable (*Nancy Larkin*), Jack Whiting (*Walter Brewster*), Clarence Kolb (*Captain Tallant*), J.C. Nugent (*Mr. Larkin*), Bonnie Jean Churchill (*Ethel May Brewster*), Nana Bryant (*Minnie Brewster*), John Hubbard (*Rodney Weatherwax*), John Henry Allen (*Messenger Boy*), Fred Graham (*Deliveryman*), Ralph Sanford (*Iceman*), Irving Bacon

(*Druggist*), Phil Warren (*Smitty*), Tom Hanlon (*Norville Goodload*), George Guhl (*Bill*), Scott Groves (*Bellhop*), George Magrill (*Orderly*), Ray Teal (*Sailor with Clarinet*), Edward Earle, Eddie Kane, Archie Twitchell (*Businessmen*)

Crew: Elliott Nugent (*Director*), Harold Hurley, Jeff Lazarus (*Producers*), Frank Butler, Doris Anderson (*Screenplay*), Victor Milner (*Photography*), Paul Jones (*Associate Producer*), Hans Dreier, Earl Hedrick (*Art Directors*), William Shea (*Editor*), Boris Morros (*Musical Director*), Phil Boutelje (*Musical Advisor*), LeRoy Prinz (*Choreographer*), Edith Head (*Costume Designer*), A.E. Freudeman (*Interior Decorator*), Karl Herlinger (*Makeup*), Harry Lindgren, Richard Olson (*Sound Recorders*)

Synopsis: Sailor Jim Brewster and his brother Walter are set to go ashore for leave at San Francisco, where Walter intends to propose to his beautiful girlfriend Nancy Larkin. For the past ten years, Jim has been scheming to have Nancy for himself, while Nancy's unglamorous, workhorse sister Letty pines for Walter. Jim issues an SOS in code to Letty, and they agree to work together toward their common goal, as they have since they were kids. Letty stows away in the trunk when Walter takes off for a mountain cabin on an errand for his commander, conspiring

Give Me a Sailor co-starred Martha with Bob Hope, a team Paramount executives considered quite prominent in the late 1930s. Soon, however, Hope's movie career would eclipse hers.

to strand the two of them together, so that Walter will have time to appreciate her superior qualities, especially her cooking. Instead, Nancy convinces Jim to take Walter's place on the trip, causing Jim and Letty to be trapped together by an approaching storm. Caught in a compromising position together, Jim has no choice but to make an honest woman of Letty, but before the wedding can take place, she unexpectedly wins a contest for her beautiful legs. Dubbed "Legs" Larkin by the press, newly wealthy via promotional contracts, and glamorized, Letty no longer needs to marry Jim. She finally attracts the attention of Walter, who's beginning to doubt Nancy's suitability as a wife and proposes to Letty instead. Thanks to Walter's commanding officer, he and Letty are all set for a large-scale wedding with all the accouterments the Navy can provide—but there may be a last-minute change of plans.

Notes: Top-billed for the first time under her Paramount contract, Martha has one of her best showcases in this lively comedy that teams her with Bob Hope. Paramount head Adolph Zukor bought the rights to the short-lived 1919 Broadway musical comedy *Linger Longer Letty,* a vehicle for comedienne Charlotte Greenwood, in the summer of 1937 with the idea of making it a Raye vehicle. The film's working title was *The Wallflower.* Often described as the female counterpart to comic Joe E. Brown (with whom she later co-starred in *$1,000 a Touchdown*), Martha is given a role here that is similar in structure to many of Brown's 1930s pictures: the poor schnook who seemingly lacks the attributes to be a great lover, but proves over the course of the story to be a better and more accomplished person than a more comely rival. Though Letty mostly proves her worthiness with domestic skills, as might be expected of the period, she is presented in the end as a far more attractive marital option than her sister.

The re-teaming of Raye and Hope was announced by studio publicists in April 1938; according to *Daily Variety* (April 14, 1938), it was "a reward for their work in *College Swing.*" The film is skillfully paced by director Elliott Nugent, who keeps the story moving and stages the comedy sequences effectively.

Martha's best comedy scenes are mostly in the first reel, as she struggles with a slippery block of ice, a telephone that seldom stops ringing, and the unexpected appearance of a frog in her kitchen. Later, wanting to doll herself up for Walter's impending visit, she applies a beauty mask that works all too well, ultimately requiring Jim to crack her "facial straitjacket" with a fist to her chin.

Betty Grable, making her second film with Martha, is stuck with a remarkably unlikable character, as Nancy takes her sister for granted, toys with Walter's affections, and generally presents herself as completely self-absorbed. To her credit, she plays it as it's written, letting herself be seen as what amounts to the evil stepsister in a Cinderella story. She's given one solo musical number. Clarence Kolb, perhaps best-known as grumpy boss Mr. Honeywell on TV's *My Little Margie,* has one of his larger character roles here as Walter's commanding officer, who's perhaps the first person to look at Letty Larkin and see her best qualities.

Paramount flacks promoted the film by sending complimentary cakes to exhibitors across the country. Accompanying the baked goods were signed notes from Martha, reading, "This is a sample of the cake I baked in *Give Me a Sailor,* when I won a beautiful legs contest by mistake." The movie's trailer placed heavy emphasis on the studio's wish to glamorize Martha, billing her as "Martha 'Legs' Raye—The Gal with the Gorgeous Gams" and using the slogan, "Martha Hits the Deck ... on the Swellest Pair of See-Legs the Navy Ever Saw!"

Judging from audience response, *Give Me a Sailor* seemed not to present Martha as many of her fans wished to see her. Before long, second-billed Bob Hope would become a much more viable comedy star for Paramount than Martha, while she would return to supporting roles.

Reviews: "Business and lines meted out to both Miss Raye and Hope are mediocre, and what scoring is done and laughs levied are occasioned by her bag of trouping tricks and his facility at handling light lines and situations." *Variety,* July 27, 1938

"Martha is more subdued in comedy antics, but manages to get in some familiar mannerisms, just so her fans won't be too amazed at the transformation. She is very much up to her role." John Scott, *Los Angeles Times,* July 22, 1938

"It's a pleasant farce comedy interpreted by pleasing people; generous with its laughs and stressing what has been increasingly apparent—the fact that, allowed to be faintly natural, Martha Raye has charm, considerable good looks and a disarming wistful appeal." Mae Tinée, *Chicago Tribune,* September 3, 1938

Never Say Die (Paramount)

Release: April 14, 1939

Running Time: 82 minutes

Cast: Martha Raye (*Mickey Hawkins*), Bob Hope (*John Kidley*), Andy Devine (*Henry Munch*), Alan Mowbray (*Prince Alexis Smirnov*), Gale Sondergaard (*Juno Marko*), Sig Rumann (*Poppa Ingleborg*), Ernest Cossart (*Jeepers*), Paul Harvey (*Jasper Hawkins*), Ivan Simpson (*Kretsky*), Monty Woolley (*Dr. Schmidt*), Foy Van Dolsen (*Kretsky's Bodyguard*), Christian Rub (*Mayor*), William Burress (*Customer with Dog*), Hobart Cavanaugh (*Druggist*), Donald Haines (*Julius*), Hans Conried (*Accordionist*), Janet Elsie Clark (*Hannah*), James B. Carson (*Hotel Proprietor*), Harriette Haddon (*Telephone Operator*), Harold Entwistle (*Dyspeptic*), Oscar Rudolph (*Ambulance Attendant*), Frank Reicher (*Man in Charge of Duel*), Paul Weigel (*Concierge*)

Crew: Elliott Nugent (*Director*), Paul Jones (*Producer*), Don Hartman, Frank Butler, Preston Sturges (*Screenplay*), William H. Post (*Play*), Leo Tover (*Photography*), Farciot Edouart (*Special Photographic Effects*), Hans Dreier, Ernest Fegté (*Art Directors*), Edith Head (*Costumes*), James Smith (*Editor*), Philip Wisdom, Walter Oberst (*Sound Recorders*), A.E. Freudeman (*Interior Decorator*), Boris Morros (*Musical Director*)

Synopsis: Wealthy hypochondriac John Kidley is the object of much female attention at the Swiss health spa where he's staying, as women have heard that he has $20 million and only a short time to live. Most aggressively in pursuit of him is much-married Juno Marko, a "black widow" whose husbands tend to die in fairly short order. Another guest is good-hearted Mickey Hawkins from Eagle Heights, Texas, accompanied by her father. The Hawkins family is newly rich with oil money, and Mickey's father wants her to enhance their social position by an arranged marriage with well-connected Prince Smirnov. Mickey, who's in love with bus driver Henry Munch, rebels at marrying into royalty to please her father, and the prince is wedding her only to earn a dowry that will settle his numerous debts. When Mickey and John meet, he suggests that they solve both their problems by marrying each other. Since he expects to die soon, he offers to clear the way for Mickey to live happily ever after with Henry and the Kidley fortune. But Mickey and John's spurned lovers don't intend to give up quite that easily.

Notes: For the first reel, this looks more like a Bob Hope picture than a Martha Raye picture, as she doesn't make her entrance until nearly 20 minutes into the film, cast as the gawky daughter of a *nouveau riche* family. As she complains to her social-climber father, "Ever since we struck oil and got to wearing shoes, you been getting mighty nose-high, Pa!"

Paramount reached back a ways to dig out *Never Say Die,* a comedy originally staged on Broadway in 1912 and '13. Martha is directed here for the second time by Elliott Nugent, who previously helmed *Give Me a Sailor.* She performs the only musical number in the picture. According to *Daily Variety* (November 2, 1938), an "epidemic of colds" threatened to slow *Never Say Die* production, with Martha, Hope and Nugent among the chief sufferers.

It wouldn't be a Martha Raye Paramount picture if she didn't take a plunge into water; here, it's done in a half-hearted attempt at suicide after her father insists she marry the prince, and results in her meeting Hope's character. Lest we think that Mickey and John are taking full advantage of their marital privileges, we're treated (if that's the word) to the sight of Hope and Andy Devine sharing a hotel bed. Some of Paramount's newspaper ads spotlighted these scenes, saying, "You may die laughing when Bob and Andy play footie in a Swiss feather bed, but remember, we warned you!"

Notable among the supporting cast is Gale Sondergaard (1899–1985), who ably instills her comic role with just the right amount of genuine menace, as befitting a woman whose last husband purportedly "fell off the Matterhorn" as she stood nearby. John Kidley's relationship with his loyal manservant Jeepers (well-played by Ernest Cossart) is slightly reminiscent of that between the spoiled title character of *Arthur* (1981), played by Dudley Moore, and his dry-witted butler (John Gielgud).

In later years, Hope was known to give his movie scripts to his own staff of writers for a once-over, adding extra jokes and bits of business that (usually) strengthened the picture. A little of that might have helped *Never Say Die,* which is amusing and pleasant entertainment, but a bit light on full-out laugh lines. Some reviewers in 1939 thought Martha was trying too hard to play leading-lady roles, at the expense of her comedy. However, in *Motion Picture Herald*'s "What the Picture Did for Me" column (May 4, 1940), a Kansas movie house owner reported, "This is the best picture we have ever shown with Martha Raye in it…. The box office shows up well on this one."

This proved to be the last Raye-Hope teaming at Paramount. Early reports indicated that she would appear in his next film, *Some Like It Hot,* but this didn't pan out. Her Paramount career soon came to an inglorious close, while he went on to become one of the biggest box office names of the 1940s.

Reviews: "Picture has a few funny moments, but on the whole is just a mild farce…. [It] unfolds at a slow pace, with script losing many opportunities for laughs in dialog…. Both Martha Raye and Hope play too straight and dramatic." *Variety,* March 8, 1939

"The first two or three reels keep you chuckling practically all the time. Clever, amusing acting and good dialog—droll, you know. Then there's a short arid stretch. But, zippy!—things pick up and you're off to a good finish. Miss Raye and Mr. Hope make a delightful comedy team." Mae Tinée, *Chicago Tribune,* May 16, 1939

"Gags flow freely throughout *Never Say Die,* some hilarious, others unfunny. But the average is pretty good…. Devotees of Miss Raye and Hope will like *Never Say Die.* The two are well matched." John L. Scott, *Los Angeles Times,* March 17, 1939

$1,000 a Touchdown (Paramount)
Release: October 4, 1939
Running Time: 71 minutes
Cast: Joe E. Brown (*Marlow Mansfield Booth*), Martha Raye (*Martha Madison*), Eric Blore (*Henry*), Susan Hayward (*Betty McGlen*), John Hartley (*Bill Anders*), Syd Saylor (*Bangs*), Joyce Mathews (*Lorelei*), Tom Dugan (*Popcorn Vendor*), Matt McHugh (*Brick Benson*), Don Wilson (*Announcer*), George McKay (*Cyrus Fishbeck*), William Haade (*Guard*), Wanda McKay (*Babe*), Grace Goodall (*Nurse*), Charles Middleton (*Stage Manager*), John Hart (*Buck*), Jimmy Conlin (*Sheriff*), Josef Swickard (*Hamilton McGlen, Sr.*), Emmett Vogan (*Coach*), Dewey Robinson (*Cab Driver*), Jack Shea (*Dimples*), Johnnie Morris (*Newsboy*), Cheryl Walker (*Blondie*), Jane Webb (*Billie*), Adrian Morris (*Two-Ton Terry*), Hugh Sothern (*King Richard*), Patsy Mace (*Ginger*), George Barton (*Truck Driver*), Paula DeCardo (*Dora*), Don Evan Brown (*Jack*), Linda Brent (*Bertie*), Maxine Conrad (*Sally*), Dorothy Dayton (*Gen*), Judy King (*Honey*), Jolly Rowlings (*Harry*)
Crew: James P. Hogan (*Director*), Delmer Daves (*Screenplay*), William C. Mellor (*Photography*), Hans Dreier, William Flannery (*Art Directors*), Chandler House (*Editor*), George Dutton, Glenn Rominger (*Sound Recorders*), A.E. Freudeman (*Interior Decorator*)
Synopsis: Marlow Mansfield Booth comes from a family of distinguished actors, but suffers so badly from stage fright that he can't even handle a spear-carrying bit part in a play. His neurosis is also characterized by an inability to remember faces, even after meeting people multiple times, as well as a panicked reaction to being in a room filled with people. Sent to a psychiatrist, Dr. Grail, Marlow meets another patient, Martha Madison, who's suffering under the tension of operating Madison University, the college her grandfather founded in the town of Madison Junction.

Although Martha takes an immediate shine to Marlow, he keeps forgetting who she is, until a motorcycle accident unexpectedly restores his long-term memory. Marlow volunteers to help Martha solve her problems with the university, which is so far in arrears that it is danger of being repossessed and converted into a shoe factory. They transform Madison U into an acting school, with Marlow as its president and Martha as dean of women. When initial enrollment is sluggish, they decide that the school needs a football team as a draw. Also popular with the aspir-

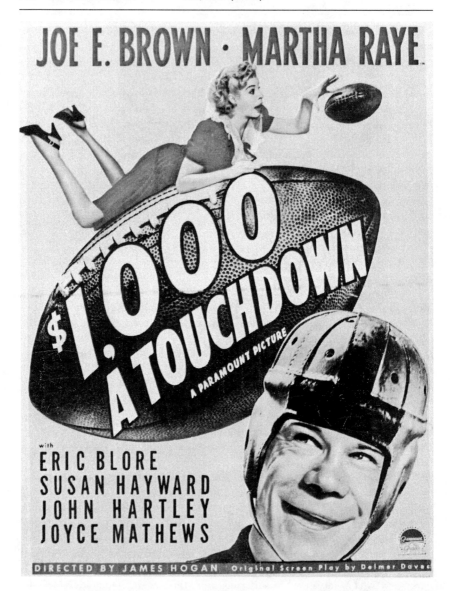

Poster art for *$1,000 a Touchdown* spotlights stars Martha Raye and Joe E. Brown. He later lambasted the picture as "terrible."

ing actors who enroll in school is the class in romantic techniques taught by beautiful Betty McGlen. After bribing a group of All-American players to transfer to Madison U, and assigning Marlow to serve as their coach, Martha tries to put the school on the map by challenging reigning football champions the Green Tree Pickers. Although the Madison boys give it their all, they aren't equipped to take on the Pickers, and go into halftime losing 27–0, leaving Martha to devise a solution to win the game and save the school—as long as her cash holds out.

Notes: "A volcano of fun" (according to studio publicists), this film pairs Martha with a comedian often described as her male counterpart. Like Martha, Joe E. Brown had long gotten laughs with his oversized mouth. Past the peak of his movie fame, however, he (like Martha) needed a hit in order to stay in the game. "This picture marks the first joint starring appearance of Joe and Martha," crowed Paramount copywriters, "and turns them loose in a story which packs amiable antics, romance and football thrills, combined in just the proper portions to suit the talents of the two comedians."[13]

Delmer Daves (1904–1977) enjoyed a long career as a writer and director. (He also had a hand in writing Martha's next Paramount feature, *The Farmer's Daughter*.) His *$1,000 a Touchdown* screenplay uses a variation on the central gimmick from *Mountain Music*. Here, Marlowe Booth keeps forgetting Martha every time he's out of her sight, until a plunge into a lake abruptly cures his memory malady. It later develops that Martha's kisses also have a curative effect on Marlow, albeit temporary.

The script takes a dated view of women's roles in higher education. The announcement that Martha has succeeded in signing up several noteworthy football players for the university is followed by a newspaper headline reading, "Madison University Enrolls Two Hundred Girls This Week." Thanks to some sloppy continuity, Brown's character name is variously spelled as Marlow and Marlowe when seen in writing on his office door and on telegrams.

Brown had long been known for his sports-flavored comedies (sports was his passion off-screen as well), but it's not until nearly halfway through its brief running time that *$1,000 a Touchdown* begins to focus on matters athletic. Here, however, Joe E. is playing a man who knows about football only what he read in a book, leaving him ill-equipped to serve as the team's coach. (Brown was disappointed in *$1,000 a Touchdown*, describing it in his autobiography as "terrible.") The name of the rival football team here is a riff on the Green Bay Packers, the National Football League's championship team in 1939.

Featured in the film's second half is a 22-year-old Susan Hayward (1917–1975), in one of her first sizable roles. Seen onscreen announcing the climactic football game is longtime Jack Benny player Don Wilson (1900–1982), who indeed had been known as a sportscaster prior to joining radio's premier comedy show. Joe E. Brown's 22-year-old son, Don Evan Brown, has a bit part here. Don, enlisted as a pilot in the U.S. Air Force, was killed in 1942 during a training maneuver.

Touchdown director James P. Hogan (1890–1943), whose credits dated back to the silent era, would also helm Martha's next picture, *The Farmer's Daughter*.

Reviews: "It's a hokey and innocuous comedy that secures laughs from elemental and obvious situations aimed at the family and juve[nile] trade…. [Raye] does as well as she can with the limited material at hand." *Variety,* September 27, 1939

"Miss Raye, considerably more ladylike than usual in a blonde wig and some really nifty clothes, is amusing and, do you know it, sometimes downright appealing. She and Mr. Brown hilariously head an able and enthusiastic cast." Mae Tinée, *Chicago Tribune,* October 18, 1939

"[A] rather plaintive comedy. These two comics whose characteristics would seem to make them a natural for success found a commonplace football yarn a tremendous obstacle. They did what they could with a fifth-rate piece, but that wasn't enough." Wood Soanes, *Oakland Tribune,* October 6, 1939

The Farmer's Daughter (Paramount)
Release: March 29, 1940
Running Time: 60 minutes
Cast: Martha Raye (*Patience Bingham*), Charles Ruggles (*Nicholas "Nicksie" North*), Richard Denning (*Dennis Crane*), Gertrude Michael (*Clarice Sheldon*), William Frawley (*Scoop Trimble*), Inez Courtney (*Emily French*), William Demarest (*Victor Walsh*), Jack Norton (*Shimmy Conway*), William Duncan (*Tom Bingham*), Ann Shoemaker (*Lucy Bingham*), Benny Baker (*Monk Gordon*), Tom Dugan (*Forbes*), Lorraine Krueger (*Valerie*), Betty McLaughlin [Sheila Ryan] (*Dorinda*), Anne Harrison (*Rosalie*), John Hartley (*Barney Bingham*), Darryl Hickman (*Billy Bingham*), Etta McDaniel (*Anna*), Pat West (*Chuck Stevens*), Nick Moro (*Sound Effects Man*), Wanda McKay, Jane Webb (*Cashiers*), Janet Waldo (*Switchboard Operator*), George McKay (*Process Server*), Grace Hayle (*Columnist*)
Crew: James P. Hogan (*Director*), Lewis R. Foster (*Screenplay*), Delmer Daves (*Story*), Leo Tover (*Photography*), Hans Dreier, Franz Bachelin (*Art Directors*), Edith Head (*Costumes*), Archie Marshek (*Editing*), Harold Lewis, Don Johnson (*Sound Recorders*), A.E. Freudeman (*Interior Decorator*)
Synopsis: Stage producer "Nicksie" North is delighted to secure financing for his newest show, a musical comedy called *Voodoo Girl,* even though it comes with a few strings attached. Backer Bobby Decker wants the show to star his girlfriend, hot-tempered Clarice Sheldon (described as "that blonde-headed stick of dynamite"), and to keep the show out of New York for at least three months. Nicksie and his press agent, Scoop Trimble, decide to stage the show on the "straw hat circuit" before bringing it to Broadway. They make arrangements to rent the barn of the Bingham family, which is only a few miles from a beach resort, and fix it up as the Cherry Tree Lane Theatre. The Binghams are a friendly bunch whose daughter Patience is an aspiring performer, but known to locals as a jinx. (Patience's mother puts it more kindly when she says, "Life with Patience is very much like true love: It never runs smooth.") Patience and the show's leading man, Dennis Crane, take a shine to each other, but selfish Clarice craves Dennis' attention for herself, and Nicksie presses the actor to keep their star happy. Clarice learns that her boyfriend eloped with another woman and quits in a rage, leaving no alternative but for Patience to step into the starring role on opening night.
Notes: Evidently disappointed in their efforts to build Martha Raye to top stardom, Paramount executives dropped her into the depths of the "B" unit with a resounding crash in this nonetheless enjoyable little picture that boasts a brief running time and a small budget that's all too apparent. Billing below the title only emphasizes her fall from grace in this picture, which often occupied the lower half of double bills alongside the likes of *The Mark of Zorro* (1940) and *The Flying Deuces* (1939). Martha was notified by letter during filming that the studio had terminated her employment.

A bovine named Maude was among Martha's supporting players in *The Farmer's Daughter*.

"Martha Raye holds down the title role, but there's no holding down Martha," reported studio publicists. "She's in there swinging with both arms and a set of famed vocal chords that get over two grand numbers."[14]

Although this film presents her as a klutz, and perhaps a jinx, the screenplay lacks the disparaging comments about her looks that were so commonplace in earlier films. Martha receives perhaps the most handsome leading man of her career in Richard Denning (1914–1998), who'd previously played a bit part in *Give Me a*

Sailor. Her character recruited to help Denning's rehearse his love scenes, she makes their moments together both touching and funny, as Patience's attraction to Denny is all too apparent.

Charlie Ruggles (1886–1970) is a fine comic foil for Martha, reacting with everything from sighs to spit takes as Patience creates havoc everywhere she goes. Hattie McDaniel's sister Etta (1890–1946) has a smallish role as Clarice's long-suffering maid Anna. McDaniel gets a funny line when she delivers the news to Nicksie that his star has flown the coop. Asked why she didn't stop Clarice, Anna retorts, "Not me! I stopped a bolt of lightning once." Jack Norton (1882–1958), known for his countless minor roles as movie drunks, gets one of his bigger roles as *Voodoo Girl*'s inebriated playwright. Fans of *My Three Sons* can find both William Frawley (1887–1966) and William Demarest (1892–1983) here, with the former enjoying the larger role and the better billing.

Disappointingly, Patience's stage debut is depicted mostly in a quick montage that comes in the closing minutes, though Martha does get to perform a lovely rendition of "Jeanie with the Light Brown Hair" in an earlier scene. Her comic highlight is a drunk scene in which her inhibitions are released, causing her to hand out frank opinions ("Don't you care what anybody says. You wear that suit!") and challenge Ruggles' character to a lively game of tag.

Exhibitors' reports varied: "This pleased all and business was good," said a small-town Oklahoma theater owner, but in Georgia, "Some like it; some didn't. Fair attendance" (*Motion Picture Herald*, May 11, 1940).

Reviews: "[A] mildly amusing and obvious adventure…. It's a loosely tied series of incidents, with Miss Raye tumbling and falling all around to catch the few laughs that are present." *Variety,* February 14, 1940

"Two or three times it looks as if a spark of real humor might break through, but every time it is obliterated by Miss Raye—or somebody—going flat. Maybe a good traveling salesman might have lightened things up a bit." Frank S. Nugent, *New York Times,* February 16, 1940

"It's the old success story, with rural trimmings, and if you're willing to forget everything but laughter, you'll like it." Harold Levy, *Oakland* (CA) *Tribune,* March 8, 1940

"Film has few laughs, and the director must have thought Raye was at her funniest when falling down." Nash and Ross, *The Motion Picture Guide*

The Boys from Syracuse (Universal)
Release: July 31, 1940
Running Time: 73 minutes
Cast: Allan Jones (*Antipholus of Ephesus/Antipholus of Syracuse*), Martha Raye (*Luce*), Irene Hervey (*Adriana*), Joe Penner (*Dromio of Ephesus/Dromio of Syracuse*), Rosemary Lane (*Phyllis*), Charles Butterworth (*Duke of Ephesus*), Alan Mowbray (*Angelo*), Eric Blore (*Pinch*), Samuel S. Hinds (*Angeen*), Matt McHugh (*Bartender*), Eddie Acuff (*Taxicab Driver*), Tom Dugan (*Octavius*), Spencer Charters (*Turnkey*), Malcolm Waite (*Captain of Guards*), William Desmond (*Citizen*), Doris Lloyd, Alaine Brandes (*Women*), David Oliver (*Messenger*), Larry J. Blake (*Announcer*),

Cyril Ring (*Guard*), June Wilkins (*Secretary*), Joe Cunningham (*Foreman of Jury*), Charles Sullivan (*Policeman*), Gerald Pierce (*Newsboy*), Julie Carter (*Girl*)

Crew: A. Edward Sutherland (*Director*), Jules Levey (*Producer*), Leonard Spigelgass, Charles Grayson, Paul Gerard Smith (*Screenplay*), George Abbott (*Play*), Richard Rodgers (*Music*), Lorenz Hart (*Lyrics*), Joseph Valentine (*Photography*), Jack Otterson (*Art Director*), Martin Obzina (*Associate*), Vera West (*Gowns*), R.A. Gausman (*Set Decorator*), John P. Fulton (*Process Photographer*), Charles Previn (*Musical Director*), Frank Skinner (*Orchestrator*), Dave Gould (*Choreographer*), Milton Carruth (*Editor*), Bernard B. Brown (*Sound Supervisor*), Joseph Lapis (*Sound Technician*), Joseph A. McDonough (*Assistant Director*)

Synopsis: In ancient Asia Minor, military hero Antipholus has successfully defended his town, Ephesus, from the inhabitants of nearby Syracuse. Antipholus of Ephesus and his slave Dromio are unaware that they have lookalike twins in Syracuse, or that Antipholus' father has come to Ephesus in search of his long-missing son, believed to have been lost at sea in a shipwreck. When the boys from Syracuse unexpectedly infiltrate Ephesus, they are mistaken for their local lookalikes, causing confusion. While Antipholus of Ephesus is married, his brother is not. Likewise, dimwitted Dromio of Ephesus has a wife, Luce, who keeps him on a short leash. Mistaken for their counterparts, the boys from Syracuse spend an evening keeping company with Antipholus' wife Adriana and her slave Luce, while the fellows from Ephesus live it up at a nearby saloon.

Since it is the law of Ephesus than any visitors from Syracuse are to be executed on sight, the Duke of Ephesus has reluctantly sentenced Antipholus' visiting father to death. Likewise, the newcomers soon find themselves awaiting execution. They are kept company by impoverished tailors Angelo and Pinch, who owe a sizable amount in back taxes. Meanwhile, Adriana's sister Phyllis, who has fallen in love with her brother-in-law's twin, anxiously awaits the outcome of his trial.

Notes: Not long after being dropped by Paramount, Martha signed a deal with Universal Pictures, though at a lesser salary than she had previously enjoyed. As this film makes clear, the studio did not intend to give her starring roles, as she had enjoyed during her Paramount tenure. Still, her name value was good enough to merit billing above the title, second to singing star Allan Jones. Studio publicity told customers her "Syracuse Shuffle" was "her first complete screen dance routine…. Under the instructions of Dance Director Dave Gould, Martha rehearsed … for two weeks. Forty chorus girls dance with her in the unique routine, which begins as a Grecian ballet and then 'breaks' into a modern movement."[15]

The Boys from Syracuse was adapted from the Broadway show that ran for 235 performances during the 1938–39 season, produced by George Abbott, with Eddie Albert and Jimmy Savo in lead roles. The musical comedy was, in turn, based on Shakespeare's *The Comedy of Errors*. Wynn Murray played Martha's role of Luce in the stage production. A brief revival of *Boys from Syracuse* was on the boards in the summer of 2002. Rodgers and Hart's score included such noteworthy tunes as "This Can't Be Love."

This was the last film of comedian Joe Penner (1904–1941), who died in January 1941, a few months after its release. In Martha's featured role as the slave, she shares most of her scenes with Penner, cast as her husband. One comic scene finds her at the reins of a runaway chariot. She and Penner team for a duet of "Sing for Your Supper."

Charles Butterworth (1896–1946) has some amusing moments as the Duke of Ephesus, who rather half-heartedly rules the town with its myriad of confusing laws, and winces every time his arrival on the scene is heralded by a sour-noted fanfare.

Director A. Edward Sutherland (1895–1973) had a résumé rich in comedy, having worked with Abbott and Costello, Laurel and Hardy, Mae West, W.C. Fields *et al.* He was originally one of the Keystone Cops. The screenplay has fun with some anachronisms, and riffs on modern-day life, as in the scene where a newsboy hawks the day's happenings on freshly printed stone tablets.

Universal's ace special effects wizard John P. Fulton employs split screens and other techniques to depict the dual characters played by Allan Jones and Joe Penner, though the demands are less intense than what were required of him when Martha plays twins in her next Universal picture, *Keep 'Em Flying.* Fulton's effects were Oscar-nominated, as was Jack Otterson's art direction recreating an ancient village.

A "triple world premiere" was held on July 18, 1940, at three theaters in Syracuse, New York.

Reviews: "Martha Raye and Joe Penner are particularly outstanding in the comedy leads.... Miss Raye, provided with the swell Rodgers and Hart tunes, gets good opportunity to use her pipes as well as exhibit her broad comedy style." *Variety,* July 17, 1940

"[The movie] manages to get some delightful performances from its limited cast." Nash and Ross, *The Motion Picture Guide*

"The picture is neither the best directed nor the funniest in the world. But the contemporary gags and the expert vaudevillian clowning of Miss Raye and Mr. Penner profit from such classic trappings as chariots and togas." Cecil Smith, *Chicago Tribune,* August 16, 1940

"All in all it's a great romp, with Allan Jones, Joe Penner and Martha Raye walking off with the major acting honors." Hayden Hickok, *Syracuse* (NY) *Herald-Journal,* July 19, 1940

Navy Blues *(Warner Brothers)*

Release: September 13, 1941

Running Time: 108 minutes

Cast: Ann Sheridan (*Margie Jordan*), Jack Oakie (*Cake O'Hara*), Martha Raye (*Lilibelle Bolton*), Jack Haley (*Powerhouse Bolton*), Herbert Anderson (*Homer Matthews*), Jack Carson (*"Buttons" Johnson*), Jackie Gleason (*Tubby*), Kay Aldridge, Leslie Brooks, Georgia Carroll, Marguerite Chapman, Peggy Diggins, Claire James (*The "Navy Blues" Sextette*), William T. Orr (*Mac*), Richard Lane (*"Rocky" Anderson*), John Ridgely (*Jersey*), Tom Dugan (*Hot Dog Vendor*), William Hopper (*Ensign Walters*), Richard Travis (*Tex*), Edward Gargan (*Club Proprietor*), Selmer Jackson (*Captain Willard*), Patrick McVey, Walter Sande (*Military Policemen*), Frank Wilcox (*Inspection Officer*), Harry Strang (*Chief Petty Officer Lane*), Fred Graham (*Tough Sailor*), Edwin Stanley (*Rear Admiral*)

Crew: Lloyd Bacon (*Director*), Hal B. Wallis (*Executive Producer*), Jerry Wald, Jack Saper (*Associate Producers*), Jerry Wald, Richard Macaulay, Arthur T. Horman, Sam Perrin (*Screenplay*), Arthur T. Horman (*Story*), Tony Gaudio (*Photography*), Eddie Blatt (*Dialogue Director*), Sol Polito, James Wong Howe (*Dance Sequences Photographers*), Robert Haas (*Art Director*), Leo F. Forbstein (*Musical Director*), Seymour Felix (*Musical Numbers Director*), Ray Heindorf (*Orchestral Arrangements*), Rudi Fehr (*Editor*), J.J. Giblon (*Technical Adviser*), Howard Shoup (*Gowns*), C.A. Riggs (*Sound Recorder*), Perc Westmore (*Makeup*), H.F. Koenekamp (*Special Effects*)

Synopsis: Navy buddies Cake O'Hara and Powerhouse Bolton arrive in Honolulu for a two-week shore leave, too short on funds to have much fun. Cake concocts a moneymaking scheme when he learns that expert sharpshooter Homer Matthews is about to be transferred to their ship, the *Cleveland*. Without Homer's ability, betting odds against the *Cleveland* crew in an upcoming target practice contest are 15 to 1. Scraping together all the money they can, borrowing from shipmates like "Buttons" Johnson and hocking the ship's trophies, Cake and Powerhouse lay multiple wagers on the upcoming contest, sure they'll rake in money on a surefire win with Homer on their team. But when it develops that Homer is finishing his enlistment, two days before the contest, the scheme falls apart, leaving the boys deeply in debt.

Martha stands up to a pair of Jacks (Haley, left, and Oakie) in *Navy Blues*.

While in Honolulu, hapless Powerhouse does his best to avoid his ex-wife Lili-belle, whom he wed just before enlisting and then left behind during his tour of duty overseas. Working as a low-paid cigarette girl in a nightclub, the Honola Hut, Lilibelle tells her buddy, nightclub singer Margie, she'd "like to lay my hands on that guy I married in San Diego," who owes her back alimony. Once Lilibelle sets eyes on Powerhouse, she doggedly trails him everywhere he goes. Caught up in the boys' desperation to persuade Homer to re-enlist, Margie agrees to romance him just long enough to prevent him from going home to Iowa.

Notes: The fourth of four players billed above the title in this Warner Brothers musical comedy, Martha registers strongly as Lilibelle, who terms herself "the orig-inal kiss-less bride," and spars with ex-husband Powerhouse:

> LILIBELLE: If I knew you were so dumb, I'd never marry you.
> POWERHOUSE: You knew I was dumb when I asked you to marry me.

Seen to good advantage during the opening number "Navy Blues," where her antics include swinging from a ceiling fan, Martha resurfaces intermittently throughout the film. In her big comedy scene, she follows Powerhouse to the *Cleve-land*, where she's pushed hurriedly into a laundry bag during a surprise inspection. From there, it's only a short trip to the laundry chute, and ultimately to an unseemly landing in a garbage can. *Variety*'s reviewer didn't much care for the sight of Martha skimpily clad in the Hawaiian-themed musical numbers, though he wasn't similarly disturbed by a look at chubby Jack Oakie in a swimsuit.

Despite her top billing, there's not a lot to be seen of Ann Sheridan (1915–1967) in the film's first half, which awards most of its footage to Messrs. Oakie and Haley as an ersatz Abbott and Costello. Storywise, she becomes more important after the halfway point, but it's still not a role that likely excited the up-and-coming actress.

The film offers a good supporting role to young Herbert Anderson (1917–1994), later to be known as dad Henry Mitchell on TV's *Dennis the Menace*. Anderson was reportedly a last-minute replacement for Eddie Albert, whose abrupt departure from the *Navy Blues* cast was the subject of Hollywood gossip. In a less prominent role as another shipmate is young Jackie Gleason, billed here as "Jackie C. Glea-son."

At the time of the film's production, the United States had not yet officially entered World War II, and the main characters' military service is depicted primarily as a way to earn a living and "see the world." *Navy Blues* offers a few good songs and some amusing moments, but doesn't really have enough story to sustain a nearly two-hour running time, and probably could have been improved by some cutting.

Nothing onscreen suggests that studio executives saw any need to transport per-sonnel to Hawaii, in order to shoot a film largely set there. Indeed, studio publicity bragged about the "ten huge sets" erected on their Burbank lot, plus others set up at Laguna Beach and in San Diego. "These include authentic replicas of whole sec-tions of Honolulu, including the main street itself, as well as portions of Waikiki Beach (at Laguna) and an actual reproduction of the principal naval landing dock at Pearl Harbor, built in San Diego."[16]

One sequence finds Oakie and Haley short on clothes and taking cover underneath a pair of signboards from outside a movie theater, allowing ample opportunity to plug a couple of other then-current Warners' releases, *Manpower* and *Affectionately Yours*.

Martha reported for work on *Navy Blues* amidst plans for her marriage to hotel executive Neal Lang. Ann Sheridan served as one of Martha's bridesmaids at the ceremony, held in Las Vegas in May 1941.

Reviews: "*Navy Blues* founders on a reef of too-frequent boredom…. Miss Raye in midriff-showing costume, the hula type, is not an attractive sight." *Variety,* August 13, 1941

"Of course Martha Raye supplies a good quota of laughs. She also warbles here and there…. The production is light entertainment, not hard to take." John L. Scott, *Los Angeles Times,* September 5, 1941

"Martha Raye is happily buffoonish as Haley's sorely tried wife, undergoing notable torture during a trip in a duffle bag." Richard L. Coe, *Washington Post,* September 20, 1941

"The piece gets off to a slow start and has several tiresome stretches, but, in the main, it seemed to please the audience…. [Y]ou'll like Martha Raye." Mae Tinée, *Chicago Tribune,* November 5, 1941

Keep 'Em Flying (Universal)

Release: November 28, 1941

Running Time: 86 minutes

Cast: Bud Abbott (*Blackie Benson*), Lou Costello (*Heathcliff*), Martha Raye (*Gloria Phelps/Barbara Phelps*), Carol Bruce (*Linda Joyce*), William Gargan (*Craig Morrison*), Dick Foran (*Jinx Roberts*), Charles Lang (*Jimmy Joyce*), William Davidson (*Gonigle*), Truman Bradley (*Butch*), Loring Smith (*Major Barstow*), William Forrest (*Colonel*), Freddie Slack (*Pianist*), Richard Crane (*Cadet Stevens*), William H. O'Brien (*Waiter*), Larry Steers (*Nightclub Customer*), Phil Warren (*Bevans*), Harry Strang (*Truck Driver*)

Crew: Arthur Lubin (*Director*), True Boardman, John Grant, Nat Perrin (*Screenplay*), Edmund L. Hartmann (*Original Story*), Glenn Tryon (*Associate Producer*), Joseph Valentine (*Photography*), Ralph Ceder (*Director of Flying Sequences*), Elmer Dyer (*Aerial Photography*), John P. Fulton (*Special Photographic Effects*), Jack Otterson (*Art Director*), Harold H. MacArthur (*Associate Art Director*), Philip Cahn (*Editor*), Bernard B. Brown (*Sound Director*), William Hedgcock (*Sound Technician*), R.A. Gausman (*Set Decorator*), Joan Hathaway (*Dialogue Director*), Charles Previn (*Musical Director*), Ted Cain (*Music Supervisor*), Frank Skinner (*Musical Score*), Vera West (*Gowns*), Edward Prinz (*Choreographer*), Gil Valle (*Assistant Director*)

Synopsis: Hotshot pilot Jinx Roberts joins the military after being fired from his job as a circus stunt flyer. Tagging along to the Cal-Aero Academy are his buddies Blackie and Heathcliff, who seem to lack the ability to contribute much to the Army, but want a chance to pitch in. Impulsive, fun-loving Jinx is ill-suited to the discipline of life in the Army Air Corps and the rigors of 20 months of training. Not helping the matter is the presence of his old nemesis Craig Morrison, who's put in charge of training the newcomer.

Keep 'Em Flying cast Martha as lookalike sisters—one who liked Lou Costello's character, and one who didn't.

While Jinx romances pretty USO singer Linda Joyce, bumbling Heathcliff catches the eye of Gloria Phelps. Heathcliff can't understand why his romance with Gloria is running hot and cold, until he realizes that there are actually two lookalike Phelps sisters, only one of whom finds him appealing. Luckily, sister Barbara takes a shine to Blackie.

Jinx's unorthodox ways threaten to earn him an early discharge, and an unhappy parting with Linda, until there is an unexpected opportunity to show his mettle.

Notes: Released only a few weeks after Martha's previous military comedy *Navy Blues*, *Keep 'Em Flying* gives audiences two Marthas for the price of one, playing love interests for both Abbott and Costello in her dual role as twin sisters Gloria and Barbara Phelps. Martha is introduced in a long, precisely timed scene which finds both the Phelps sisters working the USO lunch counter when Blackie and Heathcliff first arrive at the base. Friendly, outgoing Gloria offers a hungry Heathcliff a free slice of cake, and he's bewildered every time she leaves the room and her lookalike sister appears to snatch it away.

Universal's longtime special effects ace John P. Fulton does a nice job staging the scenes of interaction between Martha's two characters. These scenes involved splitscreen effects, process photography, careful editing and a double for Raye. The results impressed 1941 audiences, and still hold up today. One especially challenging scene found Gloria and Barbara simultaneously kicking up their heels on the dance floor: "Miss Raye had a hard time matching the fast movement and tempo of her dance. Only way they could do it was to diagram the whole thing in advance with squares on the floor. Then she had to learn exactly where she was supposed to be and what she should be doing on each count. On the 37th count, for instance, she would have to be on Square 11, kicking her right foot smiling, and beginning a turn to the right."[17] Given the opportunity to solo on "Pig Foot Pete," Martha also takes part in a later rendition of "The Boy with the Wistful Eyes," shared with Carol Bruce.

According to syndicated columnist Ken Morgan, Martha had first crossed paths with Abbott and Costello three years prior to *Keep 'Em Flying*, during a personal appearance tour she organized: "One of the acts was an unknown team which proved a hit wherever they played. Now, Martha is appearing with the same pair in a motion picture—but this time they are billed over her on the marquee...."[18]

Her rambunctious clowning matches well with that of Costello, who's the wincing, sputtering recipient of a bottle she smashes over his head in one scene. Though she takes an interest in Heathcliff from their first meeting, she's also capable of exclaiming in frustration, "Why, of all the unromantic dopes!" Like Joan Davis, who proved a strong comic match for Costello in *Hold That Ghost*, Martha was not invited back for further hijinks with the popular comedian.

Reviews: "Too many of the numerous laugh routines here are only slight variations of previous material, with resultant loss of audience reaction.... Miss Raye is a good foil for the boys." *Variety,* November 26, 1941

"[T]he audience roars with mirth during the unbelievable, but nonetheless amusing tale." *Boston Globe*, December 4, 1941

"Martha Raye, in the dual role of the Phelps twins, could have afforded more fun than she does were her opportunities greater. Like her smile, they are pretty expansive as it is." Nelson B. Bell, *Washington Post,* December 4, 1941

Hellzapoppin' (Universal)

Release: December 26, 1941
Running Time: 84 minutes
Cast: Ole Olsen (*Ole*), Chic Johnson (*Chic*), Martha Raye (*Betty Johnson*), Hugh Herbert (*Quimby*), Jane Frazee (*Kitty Rand*), Mischa Auer (*Pepi*), Robert Paige (*Jeff Hunter*), Richard Lane (*Director*), Lewis Howard (*Woody*), Clarence Kolb (*Mr. Rand*), Nella Walker (*Mrs. Rand*), Shemp Howard (*Lewis*), Elisha Cook, Jr. (*Selby*), Frank Darien (*Messenger*), Katherine Johnson (*Lena*), Gus Schilling (*Orchestra Leader*), Jody Gilbert (*Louie's Girlfriend*), Andrew Tombes (*Max Kane*), Sig Arno (*Cellist*), Dave Willock (*Trombone Player*), Don Brodie (*Theater Manager*), Hal K. Dawson (*Photographer at Pool*), Charlie Hall (*Taxi Driver*), Harry Monty (*Midget Taxi Driver*), George Humbert (*Chef*), Bob Rose (*Shorty*), Samuel S. Hinds (*Showboat Captain*), Susan Miller (*Junior's Mother*), Bert Roach (*Robert T. MacChesney*), Fred Sanborn (*Tic-Tac-Toe Player*), Angelo Rossitto (*Dwarf Devil*), Dale Van Sickel (*Frankenstein's Monster*), Terry Walker (*Maid*), Gil Perkins (*Butler in Pool*), George Chandler (*Movie Cameraman*), The Harlem Congeroo Dancers, the Olive Hatch Water Ballet, The Six Hits, Slim & Slam

Crew: H.C. Potter (*Director*), Glenn Tryon, Alex Gottlieb (*Associate Producers*), Nat Perrin, Warren Wilson (*Screenplay*), Nat Perrin (*Original Story*), Woody Bredell (*Photography*), Charles Previn (*Musical Director*), Don Raye, Gene De Paul (*Words and Music*), Nick Castle, Edward Prinz (*Choreographers*), John P. Fulton (*Special Photographic Effects*), Jack Otterson (*Art Director*), Martin Obzina (*Associate Art Director*), Milton Carruth (*Editor*), Bernard B. Brown (*Sound Director*), William Fox (*Sound Technician*), Vera West (*Gowns*), R.A. Gausman (*Set Decorator*), Joseph A. McDonough (*Assistant Director*), Ted Cain (*Music Supervisor*), Frank Skinner (*Musical Score*)

Synopsis: Opening with a musical number set in Hell, where dancing devils, pretty girls and slapstick abound, *Hellzapoppin'* comes at unsuspecting viewers as a zany revue "suggested by" Olsen and Johnson's long-running Broadway show. After their Hollywood director stubbornly insists that a motion picture must have a love story, Olsen and Johnson find themselves arriving at the Long Island estate of the wealthy Rand family, where a big weekend party is underway. Ole and Chic bring along a truckload of props and costumes needed for the play that pretty Kitty Rand is staging as a Red Cross benefit, and also help along her burgeoning romance with their buddy Jeff. Jeff loves Kitty but is reluctant to let her know until he's established himself financially. Her parents urge her to accept the attentions of the socially suitable Woody.

Also among the guests is Chic's man-hungry kid sister Betty, who takes an immediate liking to impoverished nobleman Pepi and pursues him. Pepi would rather catch a wealthy young lady. Meanwhile, Jeff prepares to take the benefit show to Broadway, in hopes that it will establish him as a successful producer. When Ole and Chic wrongly think that Kitty is not the type of girl Jeff should marry, they determine to let loose on the show in hopes of preventing the marriage.

Notes: Predating by many years such later creations as *Rowan and Martin's Laugh-In, Airplane!* and the *Naked Gun* films, this is a manic, high-energy comedy. As the credits proudly announce, "any similarity between *Hellzapoppin'* and a motion picture is purely coincidental." Studio publicity described it as "a slam-bang, eye-filling, tune-filled extravaganza of gags, gals and songs." It was based on the hugely popular Broadway musical revue, which opened in September 1938 and ran 1400+ performances, closing a few days prior to the opening of Universal's film adaptation.

Despite the popularity of the stage show, which had reportedly earned something in the range of $4 million in ticket sales, observers were skeptical that its essence could be successfully captured in a film. The stage show was a free-for-all that typically spilled over into the audience, with paying customers pulled into the action. The motion picture, while succeeding admirably in capturing some of the free-form lunacy of the stage show, seemed to leave both movie goers and reviewers in 1941 a bit stunned.

A romantic musical number is interrupted periodically with slides flashed on the screen offering such messages as "Stinky Miller—Go Home!" Finally the leading man and lady stop their number and speak directly to Stinky in the audience, whereupon a silhouetted little boy stands and leaves the theater. When the film drifts away from Olsen and Johnson to a pretty young lady in a bathing suit, a stern call to Cousin Louie, in the projection room, sets the movie back on track. Later, however, a quarrel between Louie and his lady friend results in the movie being turned every which way but loose, as film is spilled all over the projection room floor and the movie in progress abruptly gives way to a Western. And then there's the fellow who walks through scenes periodically carrying a plant, a larger one each time he reappears, and calling for "Mrs. Jones."

Among the highlights for Martha, as Betty, is her energetic production number centered on the song "Watch the Birdie," as she wields a camera around a swimming pool populated with handsome young men. She's in the spotlight again in the last half hour, as her participation in Jeff's stage show unexpectedly takes a turn toward slapstick, erupting into hilarious chaos during her song number "Waiting for the Robert E. Lee." While dancing with Chic, she's asked, "Did anyone ever tell you you dance like Ginger Rogers?" She answers no, to which he retorts, "No wonder!" and earns himself a swift kick in the shins.

Though not apparent in the finished film, Martha's participation in the film was challenged by a series of ailments, among them a bout with intestinal flu. A scene in which she dodges arrows shot at a target also put her in sick bay, when a couple of the arrows found their mark in her rather than the target. But that wasn't the worst that would befall her.

In early August, she was in a car accident. Newspaper reports indicated that she "plunged 150 feet down a canyon in her automobile last night, but escaped with only a sprained ankle."[19] Said syndicated columnist Hedda Hopper (August 30, 1941), "Martha hasn't yet recovered from the accident, but she's at work in *Hellzapoppin'* in a wheelchair. Studio props have designed an invisible support to brace her when she stands for her singing scenes. That's what I call spunk, and over on the set they're calling her 'the old trouper.'" During production, Martha and then-husband Neal Lang threw a cast party at their home in Encino.

Brought to Hollywood on the strength of the long Broadway run of *Hellzapoppin'*, comics Ole Olsen and Chic Johnson would make three more pictures at Universal in the 1940s (*Crazy House, Ghost Catchers* and *See My Lawyer*) but they failed to go over big with movie audiences. Director H.C. Potter (1904–1977) went on to direct some genuine classics, including *The Farmer's Daughter* (1947, not Martha's version), and *Mr. Blandings Builds His Dream House*.

Reviews: "Here is good escapist comedy, and, as such, probably a boxoffice mop-up everywhere…. [T]he laughs are plentiful…. Martha Raye, who plays a wolf in femme clothes, scores with [her songs]." *Variety,* December 24, 1941

"[A] shambles on the screen with little rags and bits of old vaudeville gags smoking among the wreckage … chockful of an anarchic collection of unfunny gags…. Some familiar comics [Martha Raye, Mischa Auer] try desperately to fend for themselves." *New York Times,* December 26, 1941

"[I]t is bound to take your mind off the war if only to be amazed that such a thing as *Hellzapoppin'* can even exist…. Martha Raye, Mischa Auer and Hugh Herbert are very much on hand to further the antics of O. and J. and at their more fortunate moments in this 'film' they are genuinely funny." Richard L. Coe, *Washington Post,* February 20, 1942

Four Jills in a Jeep (20th Century-Fox)

Release: March 17, 1944

Running Time: 89 minutes

Cast: Kay Francis, Carole Landis, Martha Raye, Mitzi Mayfair, Jimmy Dorsey and His Orchestra (*Themselves*), John Harvey (*Ted Warren*), Phil Silvers (*Sgt. Eddie Hart*), Dick Haymes (*Lt. Dick Ryan*), Alice Faye, Betty Grable, Carmen Miranda (*Guest Stars*), George Jessel (*Master of Ceremonies*), Kirk Alyn (*Pilot*), Alec Harford (*Priest*), Lester Matthews (*Captain Lloyd*), Frances Morris (*Surgical Nurse*), Dave Willock (*Heckler*), Glenn Langan (*Captain Stewart*), Winifred Harris (*Lady Carlton-Smith*), Miles Mander (*Colonel Hartley*), Bernard Sell (*Sentry*), Ralph Byrd (*Mess Hall Sergeant*), Frank Wilcox (*Officer*)

Crew: William A. Seiter (*Director*), Irving Starr (*Producer*), Robert Ellis, Helen Logan, Snag Werris (*Screenplay*), Froma Sand, Fred Niblo, Jr. (*Story*), Jimmy McHugh, Harold Adamson (*Music and Lyrics*), Don Loper (*Musical Numbers Staging*), Emil Newman, Charles Henderson (*Musical Directors*), Peverell Marley (*Photography*), Thomas Little, Al Orenbach (*Set Decorators*), Yvonne Wood (*Costume Designer*), Ray Curtiss (*Editor*), Fred Sersen (*Special Photographic Effects*), Jesse Bastian, Murray Spivack (*Sound Recorders*), William Eckhardt (*Assistant Director*)

Synopsis: After taking part in a radio broadcast for *Command Performance, U.S.A.,* Hollywood performers Carole Landis, Martha Raye and Mitzi Mayfair express the wish to do more to support the military men overseas. Kay Francis, who emceed the program, tells them she has just received permission to take an entertainment troupe on a tour, and signs the ladies to round out her cast. They soon learn that performing on a military tour can be a decidedly unglamorous undertaking, as they experience the rigors of bouncing along a rutted road in a Jeep, navigating a camp overrun with rain and mud, and being unnerved by the enemy's presence nearby. At their first stop, Carole is drawn immediately to handsome pilot Ted Warren, while their escort Eddie Hart seems to take a shine to Martha. Mitzi is reunited with her old performing partner, singer Dick Ryan. After performing at a Red Cross fundraiser in London, the ladies are next sent to Africa, only a few hours after Carole has married Ted. In Africa, their plane is forced to make an unscheduled landing, leaving them to complete their journey on camels. Near the front line, when the ladies aren't allowed to put themselves in danger by performing, they volunteer to assist with nursing and other duties. Meanwhile, a shelling prompts Eddie and Martha to share a foxhole, where they reach a new rapprochement.

Notes: Inspired by a real-life USO tour in which the performers participated, *Four Jills in a Jeep* went before Fox cameras in 1943. (The film's title in early announcements was *Command Performance*.) Some of its plot elements are based on truth, such as Carole Landis' hasty marriage to a military man (here called Ted Warren, but in actuality Captain Thomas C. Wallace). However, there was also plenty of dramatic license, making Raye and her colleagues worry that the film, described by Fox publicists as "the maddest, merriest safari a funsome foursome ever made ... the gayest, grandest adventures four Jeep-happy girls ever met," would attract criticism. During production, Landis worked with writer Edwin Seaver on a memoir about the tour, which would carry the same title as the film. Published in 1944, it included stills from the production.

Raye devoted enormous amounts of time to entertaining troops, especially during the Vietnam War, and sometimes at the expense of furthering her own career interests. On-screen, there's a hint of what will come in Martha's real life when she tells an officer of the troupe's willingness to stray off the established USO path: "We're soldiers. And where our men go, we'll go too, if they'll let us."

The ladies are introduced to life in a military camp by their eager escort, Eddie Hart:

> EDDIE: Well, now for your first GI breakfast.
> MARTHA: Man, am I hungry!
> EDDIE: Miss Raye, won't you take my arm?
> MARTHA: I'm not that hungry!

At a performance in London, Martha performs "Mr. Paganini" (previously heard in her debut film *Rhythm on the Range*), demonstrating her unique ability to insert comedy bits into a musical number while making the most of a genuinely fine singing voice. Cut from the finished film were her solo of "Comin' in on a Wing and a Prayer," as well as her rendition, backed by the other ladies, of "It's the Old Army Game." A Christmastime scene in which she sings "Silent Night" to a room packed with soldiers also wound up on the cutting room floor.

Although relations among the four women were largely amicable during the shoot, syndicated columnist Robbin Coons reported that Martha's warmly received clowning may have aroused a bit of jealousy. Coons was present on the set while one of the film's early scenes was being shot, depicting the women newly arrived overseas, and wrote, "William A. Seiter, directing the proceedings from a high stool beside the camera, was howling. Not with rage, with laughter. Every time Miss Martha Raye did anything or said anything, Mr. Seiter was a wonderful one-man audience, and Miss Raye was doing or saying things constantly." Coons thought the atmosphere around Miss Raye's co-stars seemed "a little chilly," adding, "[F]ar be it from me to pass on the rumors that Miss Francis hadn't been happy over her role and that, to soothe her, some of Miss Landis's lines had been donated to Miss Francis, leaving Miss Landis thoroughly unsoothed. It was just an impression, too, that Miss Raye was romping off with the picture, a romp not calculated to ease anyone's tension."[20] Martha herself gave the finished picture perhaps the harshest review it ever received when she described it, some years later, as "a piece of junk."[21]

Reviews: "At best it is shallow entertainment and is unworthy of the mission that took Kay Francis, Martha Raye, Mitzi Mayfair and Carole Landis overseas. They do their utmost to raise the film above the structure of mediocrity on which it is built. Certainly the gracious dignity of Miss Francis has never been more attractive, nor Miss Raye's clowning more in the right mood to cheer soldiers." *Los Angeles Times,* April 17, 1944

"Though heavy with lightness, beauty and sex appeal, the film is only moderately entertaining. Apparently overlooked was the chancc to portray the really fine, brave and heroic work the people of the screen and stage are doing to entertain the troops on all fronts." *New York Daily Mirror,* April 6, 1944

"In Britain and Africa, the cinemactresses clearly enjoyed themselves, worked hard, and brought some pleasure to places where it was needed. But not much of the reworking of their travelogue is fun to see or hear." *Time,* April 3, 1944

"[J]ust a raw piece of capitalization upon a widely publicized affair.... It gives the impression of having been tossed together in a couple of hours." Bosley Crowther, *New York Times,* April 6, 1944

Pin-Up Girl *(20th Century-Fox)*

Release: April 25, 1944

Running Time: 84 minutes

Cast: Betty Grable (*Lorry Jones*), John Harvey (*Tommy Dooley*), Martha Raye (*Molly McKay*), Joe E. Brown (*Eddie Hall*), Eugene Pallette (*Barney Briggs*), Dorothea Kent (*Kay*), Dave Willock (*Dud Miller*), Roger Clark (*Sgt. George Davis*), Leon Belasco (*Mario*), Jesse Graves (*Porter*), Adele Jergens (*Canteen Worker*), Reed Hadley (*Radio Announcer*), Walter Tetley (*Messenger Boy*), Robert Homans (*Doorman*), Charles R. Moore, Mantan Moreland (*Redcaps*), Ruth Warren (*Scrubwoman*), J. Farrell MacDonald (*Train Conductor*), Marcel Dalio (*Pierre*), Eddie Hall (*Soldier*), Lillian Porter (*Cigarette Girl*), Charlie Spivak and His Orchestra

Crew: [H.] Bruce Humberstone (*Director*), William LeBaron (*Producer*), Robert Ellis, Helen Logan, Earl Baldwin (*Screenplay*), Libbie Block (*Story*), Mack Gordon, James Monaco (*Lyrics and Music*), Ernest Palmer (*Photography*), Hermes Pan (*Choreographer*), James Basevi, Joseph C. Wright (*Art Directors*), Thomas Little (*Set Decorator*), René Hubert (*Costume Design*), Guy Pearce (*Makeup*), Eugene Grossman, Roger Heman, Sr. (*Sound*), Fred Sersen (*Special Photographic Effects*)

Synopsis: Beautiful USO hostess Lorry Jones does her best to raise the morale of boys in uniform, handing out lovingly inscribed pictures of herself and fielding numerous proposals of marriage that she takes none too seriously. On a visit to New York, Lorry and her buddy Kay bluff their way into a nitery, the Club Chartreuse, where war hero Tommy Dooley is being feted. Tommy's attraction to Lorry, who's posing as Broadway songstress "Laura Lorraine," arouses the jealousy of the club's singer, Molly McKay. Once Lorry realizes her feelings for Tommy are genuine, she fears that her string of deceptions, and the men she has blithely led on in the past, will prevent her straight-arrow military man from giving her the happy ending she now wants.

Notes: Though Martha's figure had been praised on more than one occasion, she does not play the title role. That's Betty Grable, in what Fox publicists described as "this beauty-filled, song-crammed, laugh-packed Technicolor extravaganza." Martha is teamed once again with Joe E. Brown, her co-star in *$1,000 a Touchdown* five years earlier, and the comic pair is reduced to support here. (Martha had traded positions with Grable, who supported her only a few years earlier in *Give Me a Sailor.*) Still, the film gave audiences their first chance to see Raye in vivid Technicolor, as well as an opportunity to check out the terpsichorean talents of Nick Condos, who would soon become her fourth husband.

Martha's comedy takes a back seat to her singing, the latter being showcased in two lavish production numbers, James V. Monaco and Mack Gordon's "Red Robins, Bobwhites, and Bluebirds" and "Yankee Doodle Hayride." Her function playing Grable's jealous rival hands Martha one of the least sympathetic film roles of her career. Though her character, Molly, "love[s] heroes and she meets 'em all," she doesn't take kindly to the interest Lorry arouses in the men around them. Her competitive spirit alive and well, Molly calls Lorry's bluff about her work in a Broadway revue, gives her boss Eddie a sock in the eye when he casts "Laura Lorraine" in a show, and takes malicious pleasure in undermining the burgeoning romance between Lorry and Tommy Dooley.

According to Grable's biographer Tom McGee, production of this film was complicated by the star's pregnancy, which was announced after *Pin-Up Girl* was already underway. Some routines had to be modified or eliminated due to Grable's condition, and Martha was given an extra number to perform instead. Raye promptly rechristened the film *Pregnant Girl.*

Grable's iconic swimsuit-clad pinup photo, in which she turns her back on the camera and smiles saucily over her shoulder, features prominently in the film. It's seen behind the opening titles, illustrates a newspaper story, and is carried in the wallet of an enraptured Marine.

Director H. Bruce Humberstone is perhaps better known for directing several of Fox's "Charlie Chan" series. The film is adapted from author Libbie Block's short story *Imagine Us!,* which first appeared in the December 1942 issue of *Good Housekeeping.*

Reviews: "This movie also contains Joe E. Brown and Martha Raye, two comics who have everything in common except the material to be comic with. Miss Raye gets more of a break with her tunes." Philip K. Scheuer, *Los Angeles Times,* May 26, 1944

"The picture offers its romance and spectacle, tunes and terpings in generous sum and fulfills the theatrical function of the filmusical [sic] very well.." *Daily Variety*, April 19, 1944

Monsieur Verdoux (United Artists)

Release: April 11, 1947
Running Time: 124 minutes
Cast: Charlie Chaplin (*M. Henri Verdoux*), Martha Raye (*Annabella Bonheur*), Mady Correll (*Mona*), Allison Roddan (*Peter*), Robert Lewis (*Maurice Bottello*), Audrey Betz (*Martha*), Ada-May (*Annette*), Isobel Elsom (*Marie Grosnay*), Marjorie Bennett (*Marie's Maid*), Helene Heigh (*Yvonne*), Margaret Hoffman (*Lydia Floray*), Marilyn Nash (*The Girl*), Irving Bacon (*Pierre Couvais*), Edwin Mills (*Jean Couvais*), Virginia Brissac (*Carlotta Couvais*), Almira Sessions (*Lena Couvais*), Eula Morgan (*Phoebe Couvais*), Bernard J. Nedell (*Prefect of Police*), Charles Evans (*Inspector Morrow*), William Frawley (*Jean La Salle*), Arthur Hohl (*Real Estate Agent*), Barbara Slater (*Flower Girl*), Fritz Leiber (*Father Fareaux*), Vera Marshe (*Vicki Darwin*), John Harmon (*Joe Darwin*), Christine Ell (*Louise*), Lois Conklin (*Florist*), Wheaton Chambers (*Pharmacist*), James Craven (*Bismo*), Franklyn Farnum (*Stock Market*

Crash Victim), Addison Richards (*Bank Manager*), Herb Vigran (*Reporter*), William Self (*Max*), Lester Matthews (*Prosecutor*), Therese Lyon (*Jeannette*), C. Montague Shaw (*Mortgage Banker*), Frank Reicher (*Doctor*), Elspeth Dudgeon (*Old Woman*), Joseph Granby (*Bailiff*), Colin Kenny (*Police Detective*), Cyril Delevanti (*Postman*), Julius Cramer (*Executioner*)

Crew: Charles Chaplin (*Director-Original Story-Music Composition*), Wheeler Dryden, Robert Florey (*Associate Directors*), Roland Totheroth (*Photography*), Wallace Chewning (*Operative Cameraman*), John Beckman (*Art Director*), Rex Bailey (*Assistant Director*), Willard Nico (*Editor*), James T. Corrigan (*Sound Recorder*), Curtis Courant (*Artistic Supervisor*), Drew Tetrick (*Wardrobe*), William Knight (*Makeup*), Hedvig Mjorud (*Hair Stylist*), Rudolph Schrager (*Music Direction and Arrangement*)

Synopsis: After years of employment as a bank clerk, Henri Verdoux finds a new way to support himself and his family during the Great Depression: by "liquidating members of the opposite sex," specifically wealthy women. But Verdoux meets his match when he marries *nouveau riche* Annabella Bonheur, a woman not only lucky enough to hit the jackpot playing the lottery, but also seemingly impervious to her

Martha cuddles up to star-director Charles Chaplin in *Monsieur Verdoux,* released to differing reactions in 1947.

murderous spouse's best efforts to eliminate her. Annabella believes her husband is a sea captain, able to come ashore only for brief intervals every few weeks. She is utterly careless with her money, wasting it on fraudulent investment schemes, phony jewels and other foolish whims, but unwilling to place her husband in charge of her business affairs. When he learns that she has put the deed to her lavish house in his name, and withdrawn her money from the bank to hide it somewhere nearby, Verdoux decides it's time for Annabella to meet her maker. Unfortunately for him, his attempt to serve her poisoned wine with dinner goes awry, as does his effort to throw her overboard during a fishing trip. Having failed to dispose of Annabella, he's horrified to find her among the guests at his wedding to his next intended victim, and soon a police net is closing in on the serial killer.

Notes: Inspired by the life of Henri Désiré Landru (1869–1922), the famed "Bluebeard" who married and killed ten women during the 1910s in France, *Monsieur Verdoux* was an image-changing black comedy for Charlie Chaplin. This "comedy of murders" left many viewers in 1947 nonplused, and thanks in part to bad personal publicity surrounding Chaplin, it was a box office failure.

Martha, the only performer (besides Chaplin) to receive featured billing at the film's beginning, contributes strongly in her role as Annabella, and garnered some of the limited critical praise it attracted during its initial release. Chaplin skillfully makes use of her comic talent while integrating her broad comic tendencies into a film unlike any she had previously made.

The idea for *Verdoux* came from Orson Welles, who receives a prominent credit in the opening titles, and originally intended it as a project for himself. According to Chaplin, it was he who conceived the notion of telling the story as a comedy. Welles received a $5000 fee for the use of his concept. The film's working title was *Comedy of Murders,* and Chaplin's script under that title was the subject of a series of arguments with censor Joseph Breen over what the latter saw as violations of the Production Code.

Martha was signed to play Annabella in April 1946, and filming was underway by June. Credited as an associate director is Robert Florey, who previously directed Martha in *Mountain Music.* Both Florey and Chaplin, according to the latter's biographer Kenneth S. Lynn, believed that "Raye's knockabout vitality and brassy vulgarity recaptured the old-time spirit of silent-screen slapstick."[22] Chaplin had been impressed by her performance in *Four Jills and a Jeep.*

Although the film meets the basic Production Code requirements, in that Verdoux is condemned to the guillotine at the end, his climactic speech makes it clear that he is anything but contrite about his murderous acts. Writer-director Chaplin explicitly makes a comparison between Verdoux's killings and the many casualties brought about by war.

While Martha knew she had taken part in a well-made film, and one that showcased her very effectively, she would not receive the hoped-for career boost that her first film in three years might otherwise have provided. By the end of her life, she was aware that *Verdoux* had been reappraised by critics and attained a greater respect. But in 1947, it did her career no favors, and she would not make another film for 15 years.

Reviews: "I think that *Monsieur Verdoux* will capture audiences on an issue of curiosity, rather than anything approaching genuine satisfaction.... [A] long exposition of an unpleasant subject that is hardly exonerated by the ending." Edwin Schallert, *Los Angeles Times*, October 29, 1947

"A combination of cool cynicism and surefire slapstick.... [T]here is an underlying ugliness, an amoral quality, which is ever present.... Martha Raye is raucous and racy as one spouse who proves indestructible." Mae Tinée, *Chicago Tribune*, October 23, 1947

"Featured in support of the star is Martha Raye, at her best in rowdy and boisterous moments, such as the boat ride when she narrowly escapes being drowned." *Hollywood Reporter*, April 14, 1947

Billy Rose's Jumbo (MGM)

Release: December 6, 1962
Running Time: 123 minutes
Cast: Doris Day (*Kitty Wonder*), Stephen Boyd (*Sam Rawlins*), Jimmy Durante (*"Pop" Wonder*), Martha Raye (*Lulu*), Dean Jagger (*John Noble*), Joseph Waring (*Harry*), Lynn Wood (*Tina*), Charles Watts (*Ellis*), James Chandler (*Parsons*), Robert Burton (*Madison*), Wilson Wood (*Hank*), Norman Leavitt (*Eddie*), Grady Sutton (*Driver*), Ron Henon, The Carlisles, The Pedrolas, The Wazzans, The Hannefords, Billy Barton, Corky Christiani, Victor Julian, Richard Berg, Joe Monahan, Miss Lani, Adolph Dubsky, Pat Anthony, Janos Prohaska, The Barbettes (*Circus Performers*), John Astin (*Pilot*), Sue Casey (*Dottie*), Fred Coby (*Andy*), Olan Soule (*Ticket Agent*), Jack Boyle, Roy Engel (*Reporters*), Ralph Lee (*Perry*), Nesdon Booth, John Hart (*Marshals*), Otto Reichow (*Hans*), Robert Williams (*Deputy Sheriff*), Frank Kreig (*Second Deputy*), John Burnside (*Third Deputy*), Chuck Couch (*Mantino*), Michael Kostrick (*Michaels*)
Crew: Charles Walters (*Director*), Joe Pasternak, Martin Melcher (*Producers*), Sidney Sheldon (*Screenplay*), Ben Hecht, Charles MacArthur (*Book*), Richard Rodgers, Lorenz Hart (*Music and Lyrics*), Roger Edens (*Associate Producer*), George Stoll (*Music Supervisor-Conductor*), Conrad Salinger, Leo Arnaud, Robert Van Eps (*Orchestrators*), Bobby Tucker (*Vocal Arrangements*), William H. Daniels (*Photography*), George W. Davis, Preston Ames (*Art Directors*), Henry Grace, Hugh Hunt (*Set Decorators*), Charles K. Hagedon (*Color Consultant*), Richard W. Farrell (*Editor*), William Shanks (*Assistant Director*), A. Arnold Gillespie, J. McMillan Johnson, Robert R. Hoag (*Special Visual Effects*), Morton Haack (*Costumes*), Sydney Guilaroff (*Hair Styles*), William Tuttle (*Makeup*), Al Dobritch (*Circus Acts Coordinator*), Busby Berkeley (*Second Unit Director*), Irving Aaronson (*Assistant to the Producer*), Franklin Milton (*Recording Supervisor*)
Synopsis: In early 20th century America, Kitty Wonder and her "Pop" own and operate the traveling Wonder Circus. The circus is perpetually on the edge of financial ruin, due primarily to Pop's habit of gambling away the box office proceeds before performers and creditors have been paid. Things come to a head in Willow Falls, Iowa, when some of the performers walk out to join a rival circus. Just then, handsome Sam Rawlins arrives on the scene, asking for a job. Although Kitty ini-

"Pop" Wonder (Jimmy Durante) is ready to make Lulu an honest woman in *Billy Rose's Jumbo*.

tially refuses to hire him, he proves himself valuable when he takes up the slack at the last minute for the high-wire artist who abruptly resigned, and is soon accepted as a member of the troupe.

Unbeknownst to Kitty and her dad, Sam is actually the son of John Noble, a rival circus owner who wants to put the Wonders out of business and claim for his own their popular circus elephant Jumbo. At the urging of Pop's longtime lady friend Lulu, a fortuneteller in the circus, Kitty pursues Sam romantically. Meanwhile, Sam goes behind the Wonders' backs and pays off their creditors, in turn receiving receipts that will give his family ownership rights in their circus.

As Kitty and Sam get better acquainted, Lulu keeps up her efforts to obtain a wedding ring from her longtime beau Pop, to whom she has been engaged for 14 years. Instead of the marriage she craves, Mr. Wonder offers her the chance to be featured in a new act, a "golden opportunity to be shot out of a cannon." When a fierce thunderstorm puts both Kitty and Lulu in danger during a performance, Sam shows his mettle, and Pop realizes how important Lulu is to him. Unfortunately, just as Pop prepares to make Lulu his bride, John Noble shows up to take possession of the Wonder Circus, dealing what may be an insurmountable blow to Kitty and Sam's burgeoning relationship.

Notes: Back on the big screen for the first time in 15 years, Martha received the last top-flight opportunity of her film career with this lavish MGM musical comedy, based on a modestly successful Broadway show that ran from November 1935 through April 1936. Third-billed Jimmy Durante (1893–1980), a longtime friend of Martha's, was a veteran of the Broadway production.

The *Los Angeles Times'* Philip K. Scheuer reported in May 1961 that preparations for the film were underway, adding that Martha "will be invited to return if Charles Walters, director of *Jumbo*, has his way. The role would be opposite Red Skelton—equally tentative at the moment. The only star [producer] Joe Pasternak has officially okayed is Doris Day."[23] Thanks to cinematographer William H. Daniels, the film is visually captivating throughout: He highlighted the circus setting with vivid colors and images that made it an impressive sight in Panavision on movie screens.

Though she's billed in the circus as "The Great Indian Mystic," who "sees all" and "knows all," Lulu is at a loss to figure out what lies ahead for her and her beau, saying, "I sure wisht I knew what was gonna happen." A comic highlight is Lulu's reluctant participation in Pop's cannon act. When the trial run goes awry, Kitty chides her father for putting Lulu in danger: "The next time you try it, use a dummy." A disgusted and soot-blackened Lulu retorts, "He already did!" Like other potential love interests for Martha's characters, Pop isn't initially dazzled by her charms, saying, "And all this time I thought she looked like George Washington." But before the end credits roll, he'll find himself serenading her as "The Most Beautiful Girl in the World."

Reporters had fun with the wedding scene between Martha and Jimmy Durante, as by this time she'd been to the altar six times in real life. "I never married in most of my other pictures," she admitted good-naturedly. "But I made up for that on the outside."[24] Durante, on the other hand, had something in common with his character: Like Pop, who'd been keeping Lulu waiting a long time for a wedding ring, Durante married second wife Margie in 1960 after a 16-year courtship.

One of Hollywood's premier film clowns, Martha gets the full treatment here, decked out for the finale in a green-wigged getup that allows her full rein to show her talents. Said assistant director William Shanks, "Martha Raye has always been a broad comedienne of the baggy-pants school. I think she is unhappy unless she can amuse the crew…. Chuck's main problem is to keep her within the characterization, to cut her down a bit, and for this she is going to thank him. She'll think of herself as an actress and when she sees the picture, she'll realize he's made a whole new career for her."[25] Martha said she appreciated Walters' directorial approach. "He acts everything out, shows you just what to do, and he's understanding. He appreciates it when you do things well. That's what actors like."[26]

Billy Rose's Jumbo received mostly favorable notices, and was modestly popular at the box office, but did not sell enough tickets to recoup its sizable production cost, rendering it a failure for MGM. It would be the last musical film for Doris Day (born 1924), leaving her to concentrate on comedies for the last few years of her movie career. Although Martha was effectively showcased, *Jumbo*'s failure to make money probably contributed to her absence from movie screens until 1970.

Reviews: "[A]s corny and wonderful as the circus, and I urge you to put it down

right now as a Christmas gift for yourself and the kids … [Martha Raye is] as raucous and keyed up and screwball as ever." Philip K. Scheuer, *Los Angeles Times*,
December 21, 1962

"[O]ne of the greatest hunks of entertainment I've seen in ages, it has everything—heart, action, comedy, beauty and good taste. All your cousins, sisters and
your aunts will love it." Hedda Hopper, syndicated columnist, August 6, 1962

"[T]he story is not the reason for making *Jumbo*—in fact the plot peters out in
the smashingly spectacular conclusion. This is CIRCUS—and nobody expects reality in the face of fantasy and fun." *Boston Globe*, December 22, 1962

"Martha Raye returns to the screen after a long absence in a role that is just right
for her brand of clowning…." Mae Tinée, *Chicago Tribune*, December 23, 1962

Pufnstuf (Sid & Marty Krofft Enterprises/Universal)

Release: May 1970

Running Time: 98 minutes

Cast: Jack Wild (*Jimmy*), Billie Hayes (*Wilhelmina W. Witchiepoo*), Martha Raye
(*Boss Witch*), Mama Cass [Cass Elliot] (*Witch Hazel*), Billy Barty (*Googy Gopher/
Orville Pelican*), Jane Dulo (*Miss Flick*), Jan Davis (*Witch Way*), Sharon Baird
(*Shirley Pufnstuf*), Joy Campbell (*Orson/Cling*), Roberto Gamonet (*H.R. Pufnstuf*),
Andrew Ratoucheff (*Alarm Clock*), Angelo Rossitto (*Seymour Spider/Clang*), Felix
Silla (*Polkadotted Horse*), Johnny Silver (*Dr. Blinky*), Walker Edmiston, Joan Gerber,
Al [Allan] Melvin, Don Messick (*Character Voices*), Allison McKay, Princess Liv-
ingston, Van Snowden, Lou Wagner, Hommy Stewart, Pat Lytell, Buddy Douglas,
Jon Linton, Bob Howland, Scutter McKay, Roberta Keith, Penny Krompier, Brooks
Hunnicutt, Barrie Duffus, Evelyn Dutton, Tony Barro, Ken Creel, Fred Curt, Dennis
Edenfield

Crew: Hollingsworth Morse (*Director*), Sid and Marty Krofft (*Executive Produc-
ers*), John Fenton Murray, Si Rose (*Writers*), Si Rose (*Producer*), Kenneth Peach
(*Photography*), Malcolm Alper (*Associate Producer*), Charles Fox (*Music*), Norman
Gimbel (*Lyrics*), Alexander Golitzen, Walter Scott Herndon (*Art Directors*), Arthur
Jeph Parker (*Set Decorator*), Nicky Nadeau (*Creative Consultant*), Rolf Roediger,
Evenda Leeper, Troy Barrett (*Puppet Creations*), Paul Godkin (*Choreographer*), Wal-
don O. Watson, David H. Moriarty (*Sound*), Joseph E. Kenny (*Unit Production
Manager*), Chuck Colean (*Assistant Director*), David Rawlins (*Editor*), Donald A.
Ramsey (*Assistant to Producer*), Bud Westmore (*Makeup*), Vincent Dee (*Costume
Supervisor*), Larry Germain (*Hair Stylist*), Dell Ross (*Dialogue Coach*), Trudy Ben-
nett (*Assistant to the Executive Producers*)

Synopsis: Drummed out of his junior high school band, Jimmy, a lonely British
boy, pledges his friendship to Freddy, "a solid gold talking flute with a diamond
skin condition." Invited to take a ride on a talking boat, Jimmy and Freddy attract
the attention of the evil witch Wilhelmina Witchiepoo. She tries to steal the flute
for herself, sure it will make her the hit of the upcoming witches' convention. Jimmy
and his musical friend are rescued by Mayor H.R. Pufnstuf, a talking dragon, and
other residents of Living Island. Adopting a disguise, Witchiepoo finagles the flute
away from the trusting Pufnstuf and his friends and carries it back to her castle.

When Freddy Flute is rescued, Witchiepoo prepares to avenge herself on the people of Living Island, causing Jimmy and Freddy to conclude it would be safer for their friends if they left. But they turn back when they hear that Pufnstuf and the others have been captured, and that they must prevent the dragon from being served as the main course at the feast Witchiepoo is preparing for the visiting Boss Witch and the rest of her cohorts.

Notes: Successful children's television producers Sid and Marty Krofft brought their popular Saturday morning series *H.R. Pufnstuf* to movie theater screens in the summer of 1970. The film went into production after cast and crew completed 17 episodes of the series. The format combined live-action, costumed actors alongside oversized puppets. Drawing primarily on the performers from the weekly series, the Kroffts punched up the cast by signing Martha to play a featured role as Boss Witch, as well as casting singer Cass Elliot as Witchiepoo's rival Witch Hazel.

According to co-executive producer Sid Krofft, "It's aimed at a total family audience. It's something new and mod, full of camp dialogue, and will mean different things to different age groups. But above all, we feel it will entertain everyone."[27] The Kroffts told studio executives they could deliver the film on a budget less than $1 million, largely because it would draw on sets and costumes already created for the TV series.

Third-billed Martha, mostly absent from the film's first hour (except for a few lines of dialogue heard as a voiceover), plays a sizable part in the last 30 minutes. Wisely not attempting to top the high-camp theatrics of Billie Hayes' screechy, cackling, over-the-top Witchiepoo, she plays Boss Witch, "the commander-in-chief of all witchdom," with relative restraint. Still, she seems to be having fun with her outlandish role, and is garishly clad in a purple wig, her face accessorized with matching purple makeup as well as a hooked nose and warts. Her trademark grimaces are put to use when the grumpy Boss Witch balks at being served barbecued dragon (she had it for lunch), and freezes Witchiepoo with a glare for having the temerity to touch her royal person. Later, she takes part in a musical number, "Zap the World," one of the film's six original Charles Fox-Norman Gimbel songs. The number was included on Capitol Records' soundtrack album for the movie.

Young star Jack Wild (1952–2006), who plays Jimmy, was already an Oscar nominee for *Oliver!* Seen in a guest role as Witchiepoo's rival is Cass Elliot (1941–1974), making her feature film debut. Elliot had left The Mamas and the Papas and embarked on a solo career, and is given a musical solo here. This was her only film acting performance.

Martha was among the guests of honor at a June 1970 screening of the film (billed as its world premiere) in San Antonio, Texas, along with the Krofft brothers. The Kroffts later signed her to a starring role in their NBC-TV series *The Bugaloos,* aired in the 1970–71 season.

Reviews: "*Pufnstuf* is more puff than stuff. It probably will be a successful and profitable merchandising concept for a kidpic, but as a feature picture it is a banally written and executed effort in which all the originality is in the sets and costumes.... [Raye] is ill used." *Daily Variety,* May 28, 1970

"*Pufnstuf* is a triumphant return to the kind of old-fashioned children's stories that adults can appreciate … a great way of bringing children and their parents together on one level of understanding … the kind that's obvious when a parent laughs at the same time his child does." Bob Polansky, *San Antonio Light*, May 30, 1970

"[Raye's] appearance is too brief to make fullest possible use of her talent." Ken Sullivan, *Cedar Rapids* (IA) *Gazette*, July 3, 1971

The Phynx (Cinema Organization–Warner Brothers)

Release: Shelved after previews; never released theatrically.
Running Time: 81 minutes
Cast: Michael A. Miller, Ray Chippeway, Dennis Larden, Lonnie Stevens (*The Phynx*), Lou Antonio (*Corrigan*), Mike Kellin (*Bogey*), Michael Ansara (*Colonel Rostinov*), George Tobias (*Markevitch*), Joan Blondell (*Ruby*), Martha Raye (*Foxy*), Larry Hankin (*Philbaby*), Teddy Eccles (*Wee Johnny Wilson*), Pat McCormick (*Father O'Hoolihan*), Joseph Gazel (*Yakov*), Bob Williams (*Number One*), Barbara Noonan (*Bogey's Secretary*), Fritz Feld (*Butler*), Rich Little (*Voice in the Box*), Sue Bernard (*London Belly*), Sherry Miles (*Copenhagen Belly*), Ann Morell (*Italian Belly*), Patty Andrews, Edgar Bergen, Busby Berkeley, James Brown, Dick Clark, Xavier Cugat, Cass Daley, Andy Devine, Leo Gorcey, Huntz Hall, John Hart, Louis Hayward, George Jessel, Ruby Keeler, Patsy Kelly, Dorothy Lamour, Guy Lombardo, Trini Lopez, Joe Louis, Marilyn Maxwell, Butterfly McQueen, Pat O'Brien, Richard Pryor, Maureen O'Sullivan, Harland Sanders, Jay Silverheels, Ed Sullivan, Rudy Vallee, Clint Walker, Johnny Weissmuller (*Guest Stars*)
Crew: Lee H. Katzin (*Director*), Bob Booker, George Foster (*Producers-Story*), Stan Cornyn (*Screenplay*), Jerry Leiber, Mike Stoller (*Words and Music*), Michel Hugo (*Photography*), Stan Jolley (*Production Designer*), Dann Cahn (*Editor*), Jimmie Haskell (*Score Conductor*), Sonny Burke (*Music Supervisor*), Gordon Bau (*Makeup Supervisor*), Jean Burt Reilly (*Supervising Hair Stylist*), Al Greenway (*Makeup*), Vivianne Walker (*Hair Stylist*), John Kean, Dan Wallin (*Sound*), Ralph S. Hurst (*Set Decorator*), Les Sheldon (*Assistant Director*), Leon Chooluck (*Production Supervisor*)
Synopsis: The Super Spy Agency, working on behalf of the American government, has been trying in vain to infiltrate Communist Albania, where a number of celebrities are being held captive. The agency's computer, MOTHA ("Mechanical Oracle That Helps Americans"), recommends the creation of a pop music group, to be called The Phynx. Its four members, chosen by the computer, are agricultural college graduate Dennis, Native American Ray, African-American actor-model Lonny and handsome playboy Michael. Captured and blindfolded, the four recruits are whisked off to SSA headquarters, where they receive both musical coaching and training in espionage work, under the supervision of lead agent Bogey and his dimwitted helper Corrigan. After SSA manipulations result in the Phynx having a gold record, the performers are invited to make a goodwill tour of Albania. There they learn that the kidnapped celebrities were brought in to entertain Ruby, the American-born wife of dictator Markevitch. Although the American stars are being treated royally, they respond to The Phynx's appeal to organize an escape plan, as they are missed back home.

Notes: "*The Phynx* as a motion picture is projected as a box office hit. The Phynx as a pop musical group is projected as another rock-pop musical group as big or bigger than the Beatles, the Lovin' Spoonful, the Byrds, the Seeds, the Fugs, the Rolling Stones, the Cream, the Grateful Dead, the Yardbirds, the Jefferson Airplane."[28] So said an early 1969 press release from producers Bob Booker and George Foster, while *The Phynx* was in production. Alas, the best-laid plans of Booker and Foster went seriously awry when Warner executives opted to shelve their film, which languished in limbo until a Warner Archive DVD release in 2012.

The Phynx was manufactured much as the Monkees had been a few years earlier. Its four young members were selected after the producers interviewed hundreds of hopefuls in New York, Los Angeles, San Francisco and Boston. Unlike the Monkees, however, the four purportedly did their own singing and played their own instruments. They were to be introduced to the public via this Warner Brothers film, launching them on what was expected to be a lucrative pop music career. But, after *The Phynx* played a test engagement in Indianapolis, it was determined to be, as syndicated columnist Vernon Scott described it, one of those movies "that are so intolerably bad that studios and/or producers are too ashamed or frightened to release them."[29]

The story behind *The Phynx* is more entertaining than most of what transpires during its running time. Beyond the hype, what the film has to offer is splashes of psychedelic color, a few less-than-memorable songs and a number of pretty young ladies, including "The Belly Girls," who have top-secret military maps "tattooed on their tummies." The boys are given a few surveillance gadgets to use in their quest, including some special sunglasses that give them X-ray vision (which they mostly employ to see a handful of extras in their underwear). The script shows signs of attempting the type of free-for-all comedy that the Zucker brothers would popularize with *Airplane!* (1980), but too many of the gags fall flat.

Though a film about an up-and-coming pop music group wouldn't seem to call for the services of Martha Raye, Xavier Cugat or Guy Lombardo, they are in fact just a few of the veteran stars making cameo appearances. Most of the stars play themselves, captives of the Albanian government, and appear only in the last 15 minutes. Their roles call for them to appear onscreen, as Fritz Feld, playing the imperial family's butler, announces them by name. Dressed in evening clothes, they then take seats in the audience, listen politely to the Phynx's song, and perhaps deliver a line or two. Later, while concealed in trucks supposedly carrying a shipment of radishes out of the country, some of them are given another line or two, as when a tired-looking Johnny Weissmuller and Maureen O'Sullivan have a brief "Me Tarzan—Me Jane" exchange.

"It's an important part of the plot to have these old-time stars in the story," producer Foster told columnist Scott. Added producer Booker, "You'd be surprised how many people think some of these supporting players are dead. Most of them were delighted to be working in movies again." Booker noted that his guest stars were given "the royal treatment," with private dressing rooms, during two days of filming at Warners. Foster and Booker expressed hopes that the presence of these stars would broaden the picture's appeal beyond the youth market.[30]

Other celebrities, including Martha Raye, are seen in quick character roles earlier in the film, as when singer James Brown presents the Phynx with a gold record, or TV host Ed Sullivan (with a gun pointed at him) welcomes the unknown singers to his show. Appearing at about the 50-minute mark, Martha plays Foxy, "only the greatest super-secret double agent in the world," who meets with the Phynx in London to disclose the whereabouts of maps that will help them carry out their mission. Failing to deliver the approved code knock quickly enough, Foxy is shot through the closed door of the hotel suite by Bogey, before gaining admittance and falling dead at his feet. Martha is on-screen for no more than a minute and a half, after delivering a few unfunny lines like her aggrieved "I'm dying, he's asking where the maps are!" Joan Blondell, as Albanian first lady Ruby, gets a few more lines than most of the unfortunate captives, which may or may not have been a privilege.

While some of the guest stars seen in this ill-fated flick likely did welcome the opportunity to earn a paycheck, or to be seen in what was undoubtedly presented to them as a very *au courant* film, it's no particular credit to their filmographies, and it's difficult to see how the youth audience would have been enticed by the prospect of seeing these performers, described in dialogue as "world leaders," whom they may not even have recognized.

Director Lee H. Katzin (1935–2002) has a few feature films on his résumé (*What Ever Happened to Aunt Alice?*, *Le Mans*) but spent much of his career in television, helming episodes of *Mission: Impossible*, *The Rat Patrol*, *Miami Vice* and numerous others.

Reviews: "[A]n inept, unfunny comedy … a shelf item from the Seven Arts days.… [T]he Warner Brothers release has dreary outlook." *Variety*, May 13, 1970

The Concorde: Airport '79 (Universal)

Release: August 17, 1979
Running Time: 113 minutes
Cast: Alain Delon (*Captain Paul Metrand*), Susan Blakely (*Maggie Whelan*), Robert Wagner (*Dr. Kevin Harrison*), Sylvia Kristel (*Isabelle*), George Kennedy (*Captain Joe Patroni*), Eddie Albert (*Eli Sands*), Bibi Andersson (*Francine*), Charo (*Margarita*), John Davidson (*Robert Palmer*), Andrea Marcovicci (*Alicia Rogov*), Martha Raye (*Loretta*), Cicely Tyson (*Elaine*), Jimmie Walker (*Boisie*), David Warner (*Peter O'Neill*), Mercedes McCambridge (*Nelli*), Avery Schreiber (*Coach Markov*), Sybil Danning (*Amy*), Monica Lewis (*Gretchen*), Nicolas Coster (*Dr. Stone*), Robin Gammell (*William Halpern*), Ed Begley, Jr. (*Rescuer #1*), Jon Cedar (*Froelich*), Sheila DeWindt (*Young Girl*), Pierre Jalbert (*Henri*), Kathleen Maguire (*Mary Parker*), Macon McCalman (*Carl Parker*), Stacey Heather Tolkin (*Irina*), Brian Cutler (*Rescue Worker*), Michele Lesser (*Carla*), Conrad Palmisano (*Cooper*), Jerry M. Prell (*Passenger Agent*), Bernard "Gus" Rethwisch (*Gregori*), Dick McGarvin (*Newscaster*), George Sawaya (*Girard*), Leonora Wolpe (*Ground Hostess*), Aharon Ipale (*French Reporter*), Jean Turlier (*Robelle*), Robert Kerman (*Dulles Controller*), Doug Christenson (*Ski Patrol Leader*), Patrick Gorman (*TV Announcer*), Selma Archerd (*Passenger*), David Matthau (*Technician #1*), Frank Parker (*Technician #2*)
Crew: David Lowell Rich (*Director*), Jennings Lang (*Producer*), Philip Lathrop

(*Photography*), Lalo Schifrin (*Music*), Henry Bumstead (*Production Designer*), Burton Miller (*Costume Designer*), Dorothy Spencer (*Editor*), Rick Weaver (*Assistant Editor*), Robert Mayer (*Music Editor*), William Batliner, Robert J. LaSanka (*Casting*), Mary Ann Biddle, Mickey S. Michaels (*Set Decorators*), Connie Nichols (*Hair Stylist*), Bob Brown (*Unit Production Manager*), Newton Arnold (*First Assistant Director*), Katy Emde (*Second Assistant Director*), Bill Dietz (*Property Master*), Jim Alexander (*Sound*), Peter Albiez, Joe Goss (*Special Effects*), Peter Anderson (*Visual Effects Supervisor*), Cleo E. Baker (*Miniature Sequences*), Peter Gibbons-Fly (*Special Visual Photography*), Clifford Stine (*Special Photography*), William Johnson (*Camera Operator*), Lambert Marks, Sheila Mason (*Costume Supervisors*), Betty Abbott Griffin (*Script Supervisor*), James W. Gavin (*Helicopter Pilot*)

Synopsis: Federation World Airlines has acquired a Concorde jet, which will be employed as "America's first supersonic commercial carrier." Its first flight is Moscow-bound; manning the cockpit are American pilot Captain Joe Patroni, and French Captain Paul Metrand. Among the passengers are TV newscaster Maggie Whelan, who learns just prior to takeoff that her boyfriend, wealthy industrialist Dr. Kevin Harrison, has been illegally selling arms overseas. Knowing that Maggie will broadcast the career-ending news, Dr. Harrison arranges for a guided missile to collide with the aircraft. When Patroni and Metrand manage to avert the disaster and make a safe landing in Paris, another plan comes into play to insure that disaster strikes on the second leg of the trip.

Other passengers on this violent voyage are airline owner Eli Sands and his trophy wife, concert jazz singer Gretchen and her pot-smoking, saxophone-playing accompanist Boise, and a nervous mother awaiting the outcome of a heart transplant for her little boy. Rounding out the passenger list are the coaches and members of the Russian gymnastics team, preparing for the Olympics in Moscow. Loretta, an older woman who confides in the stewardess about a bladder problem that's exacerbated when she's nervous, finds plenty to alarm her and spends much of her time in the rest room. On the second leg of the trip, Loretta relies on a flask of liquid courage to steady her nerves.

Notes: One of the last gasps of the popular and profitable disaster movie genre of the 1970s was this fourth and final installment in the moneymaking *Airport* series which began in 1970 with the hit film based on Arthur Hailey's novel. In her final theatrical film, Martha shares alphabetical "Guest Starring" billing with a number of other players, ranging from Eddie Albert to Jimmie Walker. Although her part is relatively small, she was grateful for the opportunity to appear in a major studio release, and her doleful rendition of the line, "The bathroom is broken" after a lengthy action sequence made it into the movie's theatrical trailer.

According to producer Jennings Lang, one of the trickiest aspects of making the film was obtaining the clearance to use the brand name Concorde, whose owners "wanted to make sure that the crews were not made to look like jerks, and the plane had to survive." Regarding his cast full of celebrity names like Martha's, Lang told journalist Dick Kleiner they were employed as a shortcut. "When the audience sees a familiar face," Kleiner noted of Lang's theory, "they know pretty much what to expect, what sort of character he or she plays. So the script doesn't have to waste a whole lot of time on exposition. The star's familiar face says it all."[31] Of the scenes depicting the near-crash, shot on a mockup of the Concorde cabin erected on the Universal lot, Martha told a journalist, "It was frightening. They had doubles for all of us, but we all did it."[32]

Less than a year after this film's release, writer-directors Jim Abrahams, David Zucker and Jerry Zucker's *Airplane!* (1980) would make it virtually impossible for moviegoers to take any film in this genre seriously ever again, even borrowing and lampooning the heart-transplant story. Not that this film needed much help eliciting giggles, at least a few of which (Charo's much-quoted "You miscon-screw me!") seem to have been intentional. Campy dialogue abounds, as when a French hooker named Francine tells George Kennedy's stolid Captain Patroni, "You're adorable when you're embarrassed," or when he mutters, mid-disaster, as the flight rapidly goes to hell in a handbasket, "I'd love to see what my horoscope says for this morning." By the film's halfway point, Robert Wagner, as Dr. Kevin Harrison, shares a sentiment most of the cast could surely appreciate: "I'm gradually learning to accept most of life's humiliations."

Reviews: "As in the previous *Airports*, huge numbers of actors whirl by like targets at a skeet shoot, and with as little time to establish whole characters.... Worst off is Martha Raye. Her part consists of a bladder infection." Sheila Benson, *Los Angeles Times*, August 3, 1979

"All prints of this disastrous disaster movie should be towed back to the Universal hangar, where the studio mechanics can carefully examine how this dodo bird ever got up in the air in the first place." Michael Blowen, *Boston Globe*, August 3, 1979

"Aeronautically and otherwise, it's a bumpy trip.... Watching this crazy lineup of passengers in conversation is a lot more entertaining than watching their hand luggage whiz through the air." Janet Maslin, *New York Times News Service*, August 19, 1979

"You don't have to be stupid to write a script like this; all you have to do is take the audience for granted.... *The Concorde: Airport '79* is Hollywood filmmaking at its most venal. And I forgot to mention Martha Raye throwing up in the plane's bathroom." Gene Siskel, *Chicago Tribune*, September 3, 1979

Short Subjects

In addition to the feature films listed above, Martha Raye appeared as herself in the following shorts:

Melody Maker: Benny Davis (1932). The "Melody Makers" series of film shorts spotlighted popular songwriters. This installment was filmed while Martha was a featured singer in Benny Davis' New York stage show. Also in the cast are Roy Atwell, Charles Carlisle and Jackie Green.

Nite in a Nite Club (1934). While still a singer in New York, Martha appeared in this short directed by Milton Schwarzwald. It was one of a series of shorts produced on the East Coast by Mentone Productions, a unit of Universal Pictures. Also in the cast were the dance team of Buck and Bubbles and singer J. Harold Murray, with Harry Rose as emcee.

Cinema Circus (1937). In this MGM Technicolor short, emcee Lee Tracy introduces celebrities who perform acts under the big top. Aside from Martha, the two-reeler features her frequent co-star Bob Burns, the Ritz Brothers, Boris Karloff, Alice Faye and Mickey Rooney.

Screen Snapshots (1938). Martha is seen in footage from the radio studios of CBS, along with Joe Penner, Bette Davis, Ida Lupino and Edward G. Robinson.

No Substitute for Victory (1970). Martha speaks on behalf of servicemen in this documentary hosted by John Wayne and directed by Robert F. Slatzer.

Television Shows

Television was an important venue for Martha's work, from the late 1940s through the mid–1980s. This section provides an overview of the variety shows she hosted in the 1950s, beginning with *All Star Revue,* which evolved into *The Martha Raye Show.* It then goes on to document her many variety show guest appearances of the 1960s as well as her starring role on the Saturday morning series *The Bugaloos* (1970–71), her co-starring role in the detective drama *McMillan* (1976–77), and her multiple guest appearances in the late 1970s and early 1980s on the CBS sitcom *Alice.*

Though the primary organization of this section is roughly chronological, moving forward from her earliest appearances on *The Texaco Star Theater,* it deviates from strict date order in the interests of grouping together multiple appearances on the same program, or with the same host. For example, her multiple visits to the variety shows of Andy Williams and Carol Burnett are united under one listing, for the reader's convenience, as are her many appearances on Bob Hope specials. Likewise, the *Martha Raye Show* synopses are presented without interruption, although she occasionally made single appearances on other shows during this time period.

Where specifics about an episode are taken from newspaper listings, the name and date of the publication is given. The absence of a date indicates that it is the same as the program's air date.

This section also covers two pilot shows for unsold series in which Martha had a starring role: *Baby Snooks,* made in 1957, and *Bill and Martha,* co-starring William Bendix, made in 1964.

Following the chronological overview are two additional sections, the first listing made-for-TV movies and miniseries in which Martha appeared. The final section documents her key performances in guest roles on shows of various types over a period of 30-some years. This includes both variety and talk shows in which she appeared as herself, as well as series episodes in which she played guest characters.

Many of Raye's earliest video performances were broadcast live from New York to viewers on the East Coast. Since the nationwide coaxial cable had not yet been put into place, however, TV watchers in other time zones often didn't see the programs until three or four weeks after the original air date, when kinescopes were cycled around the country for airing. Air dates given here are of the original broadcast.

The Texaco Star Theater
a.k.a. The Buick-Berle Show

Martha's first major break as a TV performer came with her appearances on Milton Berle's NBC show, one of the fledgling medium's biggest attractions in the late 1940s and early 1950s. Berle was originally part of a rotation of hosts when the show began in the summer of 1948, and then he was named its permanent emcee that fall. His modestly budgeted program originally had no established writing staff, making it reliant on performers who could offer their own material to perform.

Though her appearances were well received, she claimed she had no interest in taking on the responsibility of her own weekly show. "If you do, you wind up a mental case," she told columnist Earl Wilson, "and that's bad when you start out a mental case."[1] Nonetheless, by early 1951, columnists reported that Berle was branching out from his starring responsibilities to pitch network executives on a Martha Raye variety show that he would produce.

In the fall of 1953, with his ratings in decline, Berle's show was revamped, with a new format and a title change to *The Buick-Berle Show* to reflect his new sponsor.

EPISODES

Texaco Star Theater. April 19, 1949. "Comedienne practically stole the show from Milton Berle with her zany singing, mugging and other antics, proving once again that a performer trained in vaude, niteries and film can make the switch to video with ease. She was on in her single spot for a full seven minutes longer than scheduled, forcing Berle to rush the remainder of the program." *Variety*, April 27, 1949

That fall, Dorothy Kilgallen reported, "Milton Berle will pay Martha Raye the biggest sum he ever parted with for a performance on his TV show."[2]

Texaco Star Theater. June 6, 1950. Guest Stars: Martha Raye, Robert Merrill, Mike Mazurki, dancers Marlowe and Laporsky.

Texaco Star Theater. June 13, 1950. Guest Star: Martha Raye; with the Seven Marvels (acrobats). "Raye, who took a terrific mauling on last week's show, comes back for more tonight" (*Los Angeles Times*). Said columnist Sheilah Graham, "Martha Raye is a howling success in television. For my money she stole the show from Milton Berle on his show, and that's supposed to be impossible."[3]

Texaco Star Theater. October 17, 1950. Guest Stars: Martha Raye, Dane Clark.

Texaco Star Theater. November 28, 1950. Guest Stars: Carmen Miranda, Eddie Fisher. Martha makes a surprise walk-on appearance during the finale.

Texaco Star Theater. January 16, 1951. Guest Stars: Martha Raye, Denise Darcel, Robert Alda, singer Don Cornell.

Texaco Star Theater. September 16, 1952. Guest Stars: Martha Raye, Dennis King. Martha sings "It's Great to Be Alive and Kicking" in Berle's season premiere. Said *Variety* (September 24, 1952), "Miss Raye ... had her shining moments, both in the vocal and clowning department. However, her major effort, extolling the virtues, pleasures and frustrations of show business, with accompanying background exposures, added up to a big disappointment, with the camera distortions as a contributory factor."

The Buick-Berle Show. November 10, 1953. Guest Stars: Martha Raye, John Payne. In a sketch, Martha accepts a date with Milton, but tries to brush him off when she gets a more appealing offer from Payne.

The Buick-Berle Show. November 2, 1954. Guest Stars: Martha Raye, singer Charlie Applewhite. Martha and Berle impersonate famous couples from history, including Mr. and Mrs. Christopher Columbus.

See also "Selected Guest Appearances" for her appearances with Milton Berle on programs of the 1960s, including *The Hollywood Palace* and *The Milton Berle Show* (1966–67).

All Star Revue

This NBC variety series was titled *Four Star Revue* when it debuted in the fall of 1950. The rotating cast during that first season consisted of Jimmy Durante, Ed Wynn, Jack Carson and Danny Thomas. Moving to a new Saturday night time slot for its second season, the show drew upon a wider range of guest hosts, necessitating the new title *All Star Revue*.

Martha, one of the most popular hosts, served as a rotating cast member for the 1951–52 and 1952–53 seasons. Following her January 1952 performance, columnist Al Morton wrote, "Martha Raye has re-established herself as one of our greatest comediennes... Uninhibited is the word for Martha, but even that becomes a diluted adjective when applied to her goings-on. After watching her in action, suffice it to say that Martha was made for television and television was made for the likes of her." Columnist John Crosby opined, "Martha Raye, a girl whose mouth can just barely be encompassed by the coaxial cable[,] is a very good comedienne indeed and who, properly handled, could be a great one.... [S]he's a very talented and multi-faceted performer."[4]

Episodes

October 20, 1951. Guest Star: Ezio Pinza; with Chandra Kaly and His Dancers, Maria Neglia, Allen Roth and His Orchestra. Director: Ezra Stone. Producers: Pete Barnum, Leo Morgan. Famed opera singer Pinza asks his maid to get him a blind date, and is fixed up with Martha. There's a culture clash when he takes her to an elegant restaurant, after which she takes him to Schulz's Stables. Songs include "Mr. Paganini" and "That Old Black Magic." Said *Variety* (October 24, 1951), "With Miss Raye's raucous buffoonery contrasting neatly with Pinza's suave charm, the two socked across a full hour's entertainment.... [This was] undoubtedly her best TV job to date."

January 5, 1952. Guest Star: Robert Cummings. Martha appears in a Cinderella sketch, as well as "singing a straight number that was styled and photographed with sensitivity and taste" (*Cedar Rapids* [IA] *Gazette*, January 13, 1952).

March 29, 1952. Guest Star: Sarah Churchill. "The storyline for the show will have Miss Raye playing a brassy nightclub singer, and her guest portraying a girl who is trying to get a part in a musical and comes to reside with Martha to learn how a girl can live in New York."[5]

May 24, 1952. Guest Star: Arthur Treacher. Treacher plays an English butler pledged to Martha through an inheritance. Martha's song numbers included "Summertime." Said *Variety* (May 28, 1952),

> Martha Raye gave every evidence that she cannot rise above the script.... When the cavernous-mouthed gal went in for straight slapstick or shenanigans, she was at her best; not so with weak dialogue and storyline where her forté as a farceuse was afforded no proper showcase.... The skits in a finishing school where she went to learn protocol in line with her newly found riches were devoid of any situations that haven't been seen and heard before—and better. Even Miss Raye's exuberance couldn't save the hour from almost total bankruptcy.

1952–53 Season

Critics applauded Martha's *All Star Revue* season opener in late September, notably the skit which found Martha and her boyfriend attending a party. "We had used, and reused, every bit of business in the act at Mack Sennett's over 30 years ago," reported columnist James Abbe, "but never with more telling effect. Never did Marie Dressler or Louise Fazenda squeeze more out of a similar situation than did Martha Raye."[6] Ratings were strong, outranking Jackie Gleason's broadcast on CBS in overnight reports.

Introduced in that September segment was former prizefighter Rocky Graziano (1919–1990), whose appearance proved such a success that he would become a mainstay of Martha's shows over the next few years. One journalist noted, "[Graziano is] not much of an actor, but with the help of the script writers and Martha, who prevents him from slipping into many a stage pitfall, he manages, by being himself, to get laughs out of almost everything he does."[7]

September 27, 1952. Guest Stars: Rocky Graziano, Cesar Romero, Risë Stevens, George Bassman Orchestra. Martha's apartment is used as the setting for the filming of a Jekyll and Hyde story. Said *Variety* (October 1, 1952), "This program was an amalgam of bigtime production, miming, casting, writing and direction. The results were as hilarious as anything she's ever done." Of the star, the review noted, "She's a genuinely funny gal and what's more, she can be tops in this field without a single blue line. She's still an actress of ability, an asset that gives greater direction to her comedy."

November 1, 1952. Guest Stars: Ezio Pinza, Milton Berle (cameo), The Kirby Stone Four; with Sara Seegar. Martha tries to help amnesiac Pinza regain his memory. *Variety* (November 5, 1952) commented, "Miss Raye had her best moments in a skit in which she gave Sara Seegar a home permanent, only to discover that she had read instructions off the back of a ready-cake mix, and in Pinza's apartment, where she was forced to impersonate the maestro of Milan's La Scala opera." Martha danced and sang "Just One of Those Things" during the show's introduction.

December 6, 1952. Guest Star: Dorothy Lamour; with Sara Seegar. Martha takes a Caribbean cruise for schoolteachers, expecting the other women aboard to be dowdy. Lamour plays herself as a fellow passenger. Sara Seegar appears as her neighbor. "Miss Raye's show all the way," *Variety* (December 10, 1952) said. "From her now-standard opening number with the male dancing chorus to the lushly produced finale, in which she amazed with a socko terp routine to a Cuban mambo, the comedienne demonstrated the socko payoff of her versatile talents."

January 17, 1953. Guest Stars: Boris Karloff, Peter Lorre. In a sketch, the two movie horror stars play owners of a tea shop, with Martha cast as the "genteel matron" who manages it. According to *Variety* (January 21, 1953), "Miss Raye abandoned temporarily the strong comedy accent and went in for a program that became oversentimental."

February 21, 1953. Guest Stars: Ezio Pinza, Rocky Graziano. *Variety* (February 25, 1953) described this as "a flashback outing pinned on mistaken identity, with the basso trying all the way to prove she was the sweetie pie waitress he married while a music student in Vienna.... [F]or Miss Raye, another opportunity to prove her mettle as an up-and-at-'em funstress." Martha's songs include "Blues in the Night." According to an item in Dorothy Kilgallen's syndicated column (February 20, 1953), Frank Sinatra was originally booked as a guest for this segment, but withdrew only days before airtime, necessitating an almost complete script rewrite.

1953–54 SEASON

In the fall of 1953, Martha's 90-minute broadcasts continued to appear under the umbrella title *All Star Revue,* although she was now the show's sole remaining headliner. Her segments were seen once per month, when *Your Show of Shows* took a week off. She continued to be enthusiastic about her flourishing video career. "Martha believes television ... is the greatest—a combination of live audience, which she needs as a performer, and a nationwide living room audience. Together they mean she can—for the first time in her life—put down some roots." Professing not to want a weekly series, she added, "I don't want to be in living rooms so much that people are sick and tired of seeing me. Just enough so they are glad. And, of course, there's the problem of getting good fresh material all the time."[8]

EPISODES

October 3, 1953. Guest Stars: Cesar Romero, Margaret Truman, Rocky Graziano, Jake LaMotta, Nov-Elites. Truman plays Martha's new roommate. In a barbershop routine, Martha and Margaret play manicurists, with Raye horrified when she thinks she has clipped off customer Romero's nose. Another routine finds Truman set up on a blind date with boxer LaMotta. Said *Variety* (October 7, 1953), "Martha Raye, on her preem for this season, established herself as the funniest lady buffoon in TV. At the same time, the excellence of the show indicated that her partnership

Martha looks askance at guest star Margaret Truman on *The Martha Raye Show.*

with director-writer Nat Hiken is one of the most potent comedy liaisons on video.... She was a sheer delight, great at lines, mugging, singing, dancing and anything that she put her efforts into. It must be remembered that 90 minutes is difficult to carry off, but here was a siege of sustained laughter, much of it resulting from Miss Raye's antics." *Billboard* (October 17, 1953) hailed it as "one of the funniest shows to hit the video waves this season. The comedy was a tour de force for Martha Raye."

October 31, 1953. Guest Stars: Eva Gabor, Zsa Zsa Gabor and Magda Gabor; Lilia Skala (as Jolie Gabor), Milton Berle, Rocky Graziano. The story finds Martha convinced that she's the long-lost sister of the glamorous Gabors. *Variety* (November 4, 1953) tagged this segment as falling short of the season opener: "a cleverly written and staged farce that missed being sock only because they tried too hard to extend the joke. …[Raye is] not only the leading lady buffoon but can give the top male funsters a good run for honors, not to mention that endurance angle." Songs included "Mr. Paganini."

December 26, 1953. Guest Stars: Bert Lahr, Ray Middleton, Rocky Graziano. Skits include a parody of *Your Hit Parade* and a spoof of *Carmen*. *Variety* (December 30, 1953) noted, "While Martha Raye has been burning up the iconoscopes as one of the hottest television personalities of the season, she's also starting to stretch her material pretty thin." Despite "some bits of comic genius," the reviewer concluded, "the high spots were all too few in the 90 minutes of program, and while it's not too likely that Miss Raye is going to run out of steam, her writers may." Syndicated columnist Jack O'Brian (December 28, 1953) added, "Oh, well; Martha Raye's shows can't always be wonderful just because she is. Bert Lahr was fine, though."

The Martha Raye Show

Raye's show continued to be seen in its Saturday night slot. However, in early 1954, her segments began to air on NBC under the title *The Martha Raye Show,* and would continue to do so until the show's cancellation in 1956. These were the final shows done under the supervision of writer-producer Nat Hiken.

EPISODES

January 23, 1954. Guest Stars: Edward G. Robinson, Cesar Romero, Rocky Graziano.

Movie star Robinson is being driven to the brink of insanity by movie fans who remember him only as gangster Little Caesar and impersonate him to his face. After a brawl, Robinson tries to recuperate in Martha's apartment with the help of his buddy Cesar Romero. When Martha's boyfriend Rocky catches wind of the two men staying with her, he sees red, forcing Romero to flee to the local YMCA. Martha is blamed when members of Robinson's fan club commemorate their anniversary by stealing a valuable piece of art he wanted from the Metropolitan Museum. Martha sings "The Man I Love." *Variety* (January 27, 1954) reported, "Miss Raye kept the entire proceedings on a high comedic level.… The final half hour was devoted to burlesques of old films. Miss Raye had a virtuoso bit with her impression of Charlie Chaplin in *The Gold Rush.*"

February 20, 1954. Guest Stars: Ezio Pinza, Eddie Fisher, Joey Faye, Rocky Graziano.

Syracuse [NY] *Post-Standard*: "The comedy plot stems from Pinza's wish to begin a new career as a pop singer and sell a million records. A new singing team of Pinza and Raye is formed."

March 20, 1954. Guest Stars: Edward Everett Horton, Buddy Ebsen, David Evans, Rocky Graziano. Martha has the deciding vote in a contest over control of a railroad company. Songs included "My Funny Valentine" and "I've Got the World on a String." *Variety* (March 24, 1954): "Her delivery and mugging brightened each line and in some instances her pantomime was strictly Chaplinesque. She was on-camera for the major part of the show but she made the herculean task seem easy and like fun."

April 17, 1954. Guest Stars: Dick Foran, Charles Ruggles, Rocky Graziano, J. Fred Muggs.

Martha undergoes a brain machine application that helps her win at gambling halls. She sings "Love Is Sweeping the Country." *Variety* (April 21, 1954) said the episode "began with enough promise but before the first ten minutes were over it took a terrible tumble…. Facial contortions were carried to excess, gross slapstick abounded—the shrill humor of the evening needed relief and in the few instances there were opportunities for some straight material somebody insisted on maintaining the aura of unbecoming nonsense."

May 15, 1954. Guest Stars: Margaret Truman, Robert Preston, Rocky Graziano, Jake LaMotta.

Highlights from previous shows were featured in Martha's season finale.

1954–55 Season

With the departure of Nat Hiken, and following a brief stint with Dickson Ward in the producer's chair, Ed Simmons and Norman Lear took over as writer-directors for Martha's shows, scheduled to air every four weeks. Commercials promoted Hazel Bishop's "long-lasting" lipsticks and other makeup products.

Critical comments continued to be favorable. "Each time Martha Raye goes on the air she further establishes herself as TV's outstanding comedienne. Nobody I have ever seen on the screen can come anywhere near matching her. Martha's specialty is slapstick but she doesn't stop there. She can sell a song along with the best of them, and when she gets all togged out in her fancy tights she can run off dance steps at a pace that makes her male chorus pant."[9]

Martha's reward for her TV success was a lucrative new contract. "In line with its policy to protect top talent against raiders or defections to rival networks, NBC has put Martha Raye under contract at an undisclosed multi-million figure," announced *Variety* (March 23, 1955). "It's the longest-term deal given any performer since Milton Berle's 20-year pact." As outlined by columnist Jack O'Brian, "She will work the next five years at $25,000 per program…. Next season the endearing big mouth does 13…. The second five years she may sit back and collect cash high up in the five-figure category even if she can't work and after the ten years have run out, she gets a retirement bundle."[10]

EPISODES

September 28, 1954. Guest Stars: Wally Cox, Paul Lynde, Charlotte Rae. *Variety*, October 6, 1954: "The storyline has a murderer on the loose with a penchant for knocking off girls named Martha…. [S]he's still the top low-comedienne on video…. [The] script showed off her special talents fairly well."

Billboard's Jane Bundy wrote (October 9, 1954), "The Charles Addams–type comedy … may have convulsed Jack the Ripper fans, but it was way out of line for TV's family audience. In view of the recent wave of brutal and senseless crimes, it is especially difficult to understand who at NBC chose to cast its beloved 'Mr. Peepers' Wally Cox as a psychopathic killer with a mania to murder girls named Martha."

October 26, 1954. Guest Stars: Louis Jourdan, Denise Darcel, Robert Clary, Charlotte Rae. "Martha Raye portrays a Parisian singer who falls for Louis Jourdan. Rocky Graziano doesn't like the idea so much until he meets Denise Darcel." Milton Berle made a brief walk-on appearance during the finale.

November 23, 1954. Guest Star: Cesar Romero (substituting for Milton Berle, who suffered a collapse from exhaustion.) The story involves a performer whose famous smile suffers when Martha accidentally belts him in the mouth.

December 21, 1954. Guest Stars: Art Carney, Reginald Owen, Jules Munshin. Paul Lynde. In what was reported as "her first departure from a full-hour storyline comedy vehicle, Martha Raye will present three distinct sketches." One of them finds Martha and Carney as members of an old vaudeville team.

January 18, 1955. Guest Stars: Cesar Romero, Rocky Graziano, Will Jordan, David Burns; with Jane Dulo. Hollywood director Darryl F. Bird (Romero) thinks he's found the perfect newcomer to star in his $2 million film *Forever Selma*. Complications ensue when his assistant accidentally signs Martha instead of the girl he wanted, and a horrified Bird is led to believe his boss loves the choice.

In sketches, Martha clowns as an incompetent diner waitress, spoofs Charlie Chaplin in *The Gold Rush,* and is taught to play Hollywood love scenes opposite a mannequin named Hubert. Comic Will Jordan impersonates "Ed Solomon," the host of "Most of the Town." Songs include "I'll Get By" and "There's a Great Day Coming, Manana."

February 15, 1955. Guest Stars: Jack E. Leonard, Rocky Graziano. *Zanesville* [OH] *Signal*: "The storyline features a cops-and-robbers motif and concerns a fast-talking gun moll who is the exact double of Martha…. Martha becomes accidentally involved with the gang who think she is their moll." Songs include "I've Got the World on a String" and "Birth of the Blues."

March 15, 1955. Guest Stars: Ricardo Montalban, Maria Riva. Montalban plays a European prince "visiting this country for the usual reason—to get a loan. Maria Riva is his sweetheart. But somehow or other Martha Raye gets publicized as the royal favorite and, for business reasons, this suits the prince." (*San Antonio* [TX] *Light*)

April 12, 1955. Guest Stars: Dennis O'Keefe, Benny Goodman, Jackie Coogan. *Long Beach* [CA] *Independent*: "O'Keefe plays a noted TV personality whom Martha seeks to impress in order to win a job. She is aided by Coogan, as her old vaudeville partner, and they do a takeoff on one of the great silent movies."

May 10, 1955. Guest Stars: Thomas Mitchell, Rocky Graziano. *Long Beach* [CA] *Independent:* "Storyline has Martha becoming involved with a group of elderly people studying American history in a night school." This episode marked a professional reunion for Martha with Mitchell, more than 20 years after he helped her develop her early comic style for the 1934 New York revue *Calling All Stars*.

June 7, 1955. Guest Stars: Errol Flynn, Rocky Graziano. "Errol Flynn, who seldom gets a chance to show his talent for comedy in the movies, will trade gags with Martha...." *San Antonio* [TX] *Light*, June 14, 1955

1955–56 Season

The Martha Raye Show returned to the airwaves in September 1955 with the first of 13 episodes she was booked to do for the season. Martha went into the season with a sense of security afforded by her longtime contract. "That contract means a lot to me," she said. "I'm 39 now—I mean really 39, not the Jack Benny kind. The next 15 years are important ones in my life. It's so great to be able to know that I'll have security for the next 15 years."[11]

But her show was plagued with troubles almost from the outset. According to *Jet* magazine (October 27, 1955), the appearance of African-American spelling champion Gloria Lockerman resulted in complaints from at least one NBC affiliate in Mississippi. A more lasting problem came from ABC and CBS offerings that siphoned away viewers, especially Nat Hiken's increasingly popular *The Phil Silvers Show*. By February 1956, Silvers' ratings had outpaced both Martha's and Milton Berle's on NBC. On March 24, 1956, *Billboard* noted that Martha's ratings now ran third to both ABC's *Warner Brothers Presents* and CBS's *The Phil Silvers Show*.

In April, trade papers reported that writer-producers Ed Simmons and Norman Lear would not be returning for Martha's fall season. *Billboard* (April 4, 1956) explained, "Simmons & Lear reported they requested the release in order to devote full time to certain NBC-TV projects now in preparation for filming by the network this summer in Hollywood.... [C]omedienne is shopping for individual scripts on the open market until status on the show is set."

Unfortunately for Martha and her fans, the question of who would write her TV comedy routines soon became a moot point, as NBC announced a fall 1956 schedule with no room for her show. Although *Variety* (April 25, 1956) reported that Martha might be back on the air soon with a 30-minute CBS show, it would in fact be many years before she again had a regular role in a weekly series.

Episodes

September 20, 1955. Guest Stars: Tallulah Bankhead, Rocky Graziano, Gloria Lockerman. Martha's season opener found her winning a chance to appear on a big-money quiz show, with Bankhead cast as a "good fairy" named "Twinkle Toes" who comes to her aid. *Variety* (September 28, 1955) found the result lacking: "Generally this lady buffoon reaches her top when she has a strong script to accompany her comedics. In her debut … she seemed abandoned by her writers." But as Jane Bundy noted in *Billboard* (October 1, 1955), "With the exception of Jimmy Durante no other TV performer today can project so much warmth, wistful earthiness and downright lovableness to an audience."

October 11, 1955. Guest Stars: Rocky Graziano, Douglas Fairbanks, Jr., the Kirby Stone Quartet; with Bill Dana, Sara Seegar. *Oakland* [CA] *Tribune*: "Douglas Fairbanks, Jr., steps out of character long enough to show his abilities in the singing and dancing departments."

November 1, 1955. Guest Stars: Paulette Goddard, Margaret Truman, Rocky Graziano, Bill Dana, Jane Dulo. *Racine Journal-Times*: "Martha and her two guests appear as wives of entertainers who are always on the road. The only way the girls will ever catch up to their husbands is to be entertainers themselves." Martha "teams with the unlikely combination of Paulette Goddard and Margaret Truman in a funny 'Kid Number.'" Songs include "Smile" and "I Wished on the Moon" (*Hammond* [IN] *Times*).

November 22, 1955. Guest Stars: Johnnie Ray, Gene Krupa, Stubby Kaye, Walter Abel, Rocky Graziano. "Martha writes a song for Johnnie which she knows will end up on the hit parade" (*Findlay* [OH] *Republican-Courier*).

December 13, 1955. Guest Stars: Jack Carson, Cesar Romero, Joe Besser, singer Julius La Rosa. "Jack Carson and Cesar Romero play two Texas millionaires who both are seeking Martha's hand in marriage" (*San Mateo* [CA] *Times*, December 10, 1955).

January 3, 1956. Guest Stars: Errol Flynn, Charles Coburn, Paul Lynde, the Bill and Cora Baird Marionettes; with Bill Dana. "Flynn portrays a scoutmaster, and Martha desires to scout him for her master" (*Long Beach* [CA] *Press-Telegram*).

January 24, 1956. Guest Stars: Gordon MacRae, Rocky Graziano, Paul Lynde, the Bill and Cora Baird Marionettes, comedian Jules Munshin; with Mary Grace Canfield. Martha's 30th anniversary as an entertainer is observed.

February 14, 1956. Guest Stars: Charlton Heston, Tim Hovey, Rocky Graziano, Hedda Hopper, Condo and Brandow (musical team). *Racine* [WI] *Journal-Times*: "Aboard a train to Hollywood, Martha Raye meets a little boy who is traveling alone. Her new friend turns out to be child actor Tim Hovey, who in turn gives Martha a helping hand in the screen capital."

March 6, 1956. Guest Stars: Buster Keaton, Paul Douglas, Harold Arlen, the Baird Marionettes. Martha and Keaton recreate a scene from Chaplin's *Limelight*, with Raye donning the Little Tramp getup. Martha sings a medley of songs by composer Arlen, including "The Man That Got Away," "Happiness Is Just a Thing Called Joe" and "C'mon, Get Happy."

March 27, 1956. Guest Stars: Peter Lawford, Mildred Natwick, Ernest Truex, Julius La Rosa. Lawford plays a detective who hires Martha as his assistant.

April 17, 1956. Guest Stars: Jean Pierre Aumont, Harpo Marx, Rocky Graziano, Risë Stevens, baseball players Jim Hearn, Duke Snider, Wes Westrum. Harpo appears as an umpire officiating at a game between the Brooklyn Dodgers and the New York Giants.

May 8, 1956. Guest Stars: Gertrude Berg, Julius La Rosa. Worn out from overwork, Martha is invited by Molly Goldberg (Berg) to rest and relax at her place in the Bronx. Said columnist Jack O'Brian, "Despite all her troubles it was Martha Raye's best telecast of the season.... The dream skit in which Martha and Molly Goldberg changed places was very funny, and Molly made it endearing... 'Every Time,' as sung by Martha, seemed to sum up all her own personal, poignant escapades.... After suffering all season from her writers' creative cramps, they came through to make it Martha's finest TV hour."[12]

May 29, 1956. Guest Stars: Constance Bennett, Cesar Romero, Robert Strauss, Fritz Feld. "Cesar Romero as a charm school operator wagers Constance Bennett as a nightclub singer that he can make a lady out of Martha" (*Oakland* [CA] *Tribune*).

The Steve Allen Show

Allen, who came to national prominence as host of *The Tonight Show,* hosted a weekly NBC variety series from 1956 to 1960, originally intended to compete with Ed Sullivan's popular Sunday night hour on CBS. Sponsored by Plymouth, Allen's show featured a number of regularly seen funnymen including Tom Poston, Don Knotts, Louis Nye, Bill Dana and Gabriel Dell. Martha was booked frequently as a guest throughout the show's four-year prime time run.

According to Allen, Martha appeared at his insistence despite some talk in network and sponsor circles that she was passé, and "had acquired a reputation for undependability."[13] Raye accepted his dictum that she would perform the material as devised by his producer and writers. A favorite device on his show was what Allen and his writers called the "Right Way/Wrong Way" formula, in which sketches showed a seemingly normal and unfunny scene followed by a second rendition in which everything possible went wrong.

In one Allen show skit, Martha starred in a live television melodrama subject to endless mishaps on the air. In another she was a Broadway star repeating her triumphant New York role in summer stock, surrounded by a less-than-professional cast and crew.

In Hollywood to make another guest appearance with Steve Allen, Martha told UPI's Joe Finnigan, "I don't know anything about Hollywood any more. It's all new to me." Her career efforts concentrated primarily on her Miami Beach nightclub. She said of comediennes, "They've always been scarce. Girls don't lean to comedy like men do. They never did."[14]

EPISODES

December 23, 1956. Guest Stars: Martha Raye, the Vienna Boys' Choir, Alan Young, Dr. Norman Vincent Peale, Ricky Vera. Martha plays a Hollywood star in a sketch.

March 10, 1957. Guest Stars: Martha Raye, Diahann Carroll, Fernando Lamas, Steve Lawrence, Jerry Lewis.

May 26, 1957. Guest Stars: Martha Raye, Andy Griffith, Dean Martin, Anna Maria Alberghetti, pianist Errol Garner, Jimmy McHugh. Martha and Steve team for "Mighty Pretty Melody."

September 8, 1957. Guest Stars: Martha Raye, Robert Young, Steve Lawrence and Eydie Gorme, Marion Lorne, Miss America Marilyn Van Derbur.

December 1, 1957. Guest Stars: Martha Raye, Errol Flynn, singer Jimmy Dean, Rita Gam and members of the Army-Navy football team. Martha plays "Kitty Carlot" in a panel-show sketch, "To Tell a Lie," trying to decide which of three men is the real Errol Flynn, and sings "Come Rain or Come Shine."

January 26, 1958. Guest Stars: Martha Raye, Charles Laughton, Jimmy Dean, Erin O'Brien. A sketch illustrates what can go wrong in shooting a movie scene.

June 1, 1958. Guest Stars: Martha Raye, Henry Fonda, Mel Torme, Shari Lewis, the Terry Gibbs Dream Band.

November 9, 1958. Guest Stars: Martha Raye, Johnny Carson, Harry Belafonte. Martha sings "Love."

February 1, 1959. Guest Stars: Martha Raye, Carl Ballantine, singer Danny Staton. The program featured a salute to jazz music.

May 31, 1959. Guest Stars: Martha Raye, Frank Gorshin, Buddy Greco. "Fearless Martha Raye poses for an assortment of crazy shots, and stars in a fairly amusing skit about a visiting Russian ballet company (resembling nothing you've ever seen)" (*Troy* [NY] *Record*, May 30, 1959). Martha sings "The Lady Is a Tramp."

February 22, 1960. Guest Stars: Martha Raye, Johnny Desmond, Maurice Evans, Tom Poston.

April 18, 1960. Guest Stars: Martha Raye, Charles Laughton, singer Mark Murphy.

Baby Snooks

After the cancellation of her NBC variety show, Martha was encouraged to turn her attention to a filmed situation comedy series, as so many of her peers had done. In 1957, she was chosen by producer Jess Oppenheimer (*I Love Lucy*) to star in his pilot for an NBC filmed sitcom. The character had been played by comedienne Fanny Brice in a long-running radio series, on which Oppenheimer had been a writer. Adapting the project to television was a project that had been underway since 1956, but was now being fast-tracked in hopes of winning a spot on the 1957–58 prime time schedule.

Reported *Daily Variety* (April 1, 1957), "After more than a year of auditioning a dozen potentials, NBC gave the nod to Martha Raye as 'Baby Snooks.' It will be piloted at California National Studio April 12 with Jess Oppenheimer producing and William Asher directing." The lead character's name, originally Minnie, was altered to Martha once Raye was aboard.

Adapting this long-running radio hit to television called for some creative thinking. In the radio *Baby Snooks,* Brice didn't have to resemble the child she was playing, and it didn't matter that a little girl was being played by an adult. Oppenheimer's concept, updated for television, circumvented this hurdle by using a show-within-

During filming of the *Baby Snooks* pilot, Martha (right) embraces child actress Ruthie Robinson (courtesy Gregg Oppenheimer).

a-show concept, making it a sitcom about an adult actress playing Baby Snooks on television, and her family.

The series pilot introduced the character of Martha Fields, a TV performer sharing her home with her sister Laurie Wheaton and her family. Laurie's husband George is a veteran currently enrolled in college on the GI Bill; he and Laurie have a young daughter, Beth. George, sensitive about having his family living in Martha's house, also finds his sister-in-law a bit disconcerting. "I was in the Normandy Invasion, Korea and the Battle of the Bulge," he says in an early version of the script, "but I never faced anything like [Martha]."

Martha, who's very fond of her niece, wants to send Beth to the exclusive Fenlake School for Girls, but George prefers that she attend public school. Martha Fields is an actress whose newest project finds her playing the character of Baby Snooks on a TV show. When little Beth accompanies her aunt to rehearsal, she sees Snooks and her Daddy in a comedy sketch about gambling on the horses.

Back at home, George is shocked and appalled by the new lingo ("tout," "betting on the bangtails") his daughter has acquired from her outing with Martha, and accuses his sister-in-law of having taken her to a racetrack. Before that misunderstanding can be put to rest, snobbish Miss Lockwood, headmistress of the Fenlake School, pays an unannounced visit. When it develops that Miss Lockwood not only disapproves of Beth's new vocabulary, but also of Martha's show business background, everyone in the family comes to the conclusion that Beth will be better off attending public school rather than the "phoney baloney" Fenlake.

Aside from Martha, the cast included Hanley Stafford (1899–1968), reprising his radio role as Snooks' Daddy, and Paul Smith (1929–2006), who would go on featured roles on *Mrs. G Goes to College* and *The Doris Day Show*, as Martha's frustrated brother-in-law. Cast as Martha's pint-sized counterpart Beth, who would exhibit some behaviors typical of Snooks, was six-year-old Ruthie Robinson (1950–2005), whose credits included playing the title character of *The Search for Bridey Murphy* (1956) as a child.

In the aftermath of *Snooks,* columnist Erskine Johnson reported another possible television project—"Martha Raye and ABC-TV are discussing a filmed comedy series"—but this failed to pan out.[15]

The Garry Moore Show

Comedian Moore (1915–1993) hosted a one-hour Tuesday night comedy-variety show on CBS from 1958 to 1964. Martha appeared twice during its inaugural season, and returned for another visit during its sixth and final year.

By far her most notorious appearance, however, was the one she didn't make in February 1959, when her illness forced her to drop out of a scheduled appearance. Carol Burnett's performance as her substitute won the younger comedienne a regular featured spot on the Moore show.

EPISODES

December 9, 1958. Guest Stars: Martha Raye, Mickey Rooney, Julius La Rosa, Errol Garner. *Pasadena* [CA] *Star-News*: "Miss Raye, a song stylist of unchallenged repute as well as a great comedienne, will show both sides of her versatile talents."

April 14, 1959. Guest Stars: Martha Raye, Diahann Carroll, Benny Fields, Blossom Seeley. The cast salutes "That Wonderful Year," 1919.

December 31, 1963. Guest Stars: Martha Raye, Melodye Condos, Chita Rivera, Roy Castle. Martha and daughter Melodye, an aspiring singer, were both booked.

Perry Como's
Kraft Music Hall

In the 1960s, Martha became a favorite guest on the variety shows of two low-key popular singers. In 1959, Como (1912–2001), who had been making frequent TV appearances since the late 1940s, became the weekly host of NBC's *The Kraft Music Hall*, produced under the auspices of the star's company Roncom Productions. Martha made her first appearance during the show's second season, and was so well-received that she was booked again less than a month later.

For the 1963–64 season, Como gave up the weekly series, but did seven specials under the same title. Martha appeared in the fifth special.

EPISODES

March 22, 1961. Guest Stars: Martha Raye, Julie Newmar, child pianist-singer Ginny Tiu. Said the syndicated *TV Key* column, "It's all-girls night tonight so Perry can hardly get a note in edgewise.... It's all in fun, the script is zippy and sprightly, the restaurant sketch is hilarious, and the solo numbers are fine." A dissenting opinion was offered by journalist William Sarmento: "Martha Raye mugged, growled and carried on in her Jerry Lewis–type way. I felt embarrassed for a woman her age. Actually Miss Raye can sing a great blues ballad but her brand of comedy left television with Milton Berle."[16] A musical medley features songs about boys and men, including "Mr. Paganini."

April 19, 1961. Guest Stars: Martha Raye, Milburn Stone (*Gunsmoke*). In a show biz retrospective, "Martha and Milburn do an old soft shoe to 'How Could You Believe Me,' and Perry floors them as the great Ziegfeld. There's a takeoff on radio, some footage of a silent film, and a visit from golf player Gary Player." (*Hutchinson* [KS] *News*). Martha duets with Como on "My Blue Heaven" and takes part in a medley of songs used as radio themes, including "Love in Bloom."

October 18, 1961. Guest Stars: Martha Raye, Rita Moreno, Ted Weems and His Quartet, Paul Lynde. Martha plays "a lunatic Peter Pan" in a sketch that also features Lynde, Kaye Ballard, and Don Adams. Wanting to take Como's kids back to Pie-in-the-Sky Land with her, Martha is thwarted by various obstacles, including an obstinate stagehand who fails to levitate her on cue. "Am I going to fly," she grumbles, looking upward, "or do I have to bring violence back to television?"

March 5, 1964. Guest Stars: Martha Raye, Mickey Rooney, Al Hirt, Jacques d'Amboise. Broadcast live from New Orleans, this installment finds Martha singing "Do You Know What It Means to Miss New Orleans?" and "Mississippi Mud," and dueting with Como on a medley of "River" tunes.

The Andy Williams Show

Martha was a favored guest in the early years of the musical variety hour hosted by singer Andy Williams (1927–2012). The show was seen weekly between 1962 and 1969 (with a revival from 1969 to 1971). The bulk of her appearances were made during its first season.

EPISODES

October 18, 1962. "Martha Raye guests in a sketch as a cleaning lady at a department store," and sings "Up a Lazy River" (*Hayward* [CA] *Daily Review*). In another sketch, Andy "seeks the secret of longevity from a 122-year-old woman, portrayed by Miss Raye" (*Dover* [OH] *Daily Reporter*, October 13, 1962). Plus, "a montage film clip of Martha making 26 costume changes in her new movie *Jumbo*" (*Indiana Evening Gazette*).

February 7, 1963. "Martha Raye and Peter Lawford join Andy in a strange version of Cinderella," with Lawford as Prince Charming (*Cedar Rapids* [IA] *Gazette*, February 3, 1963).

March 7, 1963. Guest Stars: Martha Raye, Jonathan Winters. Martha appears in a Hansel and Gretel skit and "a production number built around hats" (*Oakland* [CA] *Tribune*).

April 18, 1966. Guest Stars: Martha Raye, Red Buttons, the Arthur Lyman Quartet. Martha sings "Glory of Love"; she and Buttons play kids in a slum neighborhood, with Andy as the rich kid. Also featured: "a nostalgic look at burlesque" (*Scottsdale* [AZ] *Progress*).

The Red Skelton Hour *a.k.a.*
The Red Skelton Show

Martha was a frequent guest on Red Skelton's CBS variety show of the 1960s, and also appeared on the shorter version that ran on NBC (1970–71).

According to Skelton's producer Bill Hobin, an ideal guest for Skelton would be "an intelligent person with that [elusive] capacity to let his hair down and have fun."[17] Clearly Martha fit that bill, and she was booked repeatedly. Actress Chanin Hale, a recurring player on Skelton's shows of the 1960s, said, "We loved it when Martha Raye was a guest because she was great fun."[18] Skelton was known to enjoy having a somewhat raunchy rehearsal, and Martha was game to take part, giving as good as she got.

Appearing with Red also reunited Martha with her ex-husband David Rose, the show's musical director. By all accounts, the two worked together amicably.

Among Skelton's most popular recurring characters was the henpecked husband George Appleby, who struggled to escape from the dictates of his bossy wife Clara.

Many Skelton guest stars played Clara over the years, including Eve Arden, Vivian Vance, Audrey Meadows—and Martha.

CBS canceled *The Red Skelton Hour* in 1970 and he continued for one more year with the half-hour *The Red Skelton Show* on NBC.

Episodes

The Red Skelton Hour. CBS, January 1, 1963. "Of Mouth and Men." Guest Stars: Martha Raye, Tommy Noonan. Skelton and Raye spoof the blockbuster film *Cleopatra* in a skit with Martha assuming the role of the *femme fatale*, who describes herself as "a girl who is 36–22–36 ... and that's only my mouth!" Skelton plays the slave Nauseous, who proves resistant to the queen's charms.

"The Mouth Shall Rise Again." CBS, December 10, 1963. Guest Star: Martha Raye.

"The Mouth That Roared." CBS, October 27, 1964. Guest Star: Martha Raye. "Freddie the Freeloader is asked by government agents to get evidence against Mr. Big, boss of the racketeers. Martha Raye plays Mr. Big, whose mob is the toughest in the land." Martha sings "Money Can't Buy Me Love" and "I'll Go My Way By Myself" (*Jefferson City* [MO] *Post-Tribune*, October 23, 1964).

The Red Skelton Hour. CBS, May 4, 1965. "She's playing a TV boss who hires Clem the Idiot Kadiddlehopper and his pet goose.... Martha sings two Cole Porter numbers between sketches" (*Arizona Republic*).

The Red Skelton Hour. CBS, March 7, 1967. "Martha Raye and Mickey Rooney, as ex-burlesque players who have struck it rich, enjoy a riotous reunion with [Skelton as George Appleby].... Miss Raye sings "Happiness Is Just a Thing Called Joe" and performs "I've Got My Love to Keep Me Warm" (*Mansfield* [OH] *News-Journal*).

The Red Skelton Hour. CBS, October 15, 1968. Guest Star: Martha Raye. Martha plays "Prudence Pennyfeather, a supposedly proper Boston lady. She arrives in Deadwood, where she and Sheriff Deadeye become immediate enemies" (*Hagerstown* [MD] *Morning Herald*). She sings "How About Me?"

The Red Skelton Hour. CBS, October 14, 1969. Guest Stars: Martha Raye, The Vogues (vocalists). Martha plays a traveling saleslady who takes a shine to Clem Kadiddlehopper and sings "Watch What Happens."

The Red Skelton Show. NBC, February 15, 1971. "Appleby's Garage Sale." Unable to pay a $200 gambling debt, George Appleby tries to raise money by hosting a garage sale. Martha plays Clara Appleby.

During the CBS run of *The Red Skelton Hour,* Martha was also a guest star on his November 12, 1966, special *Clown Alley.* Skelton, as "Freddie the Freeloader," hosted this special paying tribute to the artistry of clowns, with guests Raye, Vincent Price, Audrey Meadows, Jackie Coogan, Bobby Rydell, Amanda Blake and Robert Merrill. "In music, dance and specialty acts, the variety Special will recapture highlights of the golden era of clowndom, including some of the classic 'turns' that have delighted circus audiences since the first Big Top.... Martha Raye is featured in an unusual ballet version of 'Be a Clown,' assisted by young Randy Whipple."[19]

Bob Hope Specials

Friendly since they worked together at Paramount in the 1930s, Martha and Bob Hope (1903–2003) maintained that relationship for many years. Both were heavily involved in entertaining the troops in Vietnam; she was also a frequently welcomed guest on his NBC television specials. In the mid–1960s, the specials were folded into the weekly anthology series he hosted, *Bob Hope Presents the Chrysler Theater* (1963–67).

EPISODES

Bob Hope Presents the Chrysler Theater. October 25, 1963. Bob's guests are Raye, Andy Griffith, Jane Russell, Sandy Koufax and Don Drysdale. Martha sings "I've Got My Love to Keep Me Warm." In sketches, she portrays the despotic leader of Vietnam, and spoofs *The King and I.*

Bob Hope Presents the Chrysler Theater. April 17, 1964. Guest Stars: Martha Raye, Tony Randall, Jack Jones. The fifth annual *TV Guide* Awards are presented. In a spoof of the movie *Tom Jones,* Hope and Raye "wade through a busy eating scene," while another bit finds them, along with Tony Randall, doing their version of the Beatles (*San Antonio* [TX] *Light*).

Bob Hope Presents the Chrysler Theater. December 18, 1964. Guest Stars: Martha Raye, James Garner, Nancy Wilson, Kathryn Grant. Bob's holiday special includes a skit in which he and Raye "make fun of *Peyton Place* in a silly soaper" (*Syracuse* [NY] *Post-Standard*).

Bob Hope Presents the Chrysler Theater. February 16, 1966. Guest Stars: Danny Thomas, Jill St. John, The Righteous Brothers. Martha appears in a *Batman* spoof, "in which she flies around as Batgirl while Hope, as the Lobsterman, tries to catch her with a giant flyswatter" (*Madison* [WI] *State Journal*).

Bob Hope Comedy Special. February 17, 1969. Guest Stars: Bing Crosby, George Burns, Martha Raye, Diana Ross and the Supremes. Hope's special salutes vaudeville. Martha sings "Mr. Paganini" and joins Hope in an "Oriental magic act" (*Logan* [UT] *Herald-Journal*).

Bob Hope Comedy Special. NBC, September 11, 1971. Guest Stars: Martha Raye, Angie Dickinson, Phyllis Diller, Barbara McNair, Nanette Fabray, Zsa Zsa Gabor, Imogene Coca, Sally Struthers, Jacqueline Susann, Jill St. John. The show's premise was explained in advertisements as: "One lone male on the Planet of the Shapes!" "Bob Hope made his 22nd seasonal debut without getting anyone excited" (*Waterloo* [IA] *Daily Courier*).

The Bob Hope 30th Anniversary Special. NBC, January 18, 1981. Guest Stars: Martha Raye, Milton Berle, Danny Thomas, George Burns, Marie Osmond, Rosemary Clooney. A two-hour special observing Hope's 30 years of television specials.

Women I Love: Beautiful But Funny. NBC, February 28, 1982. Guest Stars: Martha Raye, Lucille Ball, Rosemary Clooney, Pearl Bailey, Ginger Rogers, many others. The show features 100 women from Hope's films and TV shows.

Happy Birthday, Bob: A Salute to Bob Hope's 80th Birthday. NBC, May 23, 1983.

Martha made multiple appearances from the 1960s through the 1980s in Bob Hope's NBC specials. Here they enact a spoof of *The King and I.*

Guests include Martha Raye, Lucille Ball, George Burns, Phyllis Diller, Dudley Moore and Tom Selleck.

Bill and Martha

Martha and actor William Bendix (1906–1964), who'd enjoyed a long TV run with his sitcom *The Life of Riley* (NBC, 1953–58), were teamed for this proposed

situation comedy intended for CBS's 1964–65 schedule. "Format for the Bill Bendix—Martha Raye television show will have them playing a millionaire's butler and
maid,"[20] said one published account, while another described the series as "revolving
around a butler and maid who inherit a palatial home. They are able to maintain
it on a transient rental basis."[21] Comedy writer Ed Simmons, a veteran of *The Martha
Raye Show,* left his *Red Skelton Hour* post to assume the responsibilities of head
writer on the projected sitcom.

The show made it as far as CBS's announced fall schedule in the spring of 1964
before plans went awry. *Variety* (March 11, 1964) reported that CBS intended to
schedule the Bendix-Raye comedy in a Sunday evening slot, paired between 9 and
10 p.m. with another new show, producer Jack Chertok's *Living Doll* (which ultimately became *My Living Doll,* with Robert Cummings and Julie Newmar). This
would place the shows in direct competition with NBC's highly popular Western
Bonanza, not the most desirable slot.

By May, network enthusiasm for the sitcom had cooled. To columnist Cynthia
Lowry, CBS program vice-president Mike Dann said, "We found we were running
into substantial contract difficulties and decided to abandon the project."[22] Instead
of *Bill and Martha,* CBS picked up *The Joey Bishop Show,* which had been canceled
by NBC after three seasons.

Bendix believed there was another explanation for the project being terminated.
As some sources noted, "That projected series didn't materialize because of Bendix's
faltering health or contractual differences."[23] Though it was reported that his own
doctor had advised against undertaking a weekly series, Bendix, 58, took his griev-
ance to attorneys. "He had planned a new television show for this season with
Martha Raye, but it was canceled by CBS. Bendix sued CBS for $2,658,000 for
breach of contract charging CBS-TV President James Aubrey with spreading rumors
he was in ill health. The suit was settled for an undisclosed amount."[24]

Bendix did pass away on December 14, 1964, only a few months after the pilot
was rejected. He had been a patient at Los Angeles' Good Samaritan Hospital for
several days, undergoing treatment for pneumonia.

The Hollywood Palace

This ABC variety show began in 1964 as a mid-season replacement for Jerry
Lewis' unsuccessful series, using the same production facilities refurbished at considerable cost. Martha appeared several times during *Palace*'s seven-season run, as
either guest or host.

EPISODES

March 5, 1966. Guest Stars: Milton Berle (host), Martha Raye, Adam West, Henny
Youngman, Sandler and Young. In a comic-book sketch, Berle plays a beleaguered
Superman. Martha plays a villainess, the Dragon Lady, who poses as both Little
Orphan Annie and Wonder Woman to throw Superman off course, while Adam

West makes a cameo appearance as Batman. Martha sings "Taking a Chance on Love."

April 2, 1966. Guest Stars: Martha Raye (host), Ann Miller, Allen and Rossi, Chad and Jeremy, George Carlin, singer Barry Sadler. Martha sings "Lover" and "Little Girl Blue" and does a comedy skit with Marty Allen. Greeting an audience filled with servicemen, she offers one her hand to kiss, and then cracks, "You didn't learn that in basic training!"

November 30, 1968. Guest Stars: Milton Berle (host), Martha Raye, Joey Forman, Joe Besser, Barrie Chase, Rosey Grier, The Third Wave. Martha sings "Toot Toot Tootsie" and "Those Were the Good Old Days."

November 22, 1969. Guest Stars: Milton Berle (host), Martha Raye, Steve Allen, Hines, Hines and Dad, Irving Benson, The Young Bloods. Berle "plays an attorney in an old slapstick sketch, 'The Courtroom,' defending daughter Martha Raye, with Steve Allen playing the DA and Irving Benson the judge."

February 7, 1970. The series' final broadcast, hosted by Bing Crosby, features clips from previous episodes. Martha, described by Crosby as "a true star, and a great lady," is seen singing "Little Girl Blue."

The Carol Burnett Show

One of television's most popular variety shows, this CBS series ran from 1967 to 1978. Martha first turned up in the tenth episode. She was invited back for multiple appearances over the show's first several seasons, which also featured Harvey Korman, Vicki Lawrence and Lyle Waggoner as regular players. Then she was not used at all after the fourth season.

Episodes

November 20, 1967. Guest Stars: Martha Raye, Juliet Prowse. Carol introduces Martha as a "truly great lady," recounting the story of how Raye's sudden illness won Carol an early career break on *The Garry Moore Show*. Martha sings "After You've Gone." Carol and Martha play cabin-mates on a cruise ship. In another bit, Carol and Martha compare the sizes of their mouths, but Juliet Prowse is found to have one with a capacity that surpasses theirs.

February 12, 1968. Guest Stars: Martha Raye, Betty Grable. Carol and Martha sing "Flings." "The three girls get together for skits on gun molls and a funny bit about a soap opera's happy ending after 15 years of continuing catastrophes." (*North Adams* [MA] *Transcript*, February 12, 1968) Martha appears in the first-ever "As the Stomach Turns" skit, which proves so popular that it will become a recurring sketch for the remainder of the show's long run.

January 27, 1969. Guest Stars: Martha Raye, Mel Torme. *Lima* (OH) *News*: "Martha Raye is back for some slapstick and song with Carol. The two of them throw paint at each other in a silent movie sketch, and engage in a lengthy musical segment on silly songs of the '40s…. [T] cast kids the worst TV commercials of the year."

March 17, 1969. Guest Stars: Martha Raye, Mike Douglas. "...Carol and Martha [play] housewives timidly visiting a topless-waiter restaurant on their night out" (*Hayward* [CA] *Daily Review*). A sketch parodies dance marathons, with Douglas singing "Life Is Just a Bowl of Cherries."

December 8, 1969. Guest Stars: Martha Raye, Tim Conway. Sketches include "Miss Raye and Miss [Vicki] Lawrence as women seeking romance via 'Three Coins in the Fountain.'" Martha sings "If That's All There Is" and, in a duet with Burnett, "Big Beautiful Ball." In another sketch, Martha and Carol "play mothers from different sides of the track sharing a park outing with their offspring."[25] "A stageful of Shirley Temples singing and dancing 'The Good Ship Lippipop [sic]' salutes movies from 20th Century-Fox when Martha Raye and Tim Conway join Carol Burnett in a musical nightmare" (*Argus* [Fremont, CA], May 17, 1970).

March 23, 1970. *Burlington* [NC] *Daily Times*: "Martha Raye and Mel Torme join in a musical salute to Walt Disney Studios. Martha plays the owner of a mongrel dog in an encounter with the elegant owner of a toy poodle." Another sketch shows how the story of Sleeping Beauty might be told in versions rated G, PG and X.

November 16, 1970. Guest Stars: Martha Raye, Ross Martin. A comedy sketch about jury duty finds "a snooty socialite [Burnett] sharing a hotel room with a beer-swilling, uncouth type (Miss Raye)." (*Fremont* [CA] *Argus*). Another sketch, "Storefront Hospital," spoofs TV medical shows, with Martha as a wealthy and belligerent patient. Martha is also seen costumed as Benita Bizarre from *The Bugaloos*, then removing the fake nose and wig to perform a dramatic monologue.

January 25, 1971. Guest Stars: Martha Raye, New York City Ballet dancers Edward Villela and Violette Verdy. In a "Carol and Sis" segment, Martha plays the newly hired maid who isn't what the family expected. Carol and Martha do a medley of '20s and '30s songs.

March 25, 1977. This special 90-minute broadcast, commemorating the show's tenth season, features clips from previous episodes spotlighting numerous celebrity guests, including Martha.

The Bugaloos

John McIndoe (*I.Q.*), Wayne Laryea (*Harmony*), John Philpott (*Courage*), Caroline Ellis (*Joy*), Martha Raye (*Benita Bizarre*), Billy Barty (*Sparky Firefly*), Sharon Baird (*Funky Rat*), Joy Campbell (*Woofer*), Van Snowden (*Tweeter*), Joan Gerber, Walker Edmiston (*Voices*)

Si Rose (*Executive Producer*), Donald A. Ramsey (*Associate Producer*), Sid and Marty Krofft (*Creator-Producers*), Tony Charmoli (*Director*), Hal Yoergler (*Musical Director*), Charles Fox (*Music*), Charles Fox, Norman Gimbel (*Theme Song*)

This Saturday morning NBC-TV series from the prolific team of Sid and Marty Krofft was their second, following the success of *H.R. Pufnstuf* during the 1969–70 season. Both costumed actors and Krofft puppets performed in the show. The Bugaloos were a manufactured music group (much like the Monkees) consisting of four young British newcomers costumed as various insects. Reportedly more than 5000 young performers auditioned for the roles. Other recurring characters included Nutty Bird (a messenger), Magico the Magician, Bluebell Flower (who warned of impending danger), and the Grapevine (a bunch of talking grapes who passed along gossip). Although the show's primary focus was the young cast, Martha was given standout billing in the opening titles ("Starring Martha Raye as Benita Bizarre") and featured strongly in every segment.

Gleeful villainess Benita Bizarre is always frustrated in her attempts to further her musical career and win recognition from local KOOK radio disc jockey Peter Platter, who like everyone else considered her singing atrocious. She lives in a giant jukebox with her servants and minions, led by German-accented Funky Rat. She settles disputes by using her "ultrasonic, high frequency stereo zapper," which can render its victims unconscious.

Living a few miles away in Tranquility Forest ("the last of the British colonies") are lead singer Joy, singer-guitarist I.Q., and her backup musicians Courage (drums) and Harmony (keyboards), known collectively as the Bugaloos. Their pal Sparky is a firefly who is devoted to them but hopelessly clumsy. Hearing the music of the Bugaloos, Benita decides she wants "my very own British rock group," and endeavors to inveigle them into working with her. Happy with their lives in Tranquility Forest, the Bugaloos resist her every effort to infiltrate their world. Almost every episode found Benita kidnapping either one of the Bugaloos or one of their friends.

Audaciously costumed in feathers and a long, pointy nose, Benita spouts such insults as "you wacky little weirdos" or "teenage termites," as well as her frequent expression of shock, "Holy Humperdinck!" Firmly convinced of her own talent and beauty, despite prevailing opinion, she frequently tells herself things like, "Oh, Benita, you're not only a dreamboat, you're a genius!"

Variety (September 16, 1970) praised her efforts: "Miss Raye plays it with great zest and the role should be a fine vehicle for her exceptional comedic gifts…. [T]he comedy is a refreshing antidote to the banality and vulgarity of most of the cartoons."

Seventeen videotaped *Bugaloos* episodes aired during the 1970–71 season. Although plans to produce additional episodes fell through, the show continued to play in reruns for a second season. A cast album was released, and a single even charted briefly. The series saw its first DVD release in 2006.

EPISODES

"Firefly, Light My Fire." September 12, 1970. Writers: Si Rose, John Fenton Murray. The Bugaloos rescue and befriend Sparky Firefly after he's clipped by Benita's limousine. Meanwhile, wanting backup musicians for her latest record, Benita decides the Bugaloos will do nicely, and won't take a polite no for an answer.

"The Great Voice Robbery." September 19, 1970. Writer: John Fenton Murray. Frustrated when her latest record is rejected, Benita hooks Joy up to a machine that switches their voices. While the villainess launches her next recording session, the boys devise a plan to force her to restore Joy's voice.

"Our Home Is Our Hassle." September 26, 1970. Writer: Jack Raymond. Unable to write an original song for the competition Peter Platter is hosting, Benita decides the Bugaloos are being inspired by living in Tranquility Forest. After the boys are zapped unconscious, Benita moves into their digs.

"Courage Come Home." October 3, 1970. Writer: John Fenton Murray. Out flying alone in a storm, Courage hits his head and develops amnesia. Coming across the bewildered Bugaloo, Benita decides he'll make a good replacement for the household staff she just fired, and tells him he's her nephew Melvin.

"The Love Bugaloos." October 10, 1970. Writer: Elon E. Packard, Jr. Sparky falls in love with Gina Lollawattage, "The Flaming Firefly of Rock," who's in town to appear on Peter's show. While the Bugaloos try to promote a romance for Sparky, Benita plots to detain Gina so that she can replace her on the broadcast.

"If I Had the Wings of a Bugaloo." October 17, 1970. Writer: John Fenton Murray. Envious of the Bugaloos' flying ability, Benita buys her own wings, manufactured by Funky's sister. When those prove ineffectual, she kidnaps I.Q. with plans to take his wings for herself.

"Lady, You Don't Look Eighty." October 24, 1970. Writer: John Fenton Murray. The Bugaloos, celebrating Joy's 16th birthday, make a joke about her being 80 years old. Overhearing, Benita concludes that the teenagers have found the Fountain of Youth in Tranquility Forest, and kidnaps Sparky to force them to share the wealth.

"Benita the Beautiful." October 31, 1970. Writer: John Fenton Murray. Joy and Benita both plan to enter the "Miss Out of This World" beauty pageant, with the winner to receive a movie contract. Benita eliminates the competition, arranging for the other contestants to disappear before the contest begins.

"Now You See Them, Now You Don't." November 7, 1970. Writer: Elon E. Packard, Jr. The Bugaloos' "new sound," featuring a performance by Sparky, wins them the last available spot on Peter Platter's telethon. Jealous, Benita uses phony adoption papers to take Sparky home with her, so that they can sing together. With the help of a magician, the Bugaloos make themselves invisible in order to infiltrate Benita's jukebox and rescue Sparky.

"Help Wanted, Firefly." November 14, 1970. Writer: Warren S. Murray. When Peter Platter refuses to play Benita's latest record on his radio station, she plots to get even by sabotaging the circuitry to put herself on the air as "the world's most gorgeous disc jockey." This coincides with Sparky's new job at the station, where he's hoping to show he can make himself useful despite his clumsiness.

"On a Clear Day." November 21, 1970. Writer: John Fenton Murray. When Peter Platter won't let Benita perform in his upcoming Tranquility Forest rock festival, she vows to hold a rival event. Unable to line up talent, she decides instead to sabotage Peter's event by pumping smog into the forest.

"Today I Am a Firefly." November 28, 1970. Writer: Jack Raymond. Sparky decides he's reached maturity and is ready to live on his own. While he's away, the Bugaloos are shrunk to a tiny size and kidnapped by Benita's flunkies, so that they can take the place of her broken music box.

"The Bugaloos' Bugaboo." December 5, 1970. Writer: Maurice Richlin. Hearing an exaggerated account of Sparky's songwriting talent, Benita wants him to write a number she can perform at Peter Platter's talent contest. Posing as Hollywood agent J.W. Wooster, she signs Sparky to a contract, but his composition doesn't win her the acclaim she's craving.

"Benita's Double Trouble." December 12, 1970. Writer: Warren S. Murray. Peter Platter asks the Bugaloos to serve as substitute DJs on his radio station while he's away, but Benita wants the chance for herself. When she takes Peter hostage, I.Q.'s impersonation of Benita unexpectedly comes in handy.

"Circus Time at Benita's." December 19, 1970. Writer: John Fenton Murray. After Benita arranges to have a local circus canceled, the Bugaloos decide to put on a show of their own. Meanwhile, having heard that Magico the Magician has mastered the art of hypnosis, Benita wants him to make her the world's best singer.

"The Uptown 500." December 26, 1970. Writer: John Fenton Murray. Peter Platter's sponsor is hosting a road race, and the winner will get a contract to sing in TV commercials. Benita snatches Sparky and holds him hostage, in order to force the Bugaloos to throw the race.

"The Good Old Days." January 2, 1971. Writer: Warren S. Murray. Benita obtains a deed to Tranquility Forest, and gives the Bugaloos 24 hours to move out. Joy poses as a Gypsy fortuneteller to scare Benita into reconsidering. This episode features clips from previous segments.

McMillan & Wife
a.k.a. McMillan

Rock Hudson (*Commissioner Stewart McMillan*), John Schuck (*Lt. Charlie Enright*), Martha Raye (*Agatha Thornton*), Richard Gilliland (*Sgt. Steve DiMaggio*), Gloria Stroock (*Maggie*), Bill Quinn (*Chief Paulson*), Jon Epstein (*Producer*), Leonard B. Stern (*Creator-Executive Producer*), Anthony Kiser (*Associate Producer*), Jerry Fielding (*Music*)

Martha was a series regular in the sixth and final season of this popular detective series, after making a guest appearance in Season Five.

Part of the *NBC Sunday Mystery Movie*, *McMillan & Wife* was originally designed as a modern-day version of *The Thin Man*. The format had to be substantially overhauled when Susan Saint James left her role as Sally McMillan after five years (viewers were told that her character died in a plane crash).

Series creator Leonard B. Stern was familiar with Martha's talents, having written sketches for her during his days as a comedy writer for Steve Allen in the 1950s. After Martha's Emmy-nominated performance as Agatha Thornton in the February 1976 episode "Greed," she received an offer to join the regular cast for the coming season. As Martha explained her series character, "Agatha is a busybody, an eccentric, warm-hearted character who means well but is a little dingy. In other words, I'm playing my natural self."[26]

In his sixth year playing McMillan, Hudson still enacts all his scenes with professionalism, but visibly sparks when he's teamed with Martha as his exasperating housekeeper. For the sixth season, the series returned to 90-minute episodes, after a spate of two-hour segments. Hudson's deal called for this to be the series' final season, and it came to an end in the spring of 1977.

Episodes

"Greed." NBC, February 15, 1976. Writer: Virginia Aldridge. Director: Bob Finkel. Guest Stars: Martha Raye, Slim Pickens, Alejandro Rey, Nancy Malone, Nancy Morgan. This *McMillan & Wife* episode introduces the character of Agatha Thornton, sister of the McMillans' housekeeper Mildred (Nancy Walker). The plot centers on the death of a wealthy woman, and the behavior of various family members, including Agatha, who are possibly beneficiaries of her will.

"All Bets Off." NBC, December 5, 1976. Guest Stars: Jessica Walter, Dane Clark, Werner Klemperer, Jason Evers, Charles Drake, Dick Haymes, Norman Alden, Jenifer Shaw, Jeffrey Byron. Writer: Robert Swanson. Director: Jackie Cooper. Mac's lady friend Donna Drake invites him to visit her in Las Vegas, where she's playing in a championship tennis tournament. Robbed of her valuable jewels by a thief who claims to be holding her stepson hostage, Donna falls under suspicion when the robber turns up dead, shot with her gun.

This episode, although not the first filmed for the season, uses Martha more effectively than most others from this season. Initially seen helping the commissioner pack his suitcase for Vegas (hearing she's meeting a lady friend, she takes out his pajamas, saying, "You won't be needing these"), she's then absent for a lengthy stretch. In the show's second half, however, she turns up in Vegas, gives a happy squeal upon learning crime is afoot, and settles into Mac's hotel room chair for a recap ("Don't leave out a thing!"). Mac gives her an assignment: visit nearby beauty shops in search of a well-tended female suspect. She's on the scene when the drama climaxes with a shootout.

This is one of two episodes directed by former actor Jackie Cooper, an old friend of Martha's. He also appears on-camera as the desk clerk in Mac's Vegas hotel.

"Dark Sunrise." NBC, January 2, 1977. Guest Stars: Karen Valentine, Rick Lenz, Julie Adams, Dub Taylor, Kim Basinger, Antony Carbone, Stuart Nisbet. Writer: Jerry McNeely. Director: Bob Finkel. Stewart McMillan is presumed dead after his home is bombed and two bodies are found in the wreckage. Mac goes undercover to investigate, aided by a young, pretty police sergeant (the only person aware he's alive). The female victim proves to be a college student who'd uncovered some surprising facts about the current whereabouts of a long-lost cache of gold.

Seen briefly looking weepy at Mac's memorial service, Martha gets a more substantial scene to play later, when Agatha learns that her boss didn't die in the explosion. Relieved of at least one quandary ("I don't know what to do with his Dizzy Gillespie collection"), she's taken aback by the unexpected good news, which momentarily puts her into a faint. Minutes later, she finds herself and her boss under fire at the McMillan residence and has her second blackout of the day.

"Philip's Game." NBC, January 23, 1977. Guest Stars: Shirley Jones, William Windom, Tony Roberts, Nina Foch, Lloyd Bochner. Writers: Don M. Mankiewicz, Gordon Cotler, Leonard B. Stern. Director: Lou Antonio.

McMillan investigates a crooked contractor whom he believes killed a city building inspector. A hired assassin tells McMillan he has been engaged to kill him. This script provides an explanation for changes in the series since last season, alluding to Sally's plane crash death about a year ago. Agatha explains that her sister Mildred, Mac's former housekeeper, inherited a diner in the east and moved away.

As Agatha, Martha plays matchmaker for Mac and his visiting friend Ellen, a sales representative for a luggage firm. Seeing Ellen's business card, which says her specialties are "Suedes and Leather," Agatha is relieved to hear what she does for a living, saying, "I thought maybe you were kinky." Later, asked about a case on which he's working, Agatha retorts, "Listen, I don't ask you about the washing cycle, so don't give me your cops and robbers stuff."

"Coffee, Tea, or Cyanide?" NBC, January 30, 1977. Guest Stars: Julie Sommars, Robert Webber, Jack Jones, Ed Nelson, Leslie Charleson, Marisa Pavan, Tisha Sterling, Russell Johnson, Joan Pringle, Henry Beckman. Writers: Richard Bluel, Pat Fielder, Steven Bochco. Director: James Sheldon. During a two-week Hawaiian vacation, Mac's tranquility is disrupted first by a reporter (Sommars) determined to interview him, and by the murder of an airline magnate who was surrounded by colleagues and two wives.

Martha's role is relatively minor: Still eager to see her boss find "Miss Right," she impulsively invites the pesky journalist to stay in McMillan's guest room, and is delighted when the two seem to be enjoying a nice rapport. Later, prattling happily about "l'amour," she is brought back to reality by the odor of her breakfast bacon burning.

"Affair of the Heart." NBC, March 20, 1977. Guest Stars: Larry Hagman, Stefanie Powers, Barbara Bostock, Lloyd Nolan, John Kerr, Jed Allan, John de Lancie. Writer: Steven Bochco. Director: Jackie Cooper. Mac's poker buddy Wes is a successful dentist whose wife is having an affair with a local TV newsman. When the broadcaster suddenly dies in a car crash, Wes, his unfaithful wife, and his father-in-law all come under suspicion.

Martha is largely on the sidelines in this installment, but she does manage to administer some chicken soup to the hapless Sgt. DiMaggio, who's suffering from a cold, and helpfully dims the lights to further Mac's romance with a lovely assistant D.A. (Powers).

"Have You Heard About Vanessa?" NBC, April 24, 1977. Guest Stars: Joan Van Ark, JoAnna Cameron, Trisha Noble, Peter Donat, Natalie Schafer, Ron Rifkin, Roger Bowen, Gordon Jump, Francois-Marie Benard. Writer: Leonard Kantor. Director: James Sheldon.

Mac's photographer friend Georgie begs him to investigate the supposed suicide of her friend, beautiful model Vanessa Vale, who apparently jumped from the balcony of her high-rise apartment. The story has echoes of the film classic *Laura*.

The series finale finds Martha's Agatha entrusted with the care of a mysterious houseguest. Though she won't cop to listening in on phone conversations ("That would be eavesdropping!"), and allows the guest in protective custody to escape, she does provide a clue to the whereabouts of the fugitive. Later, a wincing Mac provides an impromptu critique of her telephone etiquette, which consists of answering his phone with the greeting, "Agatha!"

The Love Boat

Like many older celebrities still active in the 1970s and 1980s, Martha found work as a guest star on Aaron Spelling's long-running ABC series about romance among the passengers and crew of the *Pacific Princess*.

Her first appearance, in the segment "My Sister, Irene" (January 13, 1979), came during the second season. Martha played divorcee Irene Austin, who accepts an invitation to be reunited on the ship with her college boyfriend, a man she hasn't seen in 40 years. Catching a glimpse of her old beau Andy Hopkins (played by actor-dancer Ray Bolger) as he boards makes Irene insecure about how she looks after so many years. Posing as her own sister Althea, Irene proceeds to develop a new relationship with Andy, complicated when he begins to fall in love with her new persona. The role afforded Martha the chance to dance with Bolger in two scenes. The script was by Tony Webster, and Martha was directed by Roger Duchowny.

Martha returned to the series in the fifth-season segment "Zeke and Zelda" (December 5, 1981), this time working opposite her friend Milton Berle. The pair played a married couple, former show business performers who have fallen on hard times. After being evicted from their apartment, Zeke suggests they stow away on the *Pacific Princess*, but Zelda is overcome by guilt as she realizes that they are cheating both the cruise line and crew members like bartender Isaac. Berle and Raye do a song-and-dance number, "For My Baby and Me." The script was by Christopher Vane and Jill Baer, and was directed by Bruce Bilson.

Alice

This popular CBS sitcom, which ran from 1976 to 1985, starred Linda Lavin as Alice Hyatt, a single mother and aspiring singer who supported herself and her son waitressing in Mel's Diner, a shabby Phoenix, Arizona, eatery. The series, adapted from the 1974 Ellen Burstyn movie *Alice Doesn't Live Here Anymore,* was produced for much of its run by Bob Carroll, Jr., and Madelyn Davis, best-known for their longtime association as comedy writers for Lucille Ball, dating back to her 1940s radio show.

During the series' third season, Martha made a guest appearance as Mel's busybody mother Carrie Sharples, a character created by story editors Bob Fisher and Arthur Marx. Their first script established Carrie as a gambler who enjoys playing the horses and craps games, a jogger ("How ya think I keep this gorgeous bod?") and a fearless take-charge type who calls her son "Chubby" and keeps him in line with well-timed swats to the breadbasket. In reality, she was only about 13 years older than actor Vic Tayback, who played Mel. Subsequent appearances dealt with her marriage to a younger man and her frequent, often unexpected visits to Phoenix, where she can't resist the temptation to meddle in her son's business and cook up a storm in his diner.

The show afforded Raye a welcome opportunity to play her comedy in a multi-camera format before a live studio audience. *Alice's* broad comedy style proved a good match for Martha, and her first appearance as Carrie was so well received that she was invited back multiple times over the next several seasons. She typically made two appearances per season. Martha ultimately taped 12 *Alice* guest shots between 1979 and 1984.

EPISODES

"Mel Grows Up." February 5, 1979. Writers: Bob Fisher, Arthur Marx. Director: William Asher. Guest Stars: Martha Raye, Robert Hogan, Duane R. Campbell. Mel's mother Carrie shows up unexpectedly, telling him she's left her Brooklyn home for the winter to get reacquainted with him. Tired of his mother taking over his one-bedroom apartment, Mel enlists the help of Alice, who only succeeds in getting Carrie to invade her place. Mel ultimately learns, at age 50, to stand up to his pushy mother.

"Carrie Sharples Strikes Again." November 11, 1979. Writers: Arthur Marx, Bob Fisher. Director: Lee Lochhead. Guest Stars: Martha Raye, Michael Ballard, Duane R. Campbell, Patrick Cronin, Ted Gehring. When Mel's back gives out, Carrie temporarily takes over the cooking at Mel's Diner. To his dismay, his customers love her cooking, especially her chicken pot pie, and business booms in his absence. (When lines begin to form at the door, steady customer Henry complains, "Before Carrie, the only thing you had to wait for is indigestion.") Alice must explain to Carrie that her son feels competitive with her, and that may be causing his recurring back pains.

"Carrie's Wedding." February 3, 1980. Writers: Mark Egan, Mark Solomon. Director: Gary Shimokawa. Guest Stars: Martha Raye, Howard Witt, Duane R. Campbell, Ancel Cook, Phil Leeds, Vernon Weddle. Mel is pleased to hear that his mother is getting married—until he meets the prospective groom, Robby Mitchell, who's three years younger than Mel. ("Ain't he the bee's knees?" she says gleefully). Initially threatening to boycott the wedding, Mel shows up just in time to give his mother away. Carrie confesses to being nervous, saying, "I haven't had a honeymoon in 52 years."

Martha's facial expressions garner big laughs as Flo (Polly Holliday) whispers advice into her ear about spicing up the honeymoon.

"Carrie Sings the Blues." December 21, 1980. Writers: Mark Egan, Mark Solomon. Directors: Linda Lavin, Christine Ballard. Guest Stars: Martha Raye, Howard Witt, Dave Madden, Michael Alldredge. Carrie comes for a visit, and confesses that she has broken up with Robby. Since his mother consoles herself by baking pies, Mel is in no hurry to tell her that her errant husband called to make amends.

Along with most of the cast, Martha jumps into a physical comedy routine involving Belle's new waterbed.

"Carrie Chickens Out." February 22, 1981. Writers: Bob Fisher, Arthur Marx. Director: Marc Daniels. Guest Stars: Martha Raye, Jack Kruschen, Douglas Robinson, John Hawker. Mel doesn't want his mother in the diner kitchen, so Carrie finds

Carrie Sharples (Martha Raye, left) gets some friendly advice from Alice (Linda Lavin) in her second appearance on *Alice*.

a job at a competing restaurant, Benny's Beanery. Soon Benny's business is booming, mother and son are too stubborn to make up, and the waitresses come to work to find Mel's Diner up for sale.

"Sharples vs. Sharples." February 7, 1982. Writers: Mark Egan, Mark Solomon. Director: Linda Day. Guest Stars: Martha Raye, Edie McClurg, Rose Arrick, Lou Richards. Mel objects when Carrie wants to publish his chili recipe in her cookbook

Carrie's Continental Kitchen: Recipes from a Broad. When Mel swipes the only copy of her manuscript, and the ladies retrieve it from his apartment, they find themselves cooling their heels in jail. Martha and Linda Lavin lead a jailhouse rendition of "Lullaby of Broadway."

"My Mother the Landlord." May 16, 1982. Writers: Chet Dowling, Sandy Krinski. Director: Marc Daniels. Guest Stars: Martha Raye, Tom Williams, Susan Davis, Duane R. Campbell, Tony Longo, Jack Andreozzi. When Mel's mother buys his apartment building, he thinks he's in for a sweet deal—until she hits him with a $50 per month rent increase. He refuses to pay, and soon finds himself ejected from his domicile.

Martha gets big laughs when she searches for the missing manuscript in Mel's favored hiding place, his underwear drawer, holding up other items she finds along the way.

"Carrie on the Rebound." January 9, 1983. Writers: Bob Bendetson, Howard Bendetson. Director: Marc Daniels. Guest Stars: Martha Raye, Dave Madden, Mykel T. Williamson. Down in the dumps after her Tijuana divorce from Robby, Carrie finds diversion serving as mascot for Earl's struggling basketball team, the Coyotes. Her cheers bring the team new success, but Earl feels awkward when he thinks Carrie has fallen in love with him.

Putting Martha in a coyote costume is an engraved invitation for scene-stealing, and she makes the most of the opportunity.

"Come Back Little Sharples." April 17, 1983. Writer: Gail Honigberg. Director: Mel Ferber. Guest Stars: Martha Raye, Victoria Carroll, Merie Earle, Duane R. Campbell, Douglas Robinson. Fed up with being hounded by his waitresses for a raise, and pressured by his girlfriend and his mother to get married, Mel holes up in his apartment, existing on a diet of beer and pizza. Unable to get her son back to the diner, Carrie calls in her secret weapon, Grandma Sharples, who "swings a mean cane."

"The Over-the-Hill Girls." November 6, 1983. Writers: Mark Egan, Mark Solomon. Director: Tom Trbovich. Guest Stars: Martha Raye, Joel Brooks. Needing a new interest in life ("When you've gutted as many chickens as I have, the thrill is gone"), Carrie is encouraged by Alice and her friends to pursue her dream of becoming a professional singer. Alice lands her an audition at Vinnie's House of Veal, where she (Alice) performs occasionally. The owner decides Carrie is too old to attract the clientele he wants, and gives Alice the boot as well.

Martha receives the best musical showcase of all her *Alice* appearances here. In the finale, she and Linda Lavin team for a performance of Rod Stewart's song "Da Ya Think I'm Sexy?"

"Lies My Mother Told Me." January 29, 1984. Writers: Harvey Weitzman, Sid Dorfman. Director: Marc Daniels. Guest Stars: Martha Raye, Dave Madden, Joey D'Auria, Bob Gunter. Sobered by a near-death experience on her way to Phoenix, Carrie takes a vow to be a better mother. Aside from plying her son with gifts, Carrie upsets him by admitting that his childhood dog Buster wasn't really a war hero.

"Dollars to Donuts." March 11, 1984. Writers: David Silverman, Stephen Sustarsic. Director: Oz Scott. Guest Stars: Martha Raye, Dave Madden, Douglas Robinson. Tommy takes his winning day at the racetrack a little too seriously, and Alice worries that he will have his head turned by gambling. Successfully using his college's computers to predict winners, Tommy enlists the help of Carrie to keep his winning streak going.

In her final series appearance, Martha skillfully performs a physical comedy bit involving Alice's fold-up bed.

Made-for-TV Movies
and Miniseries

Skinflint: A Country Christmas Carol. NBC, December 18, 1979. Executive Producers: Gilbert Cates, Joseph Cates. Writer: Mel Mandel. Director: Marc Daniels. This two-hour telemovie is an original musical which transposes Charles Dickens' holiday classic to modern-day Tennessee, The cast includes a virtual who's who of contemporary country music stars, including Hoyt Axton as the Scrooge-like Cyrus Flint, Lynn Anderson and Mel Tillis as the impoverished couple, Larry Gatlin, Tom T. Hall, Barbara Mandrell, Dottie West and the Statler Brothers. Martha is cast as the Ghost of Christmas Past.

The Gossip Columnist. March 21, 1980. Writer: Michael Gleason. Director: James Sheldon. Cast: Jack Carter, Robert Vaughn, Kim Cattrall, Jayne Meadows, Bobby Sherman, Joe Penny, Bobby Vinton, Dick Sargent, Lyle Waggoner. A young journalist (Cattrall) finds her idealism challenged when she is assigned to write a gossip column. Martha gives an emotionally affecting performance as singer Georgia O'Hanlon, "an old Irish broad from the Bronx" left broke and fearful by the machinations of her crooked manager. *Daily Variety* (March 24, 1980) said this "Operation Prime Time" special "comes off as yet another 'Inside Hollywood' project, but presence of Martha Raye as a lush thrush, Sylvia Sidney as a fallen scribbler, and Robert Vaughn as an ambitious talent agency topper helps give the attempt some depth…. Raye, given a good dramatic scene and a shot at a too-brief chorus of 'Angel Eyes,' gives a strong account of herself in acting, chirping departments."

Pippin: His Life and Times. Showtime, 1981. Cast: Ben Vereen, William Katt, Chita Rivera, Leslie Denniston. Director: David Sheehan. The Tony-winning Broadway musical *Pippin* ran from 1972 to 1977, directed by Bob Fosse. This telecast was part of the "Broadway on Showtime" series, in which live performances were videotaped for replay on the pay cable channel. The performance was taped in Canada on a reported budget of $1 million. Martha, as Berthe, gets big laughs (and spontaneous audience applause) with lines like, "Men and their wars! Sometimes I think men raise flags when they can't get anything else up." She invites audience members to sing along during the choruses of her poignant yet joyful number "No Time at All." Said the *New York Times'* John J. O'Connor (February 15, 1984), "Martha Raye, as Pippin's grandmother, does enough mugging to get arrested, and her milking of the audience is a tad overdone."

Alice in Wonderland. CBS, December 9 and 10, 1985. Producer: Irwin Allen. Writer: Paul Zindel (from Lewis Carroll's book). Director: Harry Harris. Cast: Natalie Gregory, Ringo Starr, Imogene Coca, Roddy McDowall, Donald O'Connor,

Sammy Davis, Jr., Scott Baio, Red Buttons, Shelley Winters, Sherman Hemsley. The four-hour adaptation was made at a reported cost of $14.6 million. Producer Allen, the "Master of Disaster" known for *The Towering Inferno* and other action-packed movies and television shows, promised *Alice* viewers "fire, flood, hair-breadth escapes, cliffhangers, ghosts, haunted houses and all the things I've ever done in the past combined in a single production."[27] He was aided and abetted by renowned special effects artist John Dykstra, known for his work on the original *Star Wars* (1977).

Martha, cast as the Duchess, appears in the first segment, with Imogene Coca as her cantankerous cook. The comic duo teams for "There's Something to Say for Hatred," one of the original songs composed for the production by Raye's longtime friend Steve Allen. She later appears as a guest at the Queen of Hearts' soiree; the Duchess is ejected when she is slow to "grovel—right here on the gravel." Before making her exit, Martha's character imparts a bit of wisdom to Alice: "Everything has a moral—if you find it." She shares alphabetical star billing along with child actress Natalie Gregory (who played Alice), a wide array of other name performers and, because this is an Irwin Allen production, Allen's wife Sheila.

Columnist Vernon Scott, visiting the set during shooting, reported, "Martha Raye and Imogene Coca had the stagehands in stitches when they sang and pranced through a merry dance."[28] Reviewers were less enthusiastic. According to UPI's Joan Hanauer, the miniseries "gives a laundry list of grown-up stars a chance to dress up in wild costumes and have a wonderful time hamming it up," but used them in service of what she considered a "heavy-handed clumsy show" that wasn't true to the spirit of the book.[29] The Associated Press' Fred Rothenberg found it "a grand production for youngsters," but admitted that "the silliness gets tiresome."[30]

Selected Guest Appearances

Musical Comedy Time. "Anything Goes." NBC, October 2, 1950. This was the first telecast of a new series that presented adaptations of popular Broadway shows and operettas. Martha assumed Ethel Merman's 1934–35 stage role of Reno Sweeney, singing Cole Porter's music, with John Conte as her leading man. "[T]elevision has had its first real try at redoing a Broadway musical comedy of former days. Reaction was mixed…. Lacking a descriptive program, the viewer just had to figure out things for himself as the action speeded on…. Parts of the adaptation fit the new medium and parts didn't."[31] Said John Crosby, "Martha Raye, a girl of great courage, stepped into the Merman role and did a perfectly wonderful job of it. In fact, if you can't get Miss Merman, Miss Raye is certainly the best substitute around both as a comedienne and as a singer."[32]

The Colgate Comedy Hour. NBC, November 15, 1953. Martha hosted this episode of the Sunday night variety series, with guests Irene Dunne, Cesar Romero and Rocky Graziano.

The Colgate Comedy Hour. NBC, December 13, 1953. Guest Stars: Martha Raye,

Perry Como, Ben Blue, Mike Mazurki, the Fontane Sisters. In a sketch, Martha plays an inept rookie nurse, with Como as her unfortunate patient.

The Arthur Murray Party. NBC, March 1, 1954. Martha was the guest of popular dance instructor Murray and his wife Kathryn, earning what *Billboard* reported was a $15,000 appearance fee.

This Is Your Life. NBC, September 22, 1954. Host Ralph Edwards surprises Martha with her life story. Guests helping her reminisce are Milton Berle, movie director Norman Taurog, Martha's father Pete Reed and her daughter Melodye.

Person to Person. CBS, October 15, 1954. Host Edward R. Murrow interviews Martha and her husband Ed Begley from their home in Westport, Connecticut.

Producers' Showcase. NBC, December 13, 1954. This "monthly color spectacular ... present[s] a 90-minute salute to the 'Overseas Press Club" (*San Mateo* [TX] *Times*), hosted by John Daly. Guests include Martha Raye, Milton Berle, Greer Garson, Perry Como, Eddie Fisher and Darren McGavin.

Max Liebman Presents. "Big Time." NBC, February 27, 1955. Martha co-starred with Milton Berle and Ray Bolger in this color "spectacular." *Daily Variety* (February 28, 1955) wasn't impressed: "With such a trinity of talent ... fronting his 90-min. colorama there was little left for Max Liebman to do but play it for laughs and save the big production numbers for another time.... Miss Raye saw plenty of action but it still doesn't seem good taste to get messy with food. She also sloshed around with hands full of cold cream and managed most of her mugging tricks to force laughs. It might well have been a cold audience but at this end of the line the big yocks still weren't there."

What's My Line? CBS, December 11, 1955. Martha appears as the mystery guest, receiving a rousing welcome from the audience. Her identity is quickly guessed by the panel, with Dorothy Kilgallen correctly identifying her.

The Walter Winchell Show. NBC, October 12, 1956. Martha Raye, Melodye Condos, the Bill and Cora Baird Marionettes. According to *Variety* (October 17, 1956), Martha sang "Taint Necessarily So" with "sensitivity and style" and dueted with daughter Melodye on "Tonight You Belong to Me."

Can Do. NBC, November 1956. Robert Alda (host). On this short-lived game-stunt show, contestants guessed whether a celebrity "can do" or "no can do" a stunt. Guests included Martha Raye, Gypsy Rose Lee, Sal Mineo, Rocky Graziano and Polly Bergen.

The Big Record. ABC, March 5, 1958. Host, Patti Page. Guest Stars: Martha Raye, Hugh O'Brian, Connie Francis, Frankie Vaughan. "Miss Raye sets a jovial mood with a medley from *Annie Get Your Gun,* then challenges hostess with 'Anything You Can Do'" (*Hutchinson* [KS] *News*).

The Patrice Munsel Show. ABC, March 14, 1958. Martha was the guest of longtime Metropolitan Opera singer Munsel in this installment of her 30-minute variety show. According to *TV Key,* "The script is thinner than usual, but Pat and Martha Raye try to make up for it with a barrel of songs." Songs include "Too Marvelous for Words."

Club Oasis. ABC, May 11, 1958. Martha Raye (host). Guest Stars: Stan Freberg with his puppet Orville, The Novelties. Martha "sings songs—some straight, some peppered with gags—and serves as the mistress of ceremonies."[33]

The Patti Page Oldsmobile Show. ABC, January 5, 1959. Martha was reported to be the singing rage's favorite comedienne, and was her only guest star on this episode. "They'll sing straight and they'll sing crooked—the latter being a delicious song-and-dance spoof. And there'll be a gather-round-the-piano-and-just-sing bit with Rocky Cole at the piano" (*Miami* [FL] *Herald*).

I've Got a Secret. CBS, March 4, 1959. Panelists Bill Cullen, Jayne Meadows, Henry Morgan and Betsy Palmer try to guess Martha's secret.

The Milton Berle Show. NBC, March 11, 1959. Berle and guest star Martha appear in a parody of TV's *The Millionaire.* Impoverished Mr. and Mrs. Sidney Schlump become *nouveau riche* after a visit from the emissary of an anonymous philanthropist. Said *TV Key,* "It's a shambles, of course, and quite funny."

The Big Party. NBC, October 22, 1959. This short-lived variety show, sponsored by Revlon, was designed to simulate a glittering social occasion in which a celebrity host invited his or her friends to drop in. Greer Garson hosted this, the show's second aired episode. Guests included Martha, Sal Mineo, Peter Lind Hayes and Mary Healy, Nichols and May, Walter Slezak and John Bubbles. Garson performed a dramatic soliloquy from *Camille,* which was then parodied by Martha.

I've Got a Secret. CBS, October 30, 1961. Martha was the celebrity guest on this long-running Goodson-Todman panel show, hosted by Garry Moore.

The Roy Rogers-Dale Evans Show. ABC, December 8, 1962. "Pumping for her new release, *Jumbo,* Miss Raye, Roy and Dale put on an instant circus" (*Phoenix* [AZ] *Republic*).

The Judy Garland Show. CBS, January 26, 1964. Martha made three appearances during this hour-long episode, which also features Peter Lawford, Rich Little and Ken Murray. First, Judy introduces "my dear friend" Martha, who solos in a song-and-dance number, "Taking a Chance on Love." Judy later offers to show the audience what she purports is dress rehearsal footage of herself and Martha, saying, "We didn't know what she was going to do." What follows shows the two stars performing a medley of songs (Martha's clowning repeatedly upstages Judy's solo moments), followed by Judy doing her best to return the favor. Jazz critic Will Friedwald described this as "one of the best musical moments ever captured on videotape." In Martha's third appearance, she, Judy and Peter Lawford offer their own take on the hit songs of 1964.

Burke's Law. "Who Killed the Fat Cat?" ABC, February 10, 1965. Gene Barry starred as Amos Burke, a wealthy playboy and Los Angeles police department captain, in this series which ran from 1963 to 1965. Like many of producer Aaron Spelling's later shows, it relied heavily on guest stars, at least five per episode, playing suspects in the murders Burke investigates. Martha appeared as Beulah Brothers alongside fellow guest stars Macdonald Carey, Don Rickles, Diana Hyland and Billy De Wolfe in this segment. "Captain Burke tries to solve the murder of a millionaire financier by delving into his carnival life past" (*Des Moines* [IA] *Register,* February 7, 1965).

Password. CBS, March 25, 1965. Host Allen Ludden welcomes Martha and actor Barry Nelson as celebrity guests.

The Danny Thomas Special. "The Comics." NBC, November 8, 1965. Guest Stars:

Martha Raye, Tim Conway, Bill Cosby, the Three Stooges. With the help of some famed comedians, Thomas answers the question, "What makes people laugh?" In an interview, Stooge Moe Howard said, "That Martha Raye—she just whops you. We did two shows for the special, and after the first one we had to tell Martha not to hit so hard."[34]

The Milton Berle Show. ABC, September 23, 1966. Guest Stars: Martha Raye, Steve Allen, Jayne Meadows. Martha's friend Berle made a television comeback with this weekly variety show, which aired to marginal ratings for its first and only season. Sketches include a parody of *Who's Afraid of Virginia Woolf?* Martha returned for a second visit less than a month later.

The Milton Berle Show. ABC, October 14, 1966. Guest Stars: Martha Raye, Jayne Mansfield. The host and his guests team up for renditions of "I Enjoy Being a Girl" and "There Is Nothing Like a Dame." Cracks Martha of Jayne, "Take away her blonde hair, her beautiful face, her marvelous figure, and what've you got? … Me!"

The Jerry Lewis Show. NBC, September 19, 1967. After a live talk-variety show that was a massive failure on ABC in 1963, Lewis tried a second weekly series with this more traditional comedy-variety hour; it lasted two seasons. Guests on his second aired show were Martha, along with *Dragnet 1967* stars Jack Webb and Harry Morgan. A sketch finds Martha on a lonely USO tour of an Arctic post, with Jerry as her only enlistee to entertain.

Operation: Entertainment. ABC, September 27, 1968. Guest Stars: Martha Raye, Phil Harris, Slappy White, Nancy Ames. This variety series spotlighted performers entertaining troops at American military bases around the world. Martha was seen in the second-season opener.

The Jackie Gleason Show. CBS, November 9, 1968. Guest Stars: Martha Raye, George Burns, Jack Carter, Mel Torme. Martha sings "Pennies from Heaven," teams with Gleason for "Baby Face" and joins the other guests for a number called "Old Rockin' Chair's Got Me."

The All-American College Show. CBS, May 10, 1969. College students perform for a panel of celebrity judges, including Martha, Milton Berle and Walter Matthau.

The Mike Douglas Show. Syndicated, May 1969. Martha spent a week as Douglas' co-host, helping welcome guests such as Troy Donahue, Pete Barbutti and film historian Richard Lamparski.

Jimmy Durante Presents the Lennon Sisters. ABC, October 17, 1969. Guest Stars: Martha Raye, Buddy Ebsen, Bobby Goldsboro. Martha is seen in a riverboat comedy sketch with Durante and Ebsen.

The Barbara McNair Show. Syndicated, November 23, 1969. Guest Stars: Martha Raye, Rich Little, Slappy White, the Burgundy Street Singers, Steve Rossi.

The Kraft Music Hall. NBC, June 24, 1970. Guest Stars: Martha Raye, Phil Harris, singer Sandie Shaw. British comedian Des O'Connor hosted this summer run of *Music Hall.* Martha, backed by eight male dancers, does "Watch the Birdie," duets with Harris on "You Say the Nicest Things" and appears in a skit about a haunted castle.

"Ed Sullivan Presents the TV Comedy Years." CBS, February 20, 1973. Sullivan's

Her singing and her clowning made Martha a welcome guest on most of the popular variety shows of the 1960s, including this 1968 appearance with Jackie Gleason.

special salutes comedians past and present, including Martha, Sid Caesar, Jackie Gleason and Art Carney.

Love, American Style. "Love and the Hidden Meaning." ABC, November 30, 1973. Writers: Bernie Orenstein, Saul Turteltaub. Director: Norman Abbott. Guest Stars: Martha Raye, Jacqueline Susann, Joyce Haber, Judy Cassmore. This popular comic anthology series featured Martha as a plumber's wife who accuses bestselling author Susann (*Valley of the Dolls*) of using her husband as the basis for a sexy character in her new novel.

Steve Allen's Laugh-Back. Syndicated, 1976. Martha was a guest on this show that featured her in clips from Allen's earlier comedy sketches, as well as new material. Also featured were Jayne Meadows Allen, Don Knotts, Louis Nye and Bill Dana.

Bing! CBS, March 20, 1977. Bing Crosby's 50th anniversary in show business is commemorated in this 90-minute special, in which he's joined by Martha, Bob Hope, Paul Anka, Pearl Bailey, Donald O'Connor, Bette Midler, Debbie Reynolds and others.

Twas the Night Before Christmas. ABC, December 7, 1977. Paul Lynde, Anne Meara, Martha Raye, Alice Ghostley, Foster Brooks, George Gobel. "Paul Lynde is the father who comes home on Christmas Eve after an exhausting round of last-minute errands to find his five children awake, noisy, argumentative, demanding a pony and squabbling about the reality of Santa Claus."[35] Martha and Ghostley play the grandmothers.

Dinah! Syndicated, December 1977. Martha, Rock Hudson and Betty White are the guests on a holiday-themed episode of Dinah Shore's popular daytime show. Martha talks about her experiences starring in dinner theater productions of *Everybody Loves Opal* and the difficulties that sometimes arose working with a cat in a live stage show.

Just for Laughs. NBC, February 7, 1978. "What do you do just for laughs?" was the premise. Milton Berle, Connie Stevens, Rose Marie, Red Buttons and Jackie Mason were among the participants.

The Emmy Awards. ABC, September 19, 1982. Martha was a presenter at the 34th annual ceremony, which included a special tribute to Bob Hope.

Circus of the Stars. CBS, December 5, 1982. This installment of the annual special featuring celebrities performing circus stunts featured ringmasters Raye, Scott Baio, Morgan Fairchild, Vincent Price, Debbie Reynolds, Mickey Rooney and Isabel Sanford.

Murder, She Wrote. "Armed Response." CBS, March 31, 1985. Guest Stars: Martha Raye, Eddie Bracken, Stephen Elliott, Sam Groom, Bo Hopkins, Kevin McCarthy, Kay Lenz, Martin Kove. While being treated for a leg injury at a fashionable Dallas

Martha (left), a contestant (second from left) and Loni Anderson on *Win, Lose, or Draw,* hosted by Bert Convy.

clinic, Jessica Fletcher (Angela Lansbury) investigates the murder of a physician. Martha plays Sadie Winthrop, a well-to-do patient who appreciates both the attentions of men and a good card game.

All-Star Party for "Dutch" Reagan. CBS, December 8, 1985. This hour-long special presented by Variety Clubs International, honoring President Ronald Reagan, was a fundraiser for children's hospitals. Guests included Martha, Charlton Heston, Frank Sinatra, Dean Martin and Burt Reynolds. The special ranked among the week's Top Ten shows.

NBC's 60th Anniversary Celebration. NBC, May 12, 1986. Emceed by Milton Berle, Sid Caesar and Bob Hope, this three-hour special featured both clips from past network shows as well as celebrity guests, including Martha.

Win, Lose or Draw. Syndicated, 1987. Martha was a celebrity participant on this game show, hosted by Bert Convy.

Lifestyles of the Rich and Famous. Syndicated, 1992. Robin Leach (host). Martha and husband Mark Harris are interviewed.

Notes

Preface

1. Barbara Utley, "'Public Will Always Love Laughmakers,'" *Elyria* (OH) *Chronicle-Telegram*, July 6, 1978.

Chapter I

1. Viola Hegyi Swisher, "Getting Serious," *After Dark*, March 1980.
2. Doug McClelland, "Making the Rounds with 'Boondock Maggie,'" *After Dark*, September 1975.
3. Martha Raye, "Me and My Big Mouth," *Washington Post*, April 25, 1954.
4. Marie Torre, "Martha Raye All Mixed Up," *Boston Globe*, February 6, 1957.
5. Doug McClelland, "Making the Rounds with Boondock Maggie," *After Dark,* September 1975.
6. "Margie Won't Sing," *Emporia* (KS) *Gazette,* December 22, 1921.
7. "Litle [Sic] Movie Star Here Aagain [Sic] This Week," *Moberly* (MO) *Evening Democrat*, April 30, 1922.
8. "Young Movie Star Appears at Myers," *Janesville* (WI) *Daily Gazette*, May 5, 1923.
9. "Child Movie Star Here in Person," *Moberly* (MO) *Evening Democrat,* April 27, 1922.
10. "Children Provide Laughs," *Lima* (OH) *News*, September 7, 1928.
11. "Amusements," *Bridgeport Telegram*, February 9, 1928.
12. "Montanans Are Attraction on Myrick Bill," *Billings* (MT) *Gazette*, August 24, 1924.
13. Nancy Anderson, "Martha Raye Lives Down War Woes," *New Castle* (PA) *News*, June 27, 1979.
14. Lawrence Laurent, "Now It's More Martha than It Is Mouth," *Washington Post*, April 11, 1954.

15. Pauline Swanson, "Cry the Night," *Radio Mirror*, April 1938.
16. "At Salt Lake Theaters," *Salt Lake Tribune*, October 22, 1933.
17. Jack O'Brian, "Broadway," *Camden* (AK) *News*, February 5, 1946.
18. "Martha Raye: Comedienne Now Showing She Has a More Serious Side," *Hutchinson* (KS) *News*, December 2, 1985.
19. "Boyle's Column," *Kingsport* (TN) *News*, May 10, 1955.
20. Paul Harrison, "Hollywood," *Chester* (PA) *Times*, July 30, 1936.

Chapter II

1. Read Kendall, "Out and About in Hollywood," *Los Angeles Times*, January 17, 1936.
2. Read Kendall, "Out and About in Hollywood," *Los Angeles Times*, January 28, 1936.
3. John Scott, "Everyone Connected with Studio Turns Talent Scout," *Los Angeles Times*, May 10, 1936.
4. *Ibid.*
5. Paul Harrison, "In Hollywood," *Frederick* (MD) *News*, August 26, 1937.
6. Paul Harrison, "Hollywood," *Chester* (PA) *Times*, July 30, 1936.
7. Frederick James Smith, "Ugly Duckling," This Week, *Philadelphia Record*, September 19, 1937.
8. Robbin Coons, "Comedienne with Elastic Mouth Values Talent Over Pretty Face." *Lowell Sun*, August 19, 1936.
9. "Her Face Is Her Fortune, and She's Thankful It's a Funny One," *Montana Standard*, December 6, 1936.
10. Hugh Braly, letter to Sam D. Palmer, December 4, 1936. Martha Raye Papers, Special Collections, Margaret Herrick Library, Los Angeles, California.

11. Leo Townsend, "Hollywood's Raye of Sunshine." *Radio Stars,* April 1937.

12. Hugh Braly, letter to Chris Dunphy, December 1, 1936. Martha Raye Papers, Special Collections, Margaret Herrick Library, Los Angeles, California.

13. "Rehearsals for Al Jolson's Trocadero Club Program Have Playtime Atmosphere," *Washington Post*, February 28, 1937.

14. *Ibid.*

15. "On the Air," *Circleville* (OH) *Herald*, September 9, 1937.

16. "Martha Raye Says Engagement Over," *San Antonio Light*, June 26, 1936.

17. "Martha Raye Gets Engagement Ring," *San Antonio Light*, January 7, 1937.

18. Leo Townsend, "Hollywood's Raye of Sunshine." *Radio Stars,* April 1937.

19. Martha Raye, "Me and My Big Mouth," *Washington Post*, May 2, 1954.

20. Frank Westmore and Muriel Davidson, *The Westmores of Hollywood* (Philadelphia: Lippincott, 1976), 24.

21. "Film Star Weds Makeup Artist," *Massillon* (OH) *Evening Independent*, June 3, 1937.

22. "Martha Raye Breaks Promise to Marry," *El Paso Herald-Post*, May 31, 1937.

23. Frederick James Smith, "Ugly Duckling," This Week, *Philadelphia Record*, September 19, 1937.

24. "Mother of Martha Raye Awarded Divorce Decree," *Los Angeles Times*, March 3, 1937.

25. "Boy Friend Cause of Raye Divorce," *Hammond* (IN) *Times*, September 10, 1937.

26. Anne K. Donaghue, "Martha Raye, Filmdom's Top Comedienne, Unaffected by Success," *Lowell Sun*, July 23, 1937.

27. Martha Raye, "Me and My Big Mouth," *Washington Post*, May 2, 1954.

28. Frank Westmore and Muriel Davidson, *The Westmores of Hollywood* (Philadelphia: Lippincott, 1976), 24.

29. "Martha Raye Testifies Spouse Always Carried a Gun, Even to Bed, and Now She 'Ain't Got No Buddy.'" *Galveston* (TX) *Daily News*, September 29, 1937.

30. "Answer for Martha Raye," *Daily Variety*, September 9, 1937.

31. "Martha Raye's Mate in Fight: Divorce Suit Looms as Westmore Engages in Hollywood Café Row," *Los Angeles Times*, September 4, 1937.

32. "Martha Raye Plea Dismissed," *Los Angeles Times*, September 18, 1937.

33. Lloyd Shearer, "Martha Raye: Still Searching for Marital Happiness," *Oakland Tribune*, April 15, 1962.

34. Frank Westmore and Muriel Davidson, *The Westmores of Hollywood* (Philadelphia: Lippincott, 1976), 25.

35. *Radio Mirror*, December 1937.

36. "Takes Three Pictures to Make Star?" *Salt Lake Tribune*, April 11, 1937.

37. Richard Zoglin, *Hope: Entertainer of the Century* (New York: Simon and Schuster, 2014), 120.

38. Dwight Whitney, "Maggie of the Boondocks," *TV Guide*, November 21, 1970.

39. "Martha Raye's Mother in Alienation Suit," *Bluefield* (WV) *Daily Telegraph*, February 18, 1938.

40. Lucie Neville, "Things That Make Movie Stars Mad," *Laredo Times*, August 7, 1938.

41. "Again Martha Raye's Mother Takes Mate," *San Antonio Light*, April 19, 1938.

42. "World News in Brief," *Galveston* (TX) *Daily News*, December 7, 1938.

43. "Peter Balma Denies Love Suit Charges," *Joplin Globe*, December 6, 1938.

44. "She Was Married When Martha Raye's Father Proposed, Says Woman," *Nevada State Journal*, December 3, 1938.

45. Louella O. Parsons, "New Film Based on Trial of Hines," *Charleston* (WV) *Gazette*, August 24, 1938.

46. Read Kendall, "Around and About in Hollywood," *Los Angeles Times*, September 28, 1938.

47. Jimmie Fidler, "Jimmie Fidler in Hollywood," *Los Angeles Times*, February 5, 1942.

48. Louella O. Parsons, "Glamour-Building Task for Josef," *San Antonio* (TX) *Light*, July 20, 1938.

49. Harrison Carroll, "Behind the Scenes in Hollywood," *Massillon* (OH) *Evening Independent*, June 9, 1938.

50. "Martha Raye Engaged to Wed Music Writer," *Madison* (WI) *State Journal*, July 9, 1938.

51. Will Friedwald, *A Biographical Guide to the Great Jazz and Pop Singers* (New York: Pantheon Books, 2010), 380.

52. Louella O. Parsons, "Martha Raye Hit at Legion Meeting," *San Antonio* (TX) *Light*, September 20, 1938.

53. "Film Star Arrives in S.L. to Appear at Theater," *Salt Lake* (UT) *Tribune*, March 24, 1939.

54. Lawrence Laurent, "Now It's More Martha than It Is Mouth," *Washington Post*, April 11, 1954.

55. Marjory Adams, "'You Can Have H'wood,' Says Martha Raye; 'I'll Take the East.'" *Boston Globe*, June 28, 1950.

56. Martha Raye, "Don't Make Those Marriage Mistakes," *Radio Mirror*, June 1939.

57. Philip Chapman, "Party Girl, Home Girl," *TV-Radio Mirror,* May 1955.

58. Jimmie Fidler, "In Hollywood," *Charleston* (WV) *Daily Mail*, September 27, 1939.

59. Bob Thomas, "Martha Raye Satisfied with TV Role and Wants No More of Films," *Indiana Evening Gazette*, November 7, 1955.

60. Louella Parsons, "Laughton and Lombard in Howard Story," *Syracuse Herald-Journal*, March 19, 1940.

61. Harrison Carroll, "Behind the Scenes in Hollywood," *Las Cruces* (NM) *Sun-News*, April 24, 1940.

62. "Martha Raye Divorced," *Oakland* (CA) *Tribune*, May 18, 1940.

63. Louella O. Parsons, "Judy Garland Will Marry Martha Raye's Ex-Husband," *Charleston* (WV) *Gazette*, June 8, 1941.

64. "Jolson Comes Back in New Musical," *Life*, July 29, 1940.

65. Martin Yoseloff, "Martin Yoseloff Describes Al Jolson's Newest Success," *Mason City Globe-Gazette*, July 27, 1940.

66. Martha Raye, "Voice of Broadway," *Greenville* (PA) *Record-Argus*, June 16, 1954.

67. Richard Watts, Jr., "Al Jolson Called Back to New York Stage to Put Over New Musical Play," *Oakland Tribune*, September 29, 1940.

68. "Al Jolson Faces Suit for Closing His Show," *Madison* (WI) *State Journal*, February 3, 1941.

69. "Martha Raye Wedding Skeded [Sic] for Tomorrow," *Daily Variety*, May 23, 1941.

70. Dorothy Kilgallen, "Tales from Times Square," *Lowell* (MA) *Sun*, August 5, 1941.

71. Ken Morgan, "Hollywood Keyhole," *Big Spring* (TX) Daily Herald, August 22, 1941.

72. Dorothy Kilgallen, "Broadway," *Mansfield* (OH) *News-Journal*, November 27, 1941.

73. Lloyd Shearer, "Martha Raye: She's Still Searching for Marital Happiness," *Charleston* (WV) *Gazette Mail*, April 15, 1962.

74. Louella O. Parsons, "Republic Pays $25,000 for Song," *San Antonio* (TX) *Light*, May 8, 1942.

75. "Martha Raye to Wed Night Club Dancer," *Wichita Daily Times*, June 28, 1942.

76. Abe Lastfogel, telegram to Martha Raye, December 27, 1942. Martha Raye Papers, Special Collections, Margaret Herrick Library, Los Angeles, California.

77. Carole Landis, *Four Jills in a Jeep* (New York: Random House, 1944), 12.

78. Ernie Pyle, "Actresses at Front," *Zanesville* (OH) *Times-Recorder*, February 15, 1943.

79. Louella O. Parsons, "Paging the Stars," *Lowell Sun*, January 15, 1943.

80. Erskine Johnson, "In Hollywood," *Ironwood* (MI) *Daily Globe*, January 22, 1943.

81. "Uso-Camp Shows, Inc., Take Showmen to Army-Navy," *Greenville* (PA) *Record-Argus*, April 14, 1943.

82. Inez Robb, "Martha Raye a Pioneer," *Bakersfield Californian*, October 15, 1952.

83. Louella O. Parsons, untitled column, *Lowell* (MS) *Sun*, May 15, 1943.

84. "Martha Raye Seeks Mexican Divorce," *El Paso* (TX) *Herald-Post*, September 10, 1943.

85. "Martha Raye Reveals Marriage to Partner," *Long Beach* (CA) *Independent*, March 12, 1944.

86. Raymond Strait, *Hollywood's Star Children* (New York: SPI, 1992), 250.

87. "Martha Raye's Brother Face [Sic] Alimony Charge," *Ogden* (UT) *Standard-Examiner*, March 5, 1941.

88. Louella O. Parsons, "Sullivan, Hayward to Go to England," *San Antonio* (TX) *Light*, August 13, 1945.

89. Louella O. Parsons, "Sundstrom New Star for Selznick," *San Antonio* (TX) *Light*, June 21, 1945.

90. Abe Lastfogel, letter to Martha Raye,

March 6, 1946; letter to Nick Condos, March 6, 1946. Martha Raye Papers, Special Collections, Margaret Herrick Library, Los Angeles, California.

91. Dorothy Kilgallen, "Voice of Broadway," *Olean* (NY) *Times-Herald*, November 9, 1946.

92. Harrison Carroll, "Hollywood," Massillon (OH) *Evening Independent*, November 18, 1946.

93. "Martha Raye Pic Biog," *Variety*, December 18, 1946.

94. Leticia Kent, "A Mouthful from Martha," *New York Times*, October 29, 1972.

95. Nancy Anderson, "Big-Hearted Martha Raye," *Gastonia Gazette*, November 9, 1975.

96. "Martha Raye's Mother Dies," *Annapolis* (MD) *Capital*, October 21, 1947.

97. "Comedienne Slates Extra Appearances," *Charleston* (WV) *Gazette*, October 31, 1955.

98. "In Short," *Billboard*, May 8, 1948.

99. Richard Wall, personal interview.

Chapter III

1. Martha Raye, "Me and My Big Mouth," *Washington Post*, May 9, 1954.

2. Betty Shain, *Spiraling: A Memoir* (Bloomington, IN: Xlibris, 2009), unpaged.

3. John L. Scott, "Stage Role She Always Hankered to Play Brings Busy Martha Raye Back to Town," *Los Angeles Times*, August 19, 1951.

4. "Martha Raye Slaps Club Patron; He Slaps Back." *Long Beach* (CA) *Press-Telegram*, February 23, 1952.

5. Erskine Johnson, "Ed Wynn Wins Battle Against Trick Shots and Chalk Marks," *Redlands* (CA) *Daily Facts*, March 15, 1952.

6. Martha Raye, "Me and My Big Mouth," *Washington Post*, May 9, 1954.

7. Glenn Surendonk, "Stars to Come Out at Alpine Valley," *Racine* (WI) *Journal-Times*, May 13, 1977.

8. Erskine Johnson, "In Hollywood," *Portsmouth* (NH) *Herald*, April 15, 1952.

9. Rocky Graziano with Ralph Corsel, *Somebody Down Here Likes Me Too* (New York: Stein and Day, 1981), 96.

10. Hal Boye, "Mrs. Calls Rocky Graziano 'Capone,'" *Benton Harbor* (MI) *News-Palladium*, October 28, 1953.

11. Rocky Graziano with Rowland Barber, *Somebody Up There Likes Me* (New York: Simon and Schuster, 1955), 364.

12. Rocky Graziano with Ralph Corsel, *Somebody Down Here Likes Me Too* (New York: Stein and Day, 1981), 101.

13. Abe Lastfogel, letter to Nick Condos, October 20, 1952. Martha Raye Papers, Special Collections, Margaret Herrick Library, Los Angeles, California.

14. Hy Gardner, "Coast to Coast," *Long Beach* (CA) *Press-Telegram*, May 16, 1953.

15. "Martha Raye Granted Divorce from Her Fourth Husband," *Panama City* (FL) *News-Herald*, July 5, 1953.

16. Hy Gardner, "Martha Raye: She's One of TV's Most Courageous Troupers," *Albuquerque Journal*, April 18, 1954.

17. Hal Boyle, "Broadway Rehearsal Is Controlled Chaos," *Long Beach* (CA) *Press-Telegram*, October 28, 1953.

18. Cynthia Lowry, "Martha Raye Finally Decides That Country Life Is for Her," *Corpus Christi* (TX) *Caller-Times*, January 10, 1954.

19. John Lester, "Radio and Television," *Elyria* (OH) *Chronicle-Telegram*, October 9, 1953.

20. "Muggs and Cupid Put the Bite on Martha in a Busy Week," *Life*, May 3, 1954.

21. De Blois, Frank. "Martha Raye in Focus." *TV Guide*, November 26, 1955.

22. Boyle, "Broadway Rehearsal."

23. Jack Gould, "Martha Raye: Her Top Rating a Tribute to Resourcefulness of Program's Writers," *New York Times*, November 18, 1953.

24. Walter Ames, "Macrae Set to Produce College Dramas on TV; Martha Raye Show Hailed." *Los Angeles Times*, October 6, 1953.

25. David Everitt, *King of the Half Hour: Nat Hiken and the Golden Age of TV Comedy* (Syracuse, NY: Syracuse University Press, 2001), 95.

26. Al Morton, "Backstage Tension Causes Mass Jitters," *Chester* (PA) *Times*, February 25, 1954.

27. "Martha Raye Takes Wedding Vows 5th Time," *Monroe* (LA) *News-Star*, April 22, 1954.

28. Philip Chapman, "Party Girl, Home Girl," *TV-Radio Mirror,* May 1955.

29. Norman Lear, interview, Archive of American Television, http://www.emmytv legends.org/interviews/people/norman-lear, accessed November 12, 2014.

30. Jack Gaver, "Jacks-Of-All-Trades Hit Jackpot on Television," *Los Angeles Times,* April 29, 1955.

31. "$400,000 Suit by Martha Raye," *Oakland Tribune,* October 22, 1954.

32. Telegram to Martha Ray [sic], November 22, 1954. Martha Raye Papers, Special Collections, Margaret Herrick Library, Los Angeles, California.

33. Philip Chapman, "Party Girl, Home Girl," *TV-Radio Mirror,* May 1955.

34. Barbara Condos, *Hard Candy* (New York: Morrow, 1988), 185.

35. *Ibid.*

36. "Martha Raye in Rest Home in Cincinnati," *Joplin* (MO) *Globe,* December 28, 1954.

37. Milton Berle, "TV Is a Killer!" *Los Angeles Times,* February 6, 1955.

38. Earl Wilson, "It Happened Last Night," *Winnona* (MN) *Daily News,* March 15, 1955.

39. Marie Torre, "Martha Raye All Mixed Up," *Boston Globe,* February 6, 1957.

40. Cynthia Lowry, "Martha Raye Has Never Been So Happy," *Miami* (FL) *News,* January 16, 1954.

41. Paul Denis, "Channel: Gossip," *TV World,* October 1955.

42. Margaret McManus, "15-Year Pact Security for Martha," *Syracuse* (NY) *Post-Standard,* October 30, 1955.

43. Norman Lear, *Even This I Get to Experience* (New York: Penguin, 2014), 164.

44. Jack Gould, "TV: Martha Raye Show," *New York Times,* October 12, 1955.

45. Earl Wilson, "Martha Raye Returns to Television Tonight," *Sarasota* (FL) *Herald- Tribune,* September 20, 1955.

46. Dorothy Kilgallen, "Martha Raye Makes Up with Hiken," *Washington Post,* March 27, 1956.

47. "Westports' in News Again," *Westport* (CT) *Town Crier And Herald,* May 3, 1956.

48. "Martha Raye 'Shocked' at Alienation Suit Filed by Wife of Handsome Policeman." *Long Beach* (CA) *Independent,* April 30, 1956.

49. "'Misrepresentation of Supposed Facts'—O'shea," *Westport* (CT) *Town Crier and Herald,* May 10, 1956.

50. "Complains Wife Won't Hear His Side of Martha Raye Case," *Racine* (WI) *Journal- Times,* May 9, 1956.

51. "Picture Is Explained by Martha Raye," *Snyder* (TX) *Daily News,* May 10, 1956.

52. Hedda Hopper, "Altoona's Own Hedda Hopper Writes from Hollywood," *Altoona* (PA) *Mirror,* November 7, 1955.

53. "Actress' Counsel Denies Alienation Suit Price Tag," *Corpus Christi* (TX) *Caller-Times,* January 6, 1957.

54. "Martha Raye Is Hit with New Troubles," *Hayward* (CA) *Daily Review,* May 1, 1956.

55. "Martha Raye Offers Story on Love Suit," *Indiana Evening Gazette,* May 2, 1956.

56. Dorothy Kilgallen, "Ed Begley Uses 'Nom De Guerre,'" *Dover* (OH) *Daily Reporter,* October 20, 1956.

57. "Martha Raye Will Divorce 5th Husband," *Estherville* (IA) *Daily News,* June 14, 1956.

58. Robert O'Shea, deposition transcript, August 16, 1960. Martha Raye Papers. Special Collections, Margaret Herrick Library, Los Angeles, California.

59. Louella O. Parsons, "About Hollywood," *McKinney* (TX) *Daily Courier-Gazette,* July 11, 1956.

60. "Sleeping Pill Overdose Fells Martha Raye," *Lima* (OH) *News,* August 14, 1956.

61. "Mrs. Nick Condos Takes Overdose of Pills," *Holland* (MI) *Evening Sentinel,* December 12, 1956.

62. George Rosen, "TV's Phantom Millionaires: Those Network Pacts Deflated," *Variety,* October 31, 1956.

63. Marie Torre, "Martha Raye All Mixed Up," *Boston Globe,* February 6, 1957.

64. "Martha Raye Sets for 'Snooks' Role," *New York Times,* March 30, 1957.

65. Lee Belser, "Five-Times Wed Martha Raye Has No Time for Men," *Kingsport* (TN) *Times,* April 16, 1957.

66. Hal Humphrey, "He's Still Kicking," *Waterloo Daily Courier,* December 22, 1957.

67. Hy Gardner, "About Martha Raye," *Pasadena* (CA) *Star-News,* May 22, 1957.

68. Dave Kaufman, "On All Channels," *Daily Variety,* May 24, 1957.

69. Dorothy Kilgallen, "Martha Raye Holdout Giving Backers Jitters," *Washington Post*, August 10, 1957.

70. Marie Torre, "Martha Waits It Out," *Cedar Rapids* (IA) *Gazette*, December 12, 1957.

71. "Martha Raye Sails for Europe," *Florence* (AL) *Times Daily*, July 2, 1958.

72. Raymond Strait, *Hollywood's Star Children* (New York: SPI, 1992), 255.

73. "Comedienne Weds Again," *Centralia* (WA) *Daily Chronicle*, November 8, 1958.

74. J. Randy Taraborrelli, *Laughing Till It Hurts: The Complete Life and Career of Carol Burnett* (New York: Morrow, 1988), 109–111.

75. "Martha Raye Divorces Sixth." *Ironwood* (MI) *Daily Globe*, August 19, 1959.

76. Dorothy Kilgallen, "Martha Raye in Hospital," *Lowell* (MA) *Sun*, September 18, 1959.

Chapter IV

1. "Martha Raye's 2 Furs Found," *Chicago Tribune*, December 13, 1960.

2. "Meet Martha Raye Off-Stage," *Fitchburg* (MA) *Sentinel*, August 10, 1961.

3. "Martha Fractures Whalom Audience," *Fitchburg* (MA) *Sentinel*, August 8, 1961.

4. "Rescue Unit Revives Ill Martha Raye," March 27, 1962.

5. "Martha Raye Took Pills, Says Doctor," *Tucson* (AZ) *Daily Citizen*, March 27, 1962.

6. Lloyd Shearer, "Martha Raye: She's Still Searching for Marital Happiness," *Oakland* (CA) *Tribune*, April 15, 1962.

7. Dorothy Kilgallen, "The Voice of Broadway," *Coshocton* (OH) *Tribune*, September 9, 1962.

8. Dorothy Kilgallen, "Melodye Condos 'Onstage,'" *Lowell* (MA) *Sun*, October 27, 1962.

9. "Martha Raye Will Team Up with Andy Williams," *Anderson* (IN) *Sunday Herald*, March 3, 1963.

10. Joseph Finnigan, "Martha, Daughter Duo," *Bedford* (PA) *Gazette*, November 27, 1963.

11. Donald Freeman, "Martha Raye Talks from the Shoulder," *Chicago* (IL) *Tribune*, June 16, 1963.

12. Richard Wall, personal interview.

13. Dorothy Kilgallen, "Voice of Broadway," *Anderson* (IN) *Herald-Bulletin*, May 13, 1964.

14. Louella O. Parsons, "Ava Gardner to Get Miller or Stevenson Escort," *Anderson* (IN) *Herald-Bulletin*, June 22, 1964.

15. Dwight Whitney, "Maggie of the Boondocks," *TV Guide*, November 21, 1970.

16. Margaret Harford, "Martha Raye Steers 'Cadillac' on a Wild Ride,'" *Los Angeles Times*, January 21, 1965.

17. Walter W. O'Haire, letter to Martha Raye, August 28, 1965. Shirley Woolf, letter to Walter W. O'Haire, September 21, 1965. Martha Raye Papers. Special Collections, Margaret Herrick Library, Los Angeles, California.

18. "Theater: 'Everybody Loves Opal' at Whalom Playhouse," *Fitchburg* (MA) *Sentinel*, August 10, 1965.

19. Paul Aaron, "A Zany Martha Raye as 'Opal' at Colonie," *Bennington* (VT) *Banner*, July 29, 1965.

20. Inez Robb, "Entertainer Martha Raye Is Sweetheart of Gis," *El Paso* (TX) *Herald-Post*, November 19, 1965.

21. "Martha Raye Blasts Entertainers' 'Boycott,'" *Pacific Stars and Stripes*, October 25, 1965.

22. "Old Viet Hand Martha Raye Takes a Busman's Holiday," *Pacific Stars and Stripes*, November 26, 1965.

23. "Martha Sheds Raye of Light on Viet," *Variety*, January 21, 1966.

24. Sam Zolotow, "'Dolly!' Role Set for Martha Raye," *New York Times*, February 16, 1967.

25. Whitney Bolton, "Glancing Sideways," *Cumberland* (MD) *Evening Times*, March 8, 1967.

26. Earl Wilson, "It Happened Last Night," *Uniontown* (PA) *Morning Herald*, March 18, 1967.

27. William Glover, "'Colonel' Sings for Her Troops," *Corpus Christi* (TX) *Caller-Times*, April 23, 1967.

28. "'Den Mother of Boondocks' Martha Raye Is Back Again," *Pacific Stars and Stripes*, October 26, 1968.

29. "Singer Martha Raye Faints in Vietnam," *El Paso* (TX) *Post*, October 6, 1967.

30. Martha Ann Hemphill, "'Wildcat'

Opens at Music Theater," *Baytown* (TX) *Sun*, February 15, 1968.

31. Brent Howell, "'Wildcat' in Mid-Run at the Carousel," *Pasadena* (CA) *Independent Star-News*, March 31, 1968.

32. Carole Wells, personal interview.

33. James Betchkal, "Raye Is Shed on Mill Run Comedy," *Oak Park* (IL) *Oak Leaves*, May 1, 1968.

34. Joan Crosby, "Martha Raye: Witch with a Heart of Gold," *Mt. Vernon* (IL) *Register-News*, September 3, 1970.

35. "'Den Mother of Boondocks' Martha Raye Is Back Again," *Pacific Stars and Stripes*, October 26, 1968.

36. "Martha Raye Wins Hersholt Award for Treks to Viet," *Variety*, April 8, 1969.

37. http://www.youtube.com/watch?v=vdWO-FsbJQs, accessed October 9, 2014.

38. "Martha Raye Tries the Stage Again," *Mt. Vernon* (IL) *Register-News*, June 20, 1969.

39. "Raye, Cast Hold Up 'Hello, Sucker' Alone," *Sandusky* (OH) *Register*, August 23, 1969.

40. Richard L. Coe, "Martha Raye Shines Up Show," *Washington Post*, August 7, 1969.

41. Judy Hugg, "A New TV Adventure for Martha Raye," *Lowell* (MA) *Sun*, July 9, 1970.

42. Dwight Whitney, "Maggie of the Boondocks," *TV Guide*, November 21, 1970.

43. DVD commentary, *The Bugaloos: The Complete Series*, Rhino Home Video, 2006.

44. *Ibid.*

45. John McIndoe, interview, *The Bugaloos: The Complete Series*, Rhino Home Video, 2006.

46. "Even Martha Raye Turns to Criticizing the Army," *Burlington* (NC) *Daily Times*, April 21, 1971.

47. Doug McClelland, "Making the Rounds with 'Boondock Maggie,'" *After Dark*, September 1975.

48. Vernon Scott, "Martha Raye a Vietnam War Casualty," *Eugene* (OR) *Register-Guard*, August 28, 1979.

49. Leticia Kent, "A Mouthful from Martha," *New York Times*, October 29, 1972.

50. Fred Wright, "Everybody Loves This Opal Gem," *St. Petersburg* (FL) *Evening Independent*, June 6, 1973.

51. W.L. Taitte, "The Plate's the Thing," *Texas Monthly*, January 1975.

52. Joseph Culliton, personal interview.

53. Bill O'Hallaren, "'It's Good to Be Working." *TV Guide*, February 26, 1977.

54. Margery Byers, "A New Face in 'No, No, Nanette,'" *Life*, November 10, 1972.

55. Vernon Scott, "Young Men Visiting Martha Raye," *New Castle* (PA) *News*, November 15, 1973.

56. Bill O'Hallaren, "'It's Good to Be Working,'" *TV Guide*, February 26, 1977.

57. Jerry Oppenheimer and Jack Vitek, *Idol: Rock Hudson, the True Story of an American Film Hero* (New York: Villard Books, 1986), 127.

58. *Ibid.*

59. Douglas Brooks West, personal interview.

60. Aaron Gold, "Tower Ticker," *Chicago Tribune*, May 22, 1981.

61. Carroll Carroll, "'And Now a Word From…'" *Variety*, September 3, 1980.

62. Viola Hegyi Swisher, "Getting Serious," *After Dark*, March 1980.

63. Johna Blinn, "Foodstyles of Martha Raye," *Hutchinson* (KS) *News*, September 22, 1979.

64. Rose Marie, *Hold the Roses* (Lexington: University Press of Kentucky, 2002), 234–235.

65. *Ibid.*, 235.

66. H. Lee Murphy, "Old-Fashioned Views, Corny Style Wear Well on Martha Raye," *Chicago Tribune*, March 16, 1984.

67. Allen Hall, personal interview. All subsequent quotes from Hall are from this interview.

68. Raymond Strait, *Hollywood's Star Children* (New York: SPI, 1992), 263.

69. Ande Yakstis, "Lighthearted Annie Brightens Muny," *Alton* (IL) *Telegraph*, July 12, 1983.

70. Marlene Cook, "Audiences, Soldiers Love Martha Raye," *South Holland* (IL) *Star*, February 12, 1984.

Chapter V

1. Raymond Strait, *Hollywood's Star Children* (New York: SPI, 1992), 250.

2. "Raye Files Suit Against Letterman," *Kokomo* (IN) *Tribune*, August 22, 1987.

3. Army Archerd, "Just for Variety," *Variety*, July 20, 1988.

4. "Martha Raye Thanks Her Fans," *Spokane* (IL) *Chronicle*, July 22, 1991.

5. Bob Thomas, "Martha Raye Dead at 78 After Lengthy Illness," *Hutchinson* (KS) *News*, October 20, 1994.

6. Jane Wollman Rusoff, "Martha Raye's Warm December," *Washington Post*, December 28, 1991.

7. *Ibid.*

8. Stephanie Mansfield, "The Seventh Mr. Martha Raye," *Washington Post*, December 30, 1994.

9. Dolores Barclay, "Miss M Is Still Divine, Just a Bit More Sedate," *Santa Fe* (NM) *New Mexican*, November 10, 1983.

10. Gregg Kilday, "Martha Raye and 'For the Boys': A Newlywed Game?" *Entertainment Weekly,* December 20, 1991.

11. "Suit by Raye's Daughter 'Smokescreen,' Says Hubby," *Variety,* December 24, 1991.

12. Jeannie Park, "A Star's September Song," *People*, January 27, 1992.

13. *Ibid.*

14. Raymond Strait, *Hollywood's Star Children* (New York: SPI, 1992), 263.

15. "Doctors Amputate Martha Raye's Left Leg," *Gettysburg* (PA) *Times*, October 29, 1993.

16. "Local Author, Book Used for Profile of Martha Raye on 'Biography,'" *Daily Gazette* (Schenectady, NY), October 9, 1999.

17. "Ailing Martha Raye to Get President's Freedom Medal," *New Bern* (NC) *Sun-Journal*, November 3, 1993.

18. "Bette Midler Insists 'For the Boys' Isn't Based on Martha Raye," *Syracuse* (NY) *Post- Standard*, February 18, 1994.

19. "'For the Boys' Isn't About Martha Raye, Judge Says," *Santa Ana* (CA) *Register*, March 10, 1994.

20. "'Favorite Loudmouth' Martha Raye Dies," *Arlington Heights* (IL) *Daily Herald*, October 20, 1994.

21. John Horn, "Martha Raye, Comedian Big Mouth, Dies at 78." *Clearfield* (PA) *Progress*, October 20, 1994.

22. Bob Thomas, "Martha Raye Dead at 78," *Nashua* (NH) *Telegraph*, October 20, 1994.

23. "Martha Raye Burial: Green Berets Honor One of Their Own," *Syracuse* (NY) *Herald- Journal*, October 22, 1994.

24. Randall Rigsbee, "Aberdeen Man Is Pall Bearer at Raye Funeral," *Moore County* (NC) *Citizen News-Record*, October 23, 1994.

25. Marlene Cook, "Audiences, Soldiers Love Martha Raye," South Holland (IL) Star, February 12, 1984.

26. Kaye Ballard with Jim Hesselman, *How I Lost 10 Pounds in 53 Years: A Memoir* (New York: Back Stage Books, 2006), 13.

27. *Ibid.*, 85.

Filmography

1. Paul Harrison, "'Twas Bitter Struggle Mugging into Movies," *Sandusky* (OH) *Star Journal*, August 3, 1936.

2. Jimmie Fidler, "Hollywood Success Leaves Martha Raye Unspoiled," *Salt Lake* (UT) *Tribune*, October 6, 1936.

3. "Martha Raye New Comedienne Sensation Prominent in Film," *Edwardsville* (IL) *Intelligencer*, January 15, 1937.

4. "Martha Raye Comes on Paramount Twin Bill for Tuesday," *Cedar Rapids* (IA) *Gazette*, January 31, 1937.

5. "Movie Company Is Visited by Bad Luck," *Reno* (NV) *Evening Gazette*, September 19, 1936.

6. "Bob Burns, Martha Raye Get Star Roles in Comedy, 'Mountain Music,' at Ritz," *Big Spring* (TX) *Daily News*, June 27, 1937.

7. May Mann, "Martha Found Cinema's Cure for the Doldrums," *Ogden* (UT) *Standard-Examiner*, March 28, 1937.

8. Franklyn Frank, *Cleveland* (OH) *Call and Post*, August 12, 1937.

9. Sally Bell, "Georgia Film Critic Pans Artists, Models," *Norfolk* (VA) *Journal and Guide*, September 25, 1937.

10. "Lamour and Milland Head 'Holiday' Cast," *McKean County* (PA) *Democrat*, October 13, 1938.

11. "Hunt for Fighting Bulls Gets Director's Goat," *Los Angeles Times*, February 20, 1938.

12. "Variety Found in Week End Theatre Bills," *Idaho Falls* (ID) *Post-Register*, August 20, 1938.

13. "Joe Brown, Martha Raye in Comedy

at Paramount," *Logansport* (IN) *Press*, December 10, 1939.

14. "Whole Range Film Subjects Covered in Local Bookings This Week," *Kingsport* (TN) *Times*, April 14, 1940.

15. "'Syracuse Shuffle' in Film," *Syracuse* (NY) *Herald Journal*, July 17, 1940.

16. "Ann Sheridan in New Gay Musical," *Laredo* (TX) *Times*, January 11, 1942.

17. Paul Harrison, "Harrison in Hollywood," *El Paso* (TX) *Herald Post*, October 22, 1941.

18. Ken Morgan, "Hollywood Keyhole," *Big Spring* (TX) *Daily Herald*, October 1, 1941.

19. "Martha Raye Plunges Down Canyon in Auto," *Charleston* (WV) *Gazette*, August 10, 1941.

20. Robbin Coons, "Comedy Missed on Movie Lot," *Pulaski* (VA) *Southwest Times*, December 7, 1943.

21. Dwight Whitney, "Maggie of the Boondocks," *TV Guide*, November 21, 1970.

22. Kenneth S. Lynn, *Charlie Chaplin and His Times* (New York: Simon and Schuster, 1997), 446.

23. Philip K. Scheuer, "Widmark Gets Lead from His Ex-Lead." *Los Angeles Times*, May 2, 1961.

24. Bob Thomas, "Martha Raye Married in 'Jumbo' Scene," *Greeley* (CO) *Daily Tribune*, February 28, 1962.

25. Whitcomb, Jon. "Hollywood's Biggest Star." *Cosmopolitan*, October 1962.

26. *Ibid.*

27. Vera Servi, "A Mod Musical Film with Camp Dialog Aims for Family Trade," *Chicago Tribune*, August 2, 1970.

28. "Film Crew Shoots in Mojave." *Bakersfield* (CA) *Californian*, February 21, 1969.

29. Vernon Scott, "How Bad Can a Movie Be?" *Oakland* (CA) *Tribune*, October 17, 1971.

30. Vernon Scott, "Movie Rooted in Nostalgia," *Oakland* (CA) *Tribune*, March 28, 1969.

31. Dick Kleiner, "New 'Airport' Stars Sst Concorde," *Jacksonville* (FL) *Journal-Courier*, February 18, 1979.

32. Joan E. Vadeboncoeur, "'No Refusals' from 'Concorde' Actors in Filming Risky Scenes," *Syracuse* (NY) *Herald-Journal*, August 10, 1979.

Television Shows

1. Earl Wilson, "The Man of the Hour," *Syracuse* (NY) *Herald-Journal*, November 7, 1950.

2. Dorothy Kilgallen, "Jottings in Pencil," *Greenville* (PA) *Record-Argus,* September 23, 1950.

3. Sheilah Graham, "June Haver's Next Film Set on South Pacific Isle," *Bluefield* (WV) *Daily Telegraph*, June 24, 1950.

4. John Crosby, "Radio in Review," *East Liverpool* (OH) *Review*, January 11, 1952.

5. Peg Simpson, "Meet the Masters Tops Television's Musical Offerings," *Syracuse* (NY) *Post-Standard*, March 29, 1952.

6. James Abbe, "Rocky Graziano Stars on TV as Foil for Martha Raye," *Oakland* (CA) *Tribune*, September 29, 1952.

7. C.E. Butterfield, "Columnist Considers Miss Martha Raye Top Tv Comedienne." *Freeport* (IL) *Journal-Standard*, November 1, 1954.

8. Cynthia Lowry, "Martha Raye Is Crazy About the Country," *Cedar Rapids* (IA) *Gazette*, January 10, 1954.

9. C.E. Butterfield, "Columnist Considers Miss Martha Raye Top Tv Comedienne." *Freeport* (IL) *Journal-Standard*, November 1, 1954.

10. Jack O'Brian, "Martha Raye Gets Tv Deal," *Stars and Stripes*, May 17, 1955.

11. Bob Thomas, "Martha Raye Satisfied with TV Role and Wants No More of Films," *Indiana Evening Gazette*, November 7, 1955.

12. Jack O'Brian, "Martha Raye in Finest TV Hour," *Mansfield* (OH) *News-Journal*, May 9, 1956.

13. Steve Allen, *More Funny People* (New York: Stein and Day, 1982), 215.

14. Joe Finnigan, "Martha Raye Hollers in Famed Form," *Salt Lake City* (UT) *Tribune*, April 18, 1960.

15. Erskine Johnson, "Hollywood Today!" *Coshocton* (OH) *Tribune*, March 2, 1958.

16. William Sarmento, "How Cute Can One Really Be?" *Lowell* (MA) *Sun*, March 23, 1961.

17. Wesley Hyatt, *A Critical History of Television's the Red Skelton Show, 1951–1971* (Jefferson, NC: McFarland, 2004), 82.

18. *Ibid.*, 83.

19. "Troopers Travel Clown Alley," *Logan* (UT) *Herald-Journal*, November 7, 1966.

20. Erskine Johnson, "Kathryn Grayson: Role Takes a Toll," *Redland* (CA) *Daily Facts*, April 7, 1964.

21. "Cbs Completes Fare for Night Programming," *Dover* (OH) *Daily Reporter*, April 2, 1964.

22. Cynthia Lowry, "'Outer Limits' Finds Use for 'Grade D Movie Fodder," *Corpus Christi* (Tx) *Times*, May 5, 1964.

23. Terry Vernon, "Tele-Vues," *Long Beach* (CA) *Press-Telegram*, May 9, 1964.

24. Doris Klein, "Actor William Bendix Dies at the Age of 58," *Lowell* (MA) *Sun*, December 15, 1964.

25. "20th Century Fox Saluted on Show," *Fairbanks* (AK) *Daily News-Miner*, December 28, 1969.

26. "Martha Raye Signs with Mcmillan Series," *Florence* (SC) *Morning News*, August 7, 1976.

27. "'Alice in Wonderland' Comes to TV," *Sandusky* (OH) *Register*, December 8, 1985.

28. Vernon Scott, "Carroll Classics Coming to Tv," *New Castle* (PA) *News*, April 3, 1985.

29. Joan Hanauer, "'Alice' Has Traumatic Wonderland Trip," *New Castle* (PA) *News*, December 7, 1985.

30. Fred Rothenberg, "Alice's Musical Adventures a Child's Delight," *Medicine Hat* (Alberta, CA) *News*, December 9, 1985.

31. C.E. Butterfield, "Broadway Musical on Television; Reaction to Show Is Mixed." *Danville* (VA) *Bee*, October 5, 1950.

32. John Crosby, "Exuberant, Funny and Tuneful," *East Liverpool* (OH) *Review*), October 9, 1950.

33. "TV Scout," *El Paso* (TX) *Herald-Post,* May 10, 1958.

34. Charles Witbeck, "Danny Thomas TV Specials Premiere," *Winona* (MN) *Daily News*, November 7, 1965.

35. Joan Hanauer, "Lynde Seasons Christmas Spirit with Humbug," *Redlands* (CA) *Daily Facts*, December 6, 1977.

Bibliography

Books

Adir, Karin. *The Great Clowns of American Television*. Jefferson, NC: McFarland, 1988.

Allen, Steve. *More Funny People*. New York: Stein & Day, 1982.

Ballard, Kaye, with Jim Hesselman. *How I Lost 10 Pounds in 53 Years: A Memoir*. New York: Back Stage Books, 2006.

Berle, Milton, with Haskel Frankel. *Milton Berle: An Autobiography*. New York: Delacorte Press, 1974.

Brown, Joe E. *Laughter Is a Wonderful Thing*. New York: Barnes, 1956.

Clarke, Gerald. *Get Happy: The Life of Judy Garland*. New York: Random House, 2000.

Clooney, Rosemary, with Joan Barthel. *Girl Singer: An Autobiography*. New York: Doubleday, 1999.

Condos, Barbara. *Hard Candy*. New York: Morrow, 1988.

Erickson, Hal. *Sid and Marty Krofft: A Critical Study of Saturday Morning Children's Television, 1969–1993*. Jefferson, NC: McFarland, 2007.

Everitt, David. *King of the Half Hour: Nat Hiken and the Golden Age of TV Comedy*. Syracuse, NY: Syracuse University Press, 2001.

Fidelman, Geoffrey Mark. *The Lucy Book: A Complete Guide to Her Five Decades on Television*. Los Angeles, CA: Renaissance Books, 1999.

Fortin, Noonie. *Memories of Maggie: Martha Raye, A Legend Spanning Three Wars*. San Antonio, TX: Langmarc, 1995.

Friedwald, Will. *A Biographical Guide to the Great Jazz and Pop Singers*. New York: Pantheon Books, 2010.

Gehring, Wes D. *Joe E. Brown: Film Comedian and Baseball Buffoon*. Jefferson, NC: McFarland, 2006.

Goldman, Herbert G. *Jolson: The Legend Comes to Life*. New York: Oxford University Press, 1988.

Graziano, Rocky, with Ralph Corsel. *Somebody Down Here Likes Me, Too*. New York: Stein & Day, 1981.

Graziano, Rocky, with Rowland Barber. *Somebody Up There Likes Me*. New York: Simon & Schuster, 1955.

Hoey, Michael A. *Elvis' Favorite Director: The Amazing 52-Year Career of Norman Taurog*. Duncan, OK: BearManor Media, 2014.

Hyatt, Wesley. *A Critical History of Television's The Red Skelton Show, 1951–1971*. Jefferson, NC: McFarland, 2004.

Inman, David M. *Television Variety Shows: Histories and Episode Guides to 57 Programs*. Jefferson, NC: McFarland, 2006.

Kear, Lynn. *Kay Francis: A Passionate Life and Career*. Jefferson, NC: McFarland, 2006.

Koszarski, Richard. *Hollywood on the Hudson: Film and Television in New York from Griffith to Sarnoff*. New Brunswick, NJ: Rutgers University Press, 2008.

Lamour, Dorothy, as told to Dick McInnes. *My Side of the Road*. Englewood Cliffs, NJ: Prentice-Hall, 1980.

Landis, Carole. *Four Jills in a Jeep*. New York: Random House, 1944.

Lear, Norman. *Even This I Get to Experience*. New York: Penguin, 2014.

Lynn, Kenneth S. *Charlie Chaplin and His Times*. New York: Simon & Schuster, 1997.

Macfarlane, Malcolm, and Ken Crossland. *Perry Como: A Biography and Complete Career Record*. Jefferson, NC: McFarland, 2009.

Manvell, Roger. *Chaplin*. Boston: Little, Brown & Co., 1974.

Marx, Arthur. *The Secret Life of Bob Hope*. New York: Barricade Books, 1993.

McGee, Tom. *Betty Grable: The Girl with the Million Dollar Legs*. Vestal, NY: Vestal Press, 1995.

Neibaur, James L. *The Bob Hope Films*. Jefferson, NC: McFarland, 2005.

Oppenheimer, Jerry, and Jack Vitek. *Idol: Rock Hudson, The True Story of an American Film Hero*. New York: Villard Books, 1986.

Parish, James Robert. *The Slapstick Queens*. South Brunswick, NJ: A.S. Barnes, 1973.

_____. *The Unofficial 'Murder, She Wrote' Casebook*. New York: Kensington, 1997.

Patrick, John. *Everybody Loves Opal*. New York: Dramatists Play Service, 1962.

Phillips, Brent. *Charles Walters: The Director Who Made Hollywood Dance*. Lexington: University Press of Kentucky, 2014.

Pitrone, Jean Maddern. *Take It from the Big Mouth: The Life of Martha Raye*. Lexington: University Press of Kentucky, 1999.

Rose Marie. *Hold the Roses*. Lexington: University Press of Kentucky, 2002.

Shain, Betty. *Spiraling: A Memoir*. Bloomington, IN: Xlibris, 2009.

Shelley, Peter. *Frances Farmer: The Life and Films of a Troubled Star*. Jefferson, NC: McFarland, 2011.

Strait, Raymond. *Hollywood's Star Children*. New York: SPI, 1992.

Taraborrelli, J. Randy. *Laughing Till It Hurts: The Complete Life and Career of Carol Burnett*. New York: Morrow, 1988.

Terrace, Vincent. *Television Specials: 5,336 Entertainment Programs, 1936–2012*. 2nd ed. Jefferson, NC: McFarland, 2013.

Tucker, David C. *Joan Davis: America's Queen of Film, Radio and Television Comedy*. Jefferson, NC: McFarland, 2014.

Westmore, Frank, and Muriel Davidson. *The Westmores of Hollywood*. Philadelphia, PA: Lippincott, 1976.

Zoglin, Richard. *Hope: Entertainer of the Century*. New York: Simon & Schuster, 2014.

Articles

De Blois, Frank. "Martha Raye in Focus." *TV Guide*, November 26, 1955.

McClelland, Doug. "Making the Rounds with 'Boondock Maggie.'" *After Dark*, September 1975.

"Muggs and Cupid Put the Bite on Martha in a Busy Week," *Life*, May 3, 1954.

O'Hallaren, Bill. "'It's Good to Be Working.'" *TV Guide*, February 26, 1977.

Swisher, Viola Hegyi. "Getting Serious," *After Dark*, March 1980.

Townsend, Leo. "Hollywood's Raye of Sunshine." *Radio Stars*, April 1937.

Whitcomb, Jon. "Hollywood's Biggest Star." *Cosmopolitan*, October 1962.

Whitney, Dwight. "Maggie of the Boondocks." *TV Guide*, November 21, 1970.

Interviews

Joseph Culliton, email, September 15, 2014.
Allen Hall, telephone, October 9, 2014.
Wesley Hyatt, telephone, March 5, 2015.
Gregg Oppenheimer, email, October 15, 2014.
Richard Wall, telephone, October 15, 2014.
Carole Wells, telephone, November 4, 2014.
Douglas Brooks West, email, May 12, 2015.

Archives

Martha Raye Papers. Special Collections, Margaret Herrick Library, Los Angeles, California.

Vital Records

Peter Reed, Jr. and Maybelle Hooper Reed, marriage license #3248, filed July 19, 1916. County of Gallatin, State of Montana.

Margy Reed, birth certificate #19174, filed September 1, 1916. Board of Health, State of Montana.

Websites

www.afi.com/members/catalog
www.americanradiohistory.com
www.ancestry.com
www.archive.org
www.cinema.library.ucla.edu
www.colonelmaggie.com
www.imdb.com
www.mediahistoryproject.org
www.newspaperarchive.com
https://books.google.com/
www.radiogoldindex.com
www.tv.com
www.youtube.com

Index

Numbers in **bold italics** refer to pages with photographs.